Philosophy, Mysticism, and the Political

SUNY series in Contemporary Italian Philosophy
———
Silvia Benso and Brian Schroeder, editors

Philosophy, Mysticism, and the Political

Essays on Dante

Massimo Cacciari

Edited and with an introduction by
Alessandro Carrera

Translated by
Giorgio Mobili

The translation of this work has been funded by SEPS
SEGRETARIATO EUROPEO PER LE PUBBLICAZIONI SCIENTIFICHE

Via Val d'Aposa 7 – 40123 Bologna – Italy
seps@seps.it   www.seps.it

The production of this book has been supported by the Small Grants Program at the University of Houston.

Published by State University of New York Press, Albany

© 2021 State University of New York

All rights reserved

Printed in the United States of America

No part of this book may be used or reproduced in any manner whatsoever without written permission. No part of this book may be stored in a retrieval system or transmitted in any form or by any means including electronic, electrostatic, magnetic tape, mechanical, photocopying, recording, or otherwise without the prior permission in writing of the publisher.

For information, contact State University of New York Press, Albany, NY
www.sunypress.edu

Library of Congress Cataloging-in-Publication Data

Names: Cacciari, Massimo, author. | Carrera, Alessandro, 1954– editor, writer of introduction. | Mobili, Gigio, translator.
Title: Philosophy, mysticism, and the political : essays on Dante / Massimo Cacciari ; edited and with an introduction by Alessandro Carrera ; translated by Gigio Mobili.
Description: Albany : State University of New York Press, 2021. | Series: SUNY series in contemporary Italian philosophy | Includes bibliographical references and index.
Identifiers: LCCN 2021012591 | ISBN 9781438486895 (hardcover : alk. : paper) | ISBN 9781438486888 (pbk. : alk. paper) | ISBN 9781438486901 (ebook)
Subjects: LCSH: Dante Alighieri, 1265–1321. Divina commedia. | Dante Alighieri, 1265–1321—Political and social views. | Cacciari, Massimo—Translations into English. | LCGFT: Essays. | Literary criticism.
Classification: LCC PQ4390 .C23 2021 | DDC 851/.1—dc23
LC record available at https://lccn.loc.gov/2021012591

10 9 8 7 6 5 4 3 2 1

Contents

Introduction: Nostalgia for the Empire, or Dante's Metapolitics   1
    Alessandro Carrera

Chapter 1   Double Portrait: Saint Francis of Assisi in Dante and Giotto   21

Chapter 2   The "Sin" of Ulysses   61

Chapter 3   Dante's Divine Perception (*Aesthesis Theia*)   83

Chapter 4   The Concrete Ineffable: The Last Cantos of the *Commedia*   93

Chapter 5   Dante's *Intellectual Love*   105

Chapter 6   Latin and Vernacular in the *De vulgari eloquentia*   113

Chapter 7   On Dante's Political Theology   119

Chapter 8   A Brief Note on the German Reception of Dante   133

Chapter 9   Schelling's Dante   145

Notes   157

Chapter Sources   177

Index   179

Introduction

Nostalgia for the Empire, or Dante's Metapolitics

Alessandro Carrera

Touching Dante

Lately, every time I teach a Dante class, I must remember to warn my undergraduate students: *Beware of the Middle Ages*, the Middle Ages are *weird*, expect to be shocked! I also tell them that we are still surrounded by a mockery of Middle Ages–like mindset. Religious fundamentalism, charismatic cults, magical thinking, and nostalgia for theocracy shape our world as much as science and social sciences do, and those opposite tendencies are often at war with each other. People who speak in tongues and believe in the inerrancy of a seventeenth-century English translation of a book assembled thousands of years ago in a language they know nothing about sit side by side with those whose firm belief is that there is no other destiny than genetics, the universe is an accident, and our existence is the product of random selection and the survival of the fittest. We may study the Middle Ages; we may think that we understand the basics of the Middle Ages, we may even love the Middle Ages (they are great for mystery and intrigue), but unless we are medieval scholars, we do not *get* them. Yet anyone who knows intimately the history of Western culture can tell that modernity, *our* modernity, did not start with the Enlightenment and not even with Descartes' *Discourse on Method*. It gave its first cry centuries before, perhaps when Johannes Scotus Eriugena completed his *De divisione naturae* (867), even though the work was banned after the author's death and would not be printed until 1681. It might indeed be argued that *De divisione naturae* marked the threshold between the culmination of antiquity and the slow beginning of a new era. If we agree with this teleological overview of Western history, then the Middle Ages have always been step after step on their way to modernity, and there would be no modern science if Scotus and Aquinas had not validated human reason as necessary to understand the unfolding of God's creation. Yet we also want to think that we are luckily removed from the dark side of the Middle Ages. We want to believe that what we have in common with the Greeks and the Romans outshines everything we may owe to some obscure ninth-century monk or to some incomprehensible thirteenth-century poet. Because we believe that the philosophy, psychology, and science of the West are grounded in Sophocles, Plato, Aristotle, Cicero, and Augustine, we may have the impression that the Middle Ages are little more than an obstacle between us and the heights of classical antiquity. But that would be a mistake. The Middle Ages were a time of immense debate that laid the foundation for who we are now. The Middle Ages applied all the rationality that was available at the time to areas of human experience that modernity has left to the irrational mind and relegated to folly or superstition. The medieval men (and women too) strove to rationalize religion, mysticism, and the relation between God's plan and human politics to an extent hitherto unknown. They were obsessed with order, rules, and hierarchies from which nothing would escape, because to them everything had to *make sense*. Modern rationalism would later triumph, but it would do so by negation, having jettisoned the medieval dream that every aspect of human and superhuman experience should eventually fall into place. Modern rationalism was built on the Cartesian premise that there is a realm outside the rational mind that must be left untouched and unrationalized, or better locked away. Dreams, madness, and arcane correspondences between the human body and the body of the universe were not to become part of the modern project: they would be best left to the poets. But those were areas that the Middle Ages did not wish to abandon by the wayside. There is no "unconscious" in the Middle Ages (or rather, there is no conscious confinement of the unconscious mind), there is no psychology in the modern sense of the world (which, to a certain extent, is also the Greek sense of the word), because nothing, in the Middle Ages, lies outside God's gaze. This, among other things, is what makes it so difficult to understand those times. If nothing stands outside the mind (God's mind and man's mind) and the will (God's will and man's God-given free will), there are no excuses for what you do (not even for your *folly*)—which is precisely Dante's premise. Modernity works by exclusion; here is science, and there is what has no place in science. The Middle Ages works by inclusion. That such inclusiveness may look suspiciously "totalitarian" to us just goes to show that the totalitarianism of modernity has succeeded in its own way, making it "natural" for us to think that a very large realm of human experience does not have a proper place and is meant only to wreak havoc and increase entropy. Modernity has created an *image* of the world, and an image is always framed. The Middle Ages had a *vision* of the world (of God and the world, that is), and a vision does not have a frame (Dante's cosmology is impossible to visualize with the tools of Renaissance perspective).

Twenty years ago, my undergraduate students (who are not usually literature majors) would raise no objections to Dante. He was who he was—a man of his time, a literary authority—and that was it. But things have changed. I heard the first crack in the wall when a student began to laugh while I was explaining the geography of the *Divine Comedy*: here is Hell shaped like a funnel, here is the soil that, having recoiled in horror at the fall of Lucifer, turned into the mountain of Purgatory. . . . "But that's ridiculous," he said. Other objections were raised afterward, mostly of the kind one would expect in a gender studies class, and I had to learn how to play along. In fact, because my students seem increasingly baffled by the information I give them (believe it or not, one of their major concerns is that Beatrice is not Dante's *wife*, and the sympathy they are supposed to feel for a Platonic yet adulterous love makes them—both men and women—feel uncomfortable), I have decided that there is no point in downplaying the weirdness of the Middle Ages. When we meet Saint Bernard of Clairvaux as Dante's last guide, I show them the engraving of the Holy Mary squirting her breast milk into Bernard's eyes to heal him from what was (likely) conjunctivitis or glaucoma. I am not saying that the snake-handling preachers who were common in the United States not long ago are the modern equivalent of Saint Bernard believing he was receiving the Holy Mary's milk in his eyes. The difficult conclusion is that, compared to a snake handler or a contemporary prosperity preacher, Saint Bernard was a champion of rationality, and the same could be said of Hildegard of Bingen and her visions of God, which she dutifully transcribed. In those years, you could believe that you were physically in touch with the Holy Mary and at the same time be a very practical person, as influential in the history of Europe as any pope or king.[1] As I said before, the Renaissance and then modernity have found their spiritual ancestors in classical antiquity. Freud's rereading of Oedipus has made Sophocles our contemporary, and the satires of Juvenal may not look altogether different from, say, Kenneth Anger's *Hollywood Babylon*. Why, then, couldn't Thomas Aquinas be modernized, too?

Unfortunately, science is not on board. Geneticist and atheist *extraordinaire* Richard Dawkins, who mocks Aquinas' five demonstrations of the existence of God as an example of obscurantism and poor logic, seems to ignore that it took the almost unlimited power that Aquinas bestowed on human reason to pave the way for modern science.[2] Yet it's a fact: Aquinas, Siger of Brabant, Saint Dominic, Saint Bonaventure, Saint Francis of Assisi, Saint Clare, Saint Angela of Foligno, and any other name from the sixth century to the thirteenth will never be as proximate to us as the Greeks and the Romans are. But if that is the case, if the Middle Ages have created their own world, inaccessible to us unless we dedicate a lifetime of study to it, then the only way to teach students how to approach the subject is precisely to respect that world's radical distance.

What about Dante, then, who knew very well the difference between the old and the new, the old poetry and the new poetry of the "modern usage" ("uso moderno," *Purg.* XXVI, 113)?[3] Has the great modernization of Dante that flourished in the Anglo-Saxon world in the nineteenth and twentieth centuries come to its final chapter? After Ezra Pound, T. S. Eliot, and all the modernist poets who wrote long and complex poems in their wake, with Dante always on their mind, what will Dante's fate be now? Is it still true what I heard poet and translator Allen Mandelbaum say toward the end of the 1980s, that Dante is the poet of the future? What I know is that he is definitely not a "poet of the past." Dante is a poet who creates his own age. In this book, which collects all the articles and essays that Massimo Cacciari has written on Dante's politics of mysticism and the mysticisms of his politics, the author is very careful never to push Dante in an uncharted direction.[4] Cacciari does not force Dante into any philosophical straitjacket. He walks with Dante, takes notes, asks questions, raises issues, and tries to understand the *Divine Comedy* and other works as much as possible in Dante's terms not as a critic but from the point of view of a faithful, assiduous, perceptive, at times embedded, sometimes perplexed, and sometimes worshiping reader. If Dante belongs to the future, that is one more reason why he cannot be our contemporary. In fact, when was he? His political hopes failed in his time and were never resumed. His idea of a Christian Empire was dead on arrival. His theologization of courtly love found no followers. For centuries, and despite cores of sympathetic readers and commentators, whom he never lacked, his work was often put aside as obscure and unreadable. In the general taste, he played second (or third, or fourth . . .) fiddle to Petrarch until the nineteenth century. But he always was, and still is, a massive comet that shoots through our skies at unpredictable intervals. It never comes too close, but we feel the pull of its gravity. The best way to approach Dante is to respect the distance he keeps from us—just as he kept his distance from his own contemporaries. You can either get mad at Dante because he objectifies women by angelicizing them (such is the current wisdom of some among my female graduate students who deeply dislike the *Vita nuova*[5]) or point out that he is one of the first great Western poets to have given a voice to women who suffered abuse (Francesca, Pia, Piccarda . . .). As I said, I play along if I must, but both approaches seem quite useless to me. Both miss the point that we will never *get* Dante. He will be with us if we want him to, but we cannot touch him the way Saint Bernard was touched by the Holy Mary's milk; we cannot make him fit our standards. Dante is not one of us. He is the most powerful reminder that there will always be something eluding our assumption that we can "police" the past the way we "police" the present.[6]

The Mystery of Saint Francis

This book opens with a long chapter on Saint Francis of Assisi, a figure even more mysterious than Dante, to the point that not even Dante—such is Cacciari's argument—could figure him out. It is the most complex chapter, and Cacciari's major contribution to the understanding of Francis' uniqueness. For Francis was as incomprehensible in his own time as he is in ours. Cacciari's comparison of Dante's celebration of Francis in *Paradiso* X–XIII with Giotto's narrative of Francis' life in the Assisi frescoes and elsewhere is meant to show that both the poet and the painter failed to grasp Francis' *difference*. While they were able to highlight his historical role, his life, impact, and legend, they missed the import of his most radical message, namely, his ontology, theology, and politics of *poverty*.

What kind of narrative is Francis' life? It is a "divine comedy" in its own right, yet a comedy of suffering, the comedy of a man who imitates Christ but cannot conclude his imitation with a glorious resurrection. He is Francis *patibilis* just as Christ was *Christus patibilis*, but Francis' life can be told only in *stories*, in the plural. One all-encompassing story, one *Commedia*, was not made out of his life. Dante's philosophy fails before Francis, and even Dante's theology is not equal to the task. Francis is, as it were, another Beatrice, yet a silent Beatrice, or a silent Virgil, even more powerful because of their silence. Dante's *Paradiso* struggles under the sign of Francis, who leads the way without being the end of it. Giotto's treatment of Francis fares no better. And if both Giotto and Dante "betray" Francis (they cannot *represent* the radicalness of his *poverty*), then Francis is even more Christlike in his being betrayed.

This suggestion of betrayal may come as a surprise. After all, and to paraphrase Cacciari, Dante creates a majestic Franciscan *symphony* in *Paradiso* X–XIII, a forest of references that works as the Dantean Empire is supposed to work, being One without annihilating every singular nation or character. Because it is Thomas Aquinas who pronounces Francis' praise, we understand that Francis is indeed *primus inter pares*. But it is not pure eschatological Franciscanism that Dante has in mind; In *Paradiso* X–XIII Dante aims to reconcile theological knowledge and prophetic spirit, the power of syllogism and the harmony of eschatology. Siger, Joachim, Bonaventure, and Thomas, the great "themes" of Dante's symphony, are the four figures of Dante's *pax catholica*, which must happen *under the sign of Francis* because no one else has that power. And yet this is *Dante's* prophecy, not Francis'. It is the reformation of the Church as a precondition for renovation. Dante is a reformist (otherwise he would be a heretic who wants revolutionary renovation as condition for reformation), but a *radical* reformist, and to that extent he definitely wants to give due credit to Francis' poverty, except that Francis' difference is greater than Dante can accept.

Dante emphasizes poverty, the negotiations with the papacy, and the preaching. Giotto, for instance in the Louvre *predella*, paints the dream of Innocent III, the confirmation of the Order, and the preaching to the birds. In other words, Giotto's Francis is already being *normalized*. Providence speaks to the Pope in his dream, but not *through* Francis, and Francis is portrayed as humble and dejected before the Pope. It is true, however, that Giotto accepts Francis as a real legend while Dante essentially wants Francis to serve his idea of a Christian Empire. While

Giotto is keen on Francis' understanding of nature, Dante's Francis does not look as if he ever wrote the *Canticle of the Sun* and is not shown praising the Lord *together* with the creatures.

Dante's Francis is also above the divisions in his Order; it is not Bonaventure's Francis as it is in Giotto, because it is *Dante's* Bonaventure, not the Bonaventure of the *Legenda maior*, the most authoritative biography of Francis. However, Cacciari asks, is Giotto's cycle in Assisi that dependent on Bonaventure? In reality, it is dependent on the sacrifice that Francis and Clare had to make when they accepted a Rule for their orders. That was the great compromise that Giotto glossed over: if the life of the Brothers is a "form of life" (the life of Christ), it has to go through a constant "formation," which will never be perfect if it must follow a Rule. However, what concerns Dante is neither the Rule nor Francis as a maker of miracles. The *popular* Francis has no role in the *Commedia*. Conversely, poverty has little bearing on the Assisi frescoes (Giotto's Francis is obedient and meek, but there is no specific emphasis on his poverty), while Dante's Francis is explicitly poor. Cacciari, however, makes the point that Francis was *joyful* in his poverty, and not even Dante was able to picture the complexity of Francis' link between poverty and joy.[7] To Dante, poverty is fundamentally a theological problem that must be theologically resolved. Therefore, the question remains: why is Francis pursuing joy in poverty and poverty in joy? Which comes down to the ultimate question: who is Francis?

Francis' poverty is not a means to an end, nor is it just the virtue of renunciation. It does not result from hatred of money and possessions or a polemic against wealth. Francis' point is strictly Evangelical; the Kingdom belongs to the poor, but not on account of something that the poor do not have. The poor in spirit *lack nothing*, the poor are *perfect*, and nothing can be added to their perfection. "Poverty," Cacciari says, "is the will to conquer the Kingdom. Poor is the violence of he who wants the Kingdom. Only the poor are truly *powerful*." In other words, Francis' poverty is a political act. Centuries later, even Nietzsche was impressed by Francis' love, but he misunderstood it greatly when he rubricked it under "pity." Nietzsche overlooked that Francis' "great love" (a love full of power) was just the other side of what Nietzsche would call "great politics": a politics that *decides*, *converts*, "tames the proud" (including, we might add, the pride of the poor).

In its *destruens* part, poverty is *kenosis*, "self-emptying" of the self and the soul. Man's poverty is an *analogon* of divine *kenosis*, and thus the only real relationship man can have with God. On the Cross, God emptied himself of all divinity. Analogously, man must empty himself of his divine spark. Man must be *abandoned*, as much as Christ was abandoned on the Cross. But this self-abandonment is done out of love, it is a movement toward the Other, which becomes a necessity when we have nothing left in ourselves. We have only what we love, but we do not possess it.[8]

Cacciari has always striven to emphasize the *pars construens* of every subject matter he has tackled. The problem is that the *pars construens* requires even more violence than the *pars destruens*. In this case, contrary to what Nietzsche thought, it implies severing all ties, even the ties of pity, which is what Francis did when he rejected his father and his family. But that violence is also joy. If the *pars construens* is the poverty of self-emptying, then poverty must be *glad* to be absolutely poor, and the poor (the Brothers, the Minors) must be glad as well.[9] According to Cacciari, this is where Giotto and Dante missed the target. The joy of poverty and suffering is not visible in the Assisi frescoes. And while Dante understands poverty, he erases its merriment. Francis, together with Peter and Benedict in the Mystic Rose, is Christ reborn, but Christ as king, not Christ as poor. It must be clear that there is nothing "masochistic" in Francis' choice of poverty and suffering (as I said, there are no unconscious motivations in the Middle Ages). If that were the case, Giotto and Dante would be justified in eschewing the topic entirely. What is lacking in Giotto and Dante is Francis the joyful "jester," the "fool" (*pazzus*), and the "mother" who gives up everything for her son. We can be spouses, brothers, children, and mothers of Christ—as Francis says—and a mother follows no Rule, she already knows what needs to be done. Dante emphasizes Francis' theologico-political triumph; Giotto tells the story of a reconciliation between the Order and the Church, one that, in historical reality, was quite problematic. What is lacking in both, but especially in Dante, is Francis the *mystic*.

> α. Perhaps there was no role for Francis' brand of mysticism in Dante's idea of Empire. We have only what we love without possessing it, but there is also what we *use* without possessing it, such as the food we eat and the water we drink. The *Canticle of the Sun* tells us to love sister water, but it does not say how drinking water that is not "ours" puts us in relation with the law. According to Peter John Olivi, the

"poor use" (*usus pauper*) of what the Brother needs to keep himself alive does not fall within the jurisdiction of the law. Such *abdicatio iuris*, renunciation of the law, *de facto* puts the Brother outside the law—a position that was unacceptable to the Church. In his study on the juridical implications of Franciscan poverty, Agamben has asked, "But what is a life outside the law, if it is defined as that form of life which makes use of things without ever appropriating them? And what is use if one ceases to define it solely negatively with respect to ownership?"[10] It seems that neither the Church, nor the Order, and not even modern jurisprudence, has ever given a convincing answer to that question. Maybe it was that threshold of uncertainty between law and life that prevented Dante from fully embracing Franciscan mysticism. Life outside the law, no matter how sanctified, does not make you a citizen, neither on Earth nor in the Heavenly Jerusalem, which for Dante is essentially a Heavenly Rome. It does not make you a Roman, and you must be Roman if you want to live in Dante's Heaven, "the Rome in which Christ is / Roman." ("quella Roma onde Cristo è romano," *Purg.* XXXII, 102)

A Sin against Aristotle

For Cacciari, there is no doubt that Dante's Ulysses is a sinner and somehow deserves the place in Hell that the poet assigns to him. To determine which sin he committed, however, requires an endless analysis. Ulysses' thirst for knowledge is *lustfulness*, as the patristic literature knew well, but is this the only interpretation at our disposal? If that were the case, Ulysses would be merely a deceiver. But there is *virtue* in Ulysses' journey as there is *virtue* in Dante's journey. They are both all-questioning minds, they both think alike. Besides, why should pagan Ulysses care for the Fathers of the Church? Ulysses' journey is not intentionally blasphemous. How can his speech be fraudulent?

Was Ulysses too proud? Perhaps he was, but then he would not belong to the circle of fraudulent counselors. And his speech is melancholic, too, it is the confession of an old man. With his speech on knowledge, Ulysses deceives his sailors only indirectly, as a consequence, because, first and foremost, he deceives himself. His sin is a matter of failed *rationalism*. He is in *error*, and an error of the intellect always carries ethical and political consequences. Cacciari suggests looking at *Convivio* III, 15—Dante's theory of desire—for an answer ("And so human desire is proportioned in this life to the knowledge which we can have here, and does not go past that point except by an error which is outside the intention of nature."[11]) Natural desire is commensurate to the desirer—every being strives according to its own finality, *entelechia*. Knowledge develops in stages, from one goal to the next. When the goal pertaining to a specific desire is reached, *that* desire is completely satisfied, and *therefore* it can renew itself. Desire lacks nothing except its own satisfaction, which—contrary to what every *esprit fort* of modernity would admit—may indeed be achieved. If the journey of knowledge goes from satisfaction to satisfaction, then Ulysses' infinite longing is guilty of a radical errancy from the Aristotelian reading in the *Convivio*. Ulysses did not misinterpret the fathers of the Church, he misunderstood the *Convivio*, which means that he misunderstood Aristotle. Sure, Ulysses is the *letter* of Aristotelianism and scientific endeavor, but he is not the *spirit*. To that extent, he was a fraudulent counselor to himself, which may be the ultimate *hybris* indeed.

Infinite longing is not Aristotelian science. *Radical* Aristotelianism, however, is another matter. Radical Aristotelianism, which Dante encountered and by which, to a certain extent, he was seduced, was the Faustian pact of the Middle Ages, the belief that human intellect would have no limits whatsoever and could penetrate the archetypes, the eternal ideas inside God's mind—or even the eternal ideas *outside* of God's mind, as autonomous entities.[12] In Cacciari's *addendum* to his Ulysses chapter, Farinata's atheism, and perhaps Guido Cavalcanti's, is the foreboding of Ulysses' philosophical error. Did Guido, the *absent* Guido, whose fate in the afterlife is tragically unknown, subordinate revelation to intellect? Or did he reject revelation altogether? The shadow of Cavalcanti looms very large everywhere in the *Comedy*, and it may cover Ulysses as well. For both Guido and Ulysses, because of their *hybris*, betray Aristotle.

Obviously, Ulysses is not an Averroist. He does not syllogize; rather, he is a magician who conjures up an "unpeopled world" before his eyes and the eyes of his comrades. But science without a moral impulse toward the Good is worthless in Dante's world, and the science of the Good is Politics. In Dante, there is no will-to-know that can be abstracted from the political dimension. There is no scientific "autonomy" in Dante's universe. Yet Ulysses moves autonomously, without being part of a bigger plan. His will-to-know is not directed toward an increase in human happiness. It is not even "utilitarian"; it is utterly unpolitical.[13] He separates theory from practice as if man were not a political animal. He is a king; he is supposed to take care of himself and his associates, of his wife, of his son and father, *as a king*; to make *polis*, to rule, to do good (what Aeneas did, what Emperor Harry VII, hopefully, will do), or at least acknowledge the primacy of moral philosophy over knowledge for the sake of knowledge.

Because Ulysses is to a certain extent a *figure* of Guido (and, conversely, Guido is a figure of Ulysses), in the Addendum Cacciari briefly addresses the *vexatissima quaestio* of *Inferno* X, using Enrico Malato and Antonino Pagliaro as guides. Who is the person whom "perhaps . . . your Guido did disdain" ("forse cui Guido vostro ebbe a disdegno," *Inf.* X, 64)? According to Malato, the *cui* refers to Virgil. In Pagliaro's interpretation, the *cui* refers to Beatrice. It goes without saying that Guido would not like to be "guided" by anyone. But here the issue is not Virgil as guide but rather the nature of love, or love-passion. For Dante, we can control love-passion insofar as we have free will, whereas for Guido, we cannot. Cacciari suggests that perhaps the ambiguity of the *cui* is intentional. In that particular circumstance, Dante did not want to choose between Virgil and Beatrice, for the entire premise of the *Comedy* is that the former's teaching merges into the other's. But if there is ambiguity in Dante, it must have a purpose. One of Cacciari's favorite *tropoi* is that the origin is the most important part (*potissima pars*, in his favorite expression) of every single thing. If the beginning of love (as Francesca can attest) is entirely accidental, then how can love be controlled by free will and determination? It does not make much difference here that, to Guido, love is an "accident" ("un accidente," *Donna me prega*, 2) and, to Dante, an "accident in substance" ("uno accidente in sustanzia," *Vita nuova* XXV, 1).[14] The point has great theoretical, physiological, and ethical relevance, but it is not for Virgil to decide. On the matter of love, Virgil must remain silent and pass the baton to Beatrice, and this Guido could not accept. But Dante's ambiguity (he must keep them both, Virgil and Beatrice, without being too explicit about it) may very well be the last gesture of friendship he makes to his friend.

> β. In a way, Ulysses is the modern scholar who asks about the nature of entities but not about the essence of Being. He is the embodiment of the scientist who, in Heidegger's parlance,

"does not think." Otherwise said, the Hollywood version of Ulysses' speech is the well-known line from *Deliverance* (dir. John Boorman, 1972): "Why do you want to mess around with that river?" "*Because it's there*." But there is more: Ulysses *overhears* himself when he speaks, like a Shakespeare character who is seduced by his own words. And he falls prey to cognitive dissonance. He "knows" that what he says is deceitful, yet he believes it. It is not just his sin; this is his *tragedy* (he may be the only character in the *Comedy* who is tragic in the classical sense). Or better, his tragedy is that he has no goal. "Ulysses conceives the path of knowledge as a desiring that is never fulfilled," Cacciari says. He is not moved by *eros*; he is moved by *pothos*, by an indescribable, vague nostalgia for something that shines in the distance and can never be reached. The paradox is that Dante, by sentencing Ulysses' desire to damnation, makes us long for the same desire. Dante gives shape to *modern* desire—infinite desire, that is—the desire that will take hold of Faust and Manfred, the infinite desire theorized by Leopardi, Baudelaire, Wagner, Freud, and ultimately Lacan and Deleuze. The first infinite desire that we encounter in the *Divine Comedy* is Francesca's, "that, as you see, it has not left me yet" ("che, come vedi, ancora non m'abbandona," *Inf.* V, 105). But Francesca's desire has an object, Paolo. An object both present and eternally out of reach, but still an ideal goal. Ulysses' infinite desire, on the contrary, is bad infinity, mere accumulation of steps toward something that he cannot define. The Greeks would have punished him as well as the Fathers of the Church, yet we *modern* readers root for Ulysses because we are the spiritual heirs of Milton's Satan and of Tristan and Isolde.[15] Ulysses wants to know everything except what the Delphian oracle would command him to know, namely, himself. When Coleridge, in *Self-Knowledge*, asks, "Say, canst thou make thyself?—Learn first that trade" and ends with "Ignore thyself, and strive to know thy God!," he is updating Dante's Ulyssian spirit (to the extent that Ulysses' God is his desire, that is). Yes, there is no doubt that Dante would never acknowledge such an "irrational" God, but is Dante really that different from his Ulysses? Dante sets up his self-absolution by building the walls of God around himself, but you cannot invent Ulysses, *that* Ulysses, if he is not inside you. The *Divine Comedy* is the narrative of how Dante knew himself, yet even if we did not believe a single word he says, his poetic power would still be intact. And yet, because Ulysses not only misses Aristotelianism, but situates himself completely *outside* of it, he bursts out from the pages of the Middle Ages with irrepressible force. He does not belong in the *Divine Comedy*, and that is his scandal. His virtue and his sins are incomprehensible within the same boundaries that Dante erected around his poem and his journey. Ulysses was born from the lines of the poem to be the anti-poem, and the anti-Dante for whom Dante the poet feels the strongest *desire*. There is no question that Dante must defend himself from Ulysses, who may destroy the careful architecture of the poem just by wandering around, leaving behind everything and everyone he meets instead of carefully building up his ladder to salvation. *Ulysses does not want to be saved; he wouldn't even know what that means.* The only way Dante can prevent Ulysses from taking over the poem is to make the sea close upon him.

The Politics of Heaven

The *Divine Comedy* is truth, fiction, allegory, prophecy, and many other things. In the first of his three-part introduction to *Paradiso* (chapters 3, 4, and 5), Cacciari suggests adding *Erlebnis* to the list, a fully lived-through *experience*, not "biographical" but definitely "autobiographical." The experience of pilgrimage, that is. A pilgrimage toward a conversion-transformation that does not leave the world behind, and especially not the status of "citizen," which must be maintained on Earth as well as in Heaven. Being in Paradise means to be a citizen of Paradise, endowed with heavenly rights and duties. Dante's Paradise is *polis*, it is *civitas*, which means that there is politics in Paradise, because Paradise has a future, tied to the politics of Earth. Not even Beatrice, whose smile infinitely surpasses earthly beauty, can forget the events unfolding on Earth.

The conclusion of the pilgrimage of all souls, of which Dante's is the *exemplum*, will come at the end of time when man *touches God*, when the light of the blessed, as Solomon says, becomes stronger in the "glorified and sanctified" flesh ("gloriosa e santa," *Par.* XIV, 43) and man, in Cacciari's expression, is finally *capax Dei* (capable of God). Stronger than allegory, stronger than analogy, this is Dante's lived-through experience—the process of the sensible perception becoming *aesthesis Theia*, divine perception—of which every soul is a *sign* ("as a sign for you," "per far segno," *Par*. IV, 37–39)—a sign of the perfect joy to come. (The term "sign" has strong resonance in Cacciari's works; it can be understood as pure *index*, without symbolical and allegorical superstructures, and therefore much more direct and effectual.)

Signs of the future can be perceived on earth as well; they can be *seen*, because Paradise is the exalted mirror of the theo-drama unfolding on Earth, "the little threshing floor / that so incites our savagery" ("l'aiuola che ci fa tanto feroci," *Par*. XXII, 150). In fact, Paradise is the only place where human history can be properly understood, and whence one returns and *speaks plainly*. But how to reconcile the realm of Light, where the prophecy is spotless, and the grim reality of earthly politics? The urge to relate the vision becomes a problem of language. The vision is not incomplete; speech is. How to articulate, therefore, the *topos* of ineffability? If there is mysticism in Dante, it does not reach the point where poetry is abandoned or loses efficacy. On the contrary, the urge to make the ineffable effable is the essence of poetry. The more Dante says he cannot say, the more precise his lines are. There is no "discourse" of the final vision, but it is possible to put it into poetry. Ineffability is the impossibility of rational demonstration, *not* a failure of language. This is also where the *Divine Comedy* meets *De vulgari eloquentia*, whose importance is, to Cacciari, comparable to any other work by Dante (chapter 6). Perhaps Dante's only prophecy that was truly fulfilled is that common speech is the speech of the future.

While Heaven waits for the world to mend its ways, for the sensible to become divine, and for the final union of bodies and souls, Aristotle's political gaze joins the Neoplatonic emanation of light from the Light, and the connection between the two gives the pilgrim the strength to reflect what he sees. Imagination may fail Dante, or so he says, but his vision of the Light does not. Because God's light is physical, and it is in fact the same thing as God, Cacciari draws a "stellar" comparison between Dante and Byzantine theologian Gregory Palamas (1296–1359), a contemporary of Dante for whom poetry would have been a mere distraction but who shared with Dante the belief in the divine Light as uncreated, immaterial, sensible, and not separable from God.

However, whether Light is God or God's garment ("The Lord wraps himself in light as with a garment," Psalm 104), Love is His substance, and Love is *excessus*, Love cannot rest; it wants to create, to expand, to conquer. God appreciates the meek but is won over by those who carry the "violence of love" in them. Cacciari's philosophy has always been, by and large, a theory of the possible. There is no other category that he has investigated so deeply in his theoretical works, and with reverberations in his political philosophy. It is on the basis of his meditations on potentiality and the possible that he advances his final argument. Might the negative eschatology of *Inferno* ever give way to the *possibility* that God *might be* won over by the determination of His creatures who are violently in love with Him, to the point that He decides to put an end to the eternal damnation of the sinners? Wouldn't it be *possible* that Dante has considered such *possibility* and has left us some clues, allowing us at least the chance to formulate the thought? "In sum, that in God may live a hope for our salvation so powerful, so violent, that He himself might wish to be vanquished by it."[16]

γ. That God's light was physical, sensible, and therefore a *body*, was not a problem for the mystics, nor was it for Dante, but it was a nightmare for the theologians, because the book of Genesis does not say that God is light, it says that God *created* light, and by stating that God is light you say that God is at the same time creator and the creature. Beginning with Pseudo-Dionysius the Areopagite (whose angelology Dante follows in *Par.* XXVIII and XXIX), various authors postulated a dark light, co-substantial with God and invisible to God's creatures until it is revealed in the end time—or, in some passages by Palamas, a dark cloud that surrounds God and makes it unknowable to man. The question has ramifications that are too complex to be addressed here.[17] However, imagination and memory fail to report the final vision because they need a *distensio temporis*, but the enjoyment of the vision does not suffer because of that. In fact, we might say using contemporary jargon, enjoyment is possible precisely because it happens outside of time and speech, in an instant that is not related to either past or future—otherwise it would be caught in the rational language and it would be unsayable. The enjoyment of the final vision is the speechless *symbolon* that puts an end to the semiotic chain.

Toward a European Empire?

Is Dante a serious political prophet? And does he speak *to us* in that fashion? Of course, Cacciari does not see any "autonomy of the political" in Dante, but a relative, pragmatic autonomy may not be foreign to Dante's political thinking. The two Suns (Papacy and Empire) must illuminate, not just tolerate, each other. In fact, they *must* wish the other to be autonomous. Like Christ, who is man and God, they are one city in two persons. The universal mission of the Church needs the Empire (this was true for the early Christians as well, who did not want the dissolution of the Empire that persecuted them—a point that Cacciari stresses in *Europe and Empire*), and the Empire finds its efficient and final cause in the universalism of the Church. To maintain their relation, the two Suns must fear and hold back each other, be each other's *katechon*, the "withholding power" of Thessalonians 2:6–7.[18] Peace is possible only if the two powers are never fully at peace, never in the same bed. They must "reform" themselves autonomously, but they are connected in their autonomy. If one dies, the other dies too. That is why the Christians need dual citizenship—in the Eternal Rome and the Heavenly City. The Holy Roman Empire cannot subsist if Christ himself is not Roman (*Purg.* XXXII, 102–103). Christ's gospel is a message of salvation in Heaven and, at the same time, the announcement of an Empire that must be as lasting as the Earth will be.

From this point of view, it seems that modernity has nothing to learn from Dante's political thought. In Dante, there is no State (the Empire is the negation of the State) and no *political realism* to speak of. Is Dante, then, hopelessly unpolitical? Is this the *drama* of the *Monarchia*? According to Cacciari, we might say that Dante sees in the Empire the actualization of the Aristotelian Possible Intellect that belongs to everyone and no one in particular and ignores artificial boundaries. However (and to counterbalance every suspicion of explicit heterodoxy), Dante knows that in the end every actualization of power must be contradicted by eschatology, which ignores the human limitation of the Empire.

There is no emphasis in Dante on the *officium*, on the bureaucratic hierarchy of who does what within the structures of the Church and Empire. The elimination of enmity is what matters to him, and not just between the two Suns but between the two Cities as well. In this respect, Dante does not follow Augustine, who was the harshest critic of the Roman Empire. In Dante, the Roman Empire is the eternal model that always fails yet cannot be replaced. The *civitas Dei* does not and must not annihilate the *civitas hominis*. To Cacciari, this is where Dante is, perhaps, "modern." Because the Empire is neither a state nor a principate, it exists only for the Common Good (there is no other reason for the Empire to subsists), which is in fact a "modern" notion. When the fiction of the Common Good vanishes, the Empire crumbles.

Dante's politics is obviously not based on a social contract, nor is it a defense mechanism set up against human wickedness. Aristotle taught him that we are political animals, and politics is in our nature as much as it is in the divine will. Contrary to the well-known opinion by Passerin d'Entrèves, to whom *Monarchia* was an aberration and the *Divine Comedy* a return to the right path, Cacciari's thesis is that not only does the *Commedia* not contradict the *Monarchia*, it goes further in the same direction.[19] Following a different chronology from Passerin d'Entrèves', Cacciari tends to believe that the *Monarchia* was completed approximately when Dante was approaching the final cantos of the *Purgatorio*. Being crowned by Virgil (*Purg.* XXVII, 142) is Dante's ultimate achievement on Earth as both a poet and a philosopher. But it is just an *earthly* beatitude. To begin the *real* journey toward transhumanizing, repentance and violent conversion are necessary. Such a scenario is totally absent from the *Monarchia*, and it is in fact the next step after the *Monarchia*. Sin has broken the political order of the universe, not just the moral and theological one. To live in the perfect city, it is necessary that the citizens convert, disposing of greed, envy, and other sins, yet the city is *impotent* to convert. The *Monarchia* is not oblivious to that, but in the final cantos of the *Purgatorio* the issue is no longer politics or the Unpolitical. What is necessary (we might say) is a metapolitics of the Empire, an "event" (such as the conversion) that transcends the politics of the Empire, because the Empire is *not just a political institution*.[20] In a way, therefore, Beatrice is the real conclusion to the *Monarchia*. She is the perfect citizen of the metapolitical Empire and, in the Earthly Paradise, the perfect figure of the Empress who stands for the all-powerful Emperor (symbolized by the Griffin).

Nostalgia for the Empire is key to Dante's metapolitics, but it is a nostalgia for a *future* Empire. We must look at both sides of the issue. On the one hand, the *Commedia* does not correct the *Monarchia*'s assumption that the crucifixion of Christ was "just." It had to be, or else Jesus' sacrifice would fall under the rubric of mere human injustice. What makes Jesus' death divine is the tragic paradox at play (tragic, we might say, in a Greek sense that Dante did not know, like Socrates who was sentenced to death by the Athenian democracy and not by a tyrant). Jesus is the tragic victim of the *highest justice*—which implies that the justice of the Empire collaborates with divine justice and fails where it is supposed to fail, at the gates of metapolitics. If Jesus were not God, his death would be justice done without a remainder, but here the remainder is what counts. The Empire that Dante has in mind, however, and this is Cacciari's strong belief, is *not* like the Roman Empire. It is a federation of nations, not a superstate. And a federation of languages too, of vernaculars that must communicate with each other. Just like individuals must convert, nations must convert as well, and overcome their selfishness. Such Empire is much less hegemonical than the State and Dante, a reactionary if compared to Marsilius of Padua (the modern theorist of the State), is looking forward to a European Empire in which every nation maintains its individuality and the Empire is the guardian of their differences.

On the other hand, Cacciari's very generous, even "liberal" interpretation of the *Monarchia* does not go so far as to justify Dante's claim that the Romans had jurisdiction over all mankind and the divine right to subjugate the whole world (*Mon*. II, xi, 5, 7). In fact, Cacciari tends to agree with Dominican Friar Guido Vernani of Rimini—the fierce, "papalist" author of *De reprobatio Monarchie* (1329)—that in his Roman fury, Dante may have gone too far.[21]

German Dante

The final two chapters (8 and 9) deal with Dante's reception in Germany and Schelling's interpretation of Dante. From Goethe to Nietzsche, and from Simmel to Benjamin, Dante is a monumental figure that the German writers and thinkers have always approached with caution. It is paradoxical that the champions of German obscurity (the charge against German literature raised by generations of Italian literati) find Dante too obscure. Only Stefan George—who might have been a reactionary on many accounts but dreamed of a Europe that would include the Mediterranean world together with the German and French heritage—seemed willing to accept fully Dante's challenge, and produced a partial translation of the *Commedia* that stands as a pinnacle of twentieth century German poetry.

Ahead of George, Schelling was the only one who understood Dante as a prophet and, specifically, a prophet of *myth*. Beginning with *On Dante in Relation to Philosophy* (1803), Schelling outlines his vision of Dante as a teller of myths that are facts, because they are critical to the life of an entire people (Friedrich Schlegel, too, stresses Dante's narrative power and claims that the *Comedy* is a real "novel"). Dante is the model of the poet-teacher whose task is to create new, *rational* myths, where art and religion are combined. Dante's mythopoetic imagination is not bound by Fichtean duty or Hegelian allegory. It does not have to transcend itself. According to Schelling, it is a "symbol" the way Goethe intended it in his *Maxim* no. 752, a "live and immediate revelation of the unfathomable."[22]

But Schelling is unthinkable without Spinoza, and Dante and Spinoza would never get along. Cacciari, however, argues that because Spinoza's *amor dei intellectualis* must reside within Substance, or else it would only be accidental (and certainly not, we may add, an "accidente in sustanzia"), maybe to Schelling the freedom of Dante's transhumanizing—of "surpassing" oneself—is rooted in Substance itself, and therefore in Substance's own freedom. In Spinoza, reason and love have no place within the necessity and eternity of Substance. In Dante, however, things are different; Dante gives us the nonaccidentality of the singular, the eternity of the individual, and, with it, a model for the relationship between art, religion, philosophy, and the science of nature. If Substance is a concrete totality, then poetry, and Dante's poetry in particular, is the discipline that pierces though it, seeing the infinite in the finite, the discipline of nature in act, the conflict between gravity and light, and the harmony between their "spirits."[23] In a way, it is precisely along these lines that we still read Dante even when we cannot but disagree with him, and it will be along these lines that we will keep on reading him.

One

Double Portrait

Saint Francis of Assisi in Dante and Giotto

I

Between the great Assisi frescoes, framed by the most exquisite, mosaic-adorned, Cosmatesque spiral columns (true *stanzas* of illustrious vernacular) and the *laisses* of the *Canticle of Creatures*—a Hymn whose "assonanced prose"[1] radiates free of any theological architecture—there unfolds the drama of a century, marked by the contradictory establishment of the new Franciscan Order (a paradoxical Order, as its founder never intended there to be one) amid violent lacerations, eschatological promises, crude disenchantments, and harsh confrontations with the other "brothers," themselves mendicants and preachers, of the Dominican flock. The scene is the grandiose one of the showdowns between "the two suns" (Papacy and Empire) which betokens, in the sunset of both, the end of the dream of the Christian Republic (*respublica christiana*), and the first, irreversible installation of the power of the state—the new "mortal god" who does not recognize a superior (*superiorem non recognoscens*) and is the emperor of his kingdom (*rex est imperator in regnum suum*). Over the next centuries, no crusade will be able to impose an interval of peace to the "Christian" states. The great universalist ideal of the reduction to oneness (*ordinatio ad unum*) lies in tatters. The fall of Acre, two centuries after the conquest of Jerusalem, precedes by a mere few years the Assisi fresco about the Saint preaching to the Sultan. And Francis, too, must rush back from the Holy Land because the new, real war is now a *civil* war raging *within* the Christian family—in fact, within his own Franciscan family.

Francis is truly the harbinger (*figura futuri*) of this epoch.² He incarnates it both in his personal itinerary and in the way he foreshadows the outcome of the tensions and disagreements he experiences in his unheard-of attempt to harmonize the heart of a Christocentric mysticism (founded on the unvarnished, *sine glossa* imitation of the Model) with the awareness of a bond—indestructible and transcending any historical contingency—between *communion*, eucharistic participation,³ and Historical Church: *this* Church, of necessity only "approximable" to the spiritual one—a bond that compels one to reject any heretical temptations. This is truly the most arduous way; this is Calvary. All in all, how much easier, how much more rational, even, it would have been to be one's own party, to rise against any compromise. And how much more consistent, too, with that thirst for martyrdom that certainly burns inside Francis. Yet, he was not come to judge, but to preach the Word, in communion with all people, fleeing every separateness with the same tenacity with which others fled the world; he was come to call on everyone to make a crucial change in their life and will. Because without a will, knowledge cannot lead anywhere; it cannot *make* anything. Precisely this sense of the Franciscan *metanoia*, the *overturning of values* that it entails—starting with the meaning that *metanoia* assumes here, whereby the mind (*nous*) renounces any preeminence, empties itself of any abstraction and realizes itself in *doing* (*operari*)—is the spirit that hovers everywhere in the soul of the craftsmen of the new artistic languages.⁴ The extraordinary kind of sainthood that it expresses lives in those who are *makers* (*poietes*), in the *poets* (*poiein*) to whom a new form of love dictates to brave uncharted waters. And the navigation follows essentially one path: to represent the itinerary of the mind to God as a *historical narrative*; to express it in its temporal and perspectival depth, in its real environment; to paint the shadow that the soul casts as it goes, the traits and colors of its *complexion*—in sum: to tell of the travels/travails that everyone's *ego* must go through in order to ascend "to the divine . . . / from the human, to eternity / from time, and to a people just and sane / from Florence" ("al divino da l'umano, / a l'etterno dal tempo . . . e di Fiorenza in popol giusto e sano," *Par.* XXXI, 37–39).⁵

This story must be told to everyone, must be understood by everyone, but in forms so fully harmonized as to be able to compete with any "grammar." The classical style is authoritative only insofar as it is the principle of measure and order, not as a norm that sets unpassable limits; it is our *comedy* that we must tell today (and bring to a good end, if grace assists), not the "high tragedy" (the *Aeneid*) of "my duke" (Virgil) (*Inf.* XX, 113). "For *I* am not Aeneas, am not Paul"—remonstrates Dante ("Io non Enëa, io non Paulo sono," *Inf.*, II, 32). But is he really any less? Is it really any less *sacred* to represent the human figure in the act of *transcending* itself here-and-now, of *transhumanizing*, without it losing, even for an instant, its historical determinateness, its *proper name*? It is no longer the mere allegorical sense that speaks. Francis is a symbol of his own being there, exactly as Jesus was, whom Francis seeks to imitate. The hieratic images of the resurrected body (one with the idea) were convulsed ever since the appearance of that early, poorly realized image of Saint Francis that someone just scratched up on the bare wall of the "holy grotto" in Subiaco. The same starkly realistic traits return in Francis' portrait on wood panel attributed to Cimabue, now at the Museo di Santa Maria degli Angeli (Assisi), and then in the face of Saint Francis in Cimabue's *Madonna Enthroned with the Child, St. Francis and Four Angels*, in the lower church. The Byzantine crucifix ("calcified Greek style of the East," as Roberto Longhi once defined it) is transfigured in Francis' suffering Jesus (*Jesus patibilis*), whose revolutionary icon will go on to dominate the century, reaching its triumph in Cimabue's grandiose *requiem* located in the transept of the upper church of San Francesco in Assisi.

The *art workshop* is in Assisi. It is there that the innovators (*novatores*) from Rome and Tuscany, both masters and apprentices, congregate and react to each other's input: Pietro Cavallini, who has already frescoed a Saint Francis Cycle in the church of the Order in Rome, Jacopo Torriti, Cimabue, and, later, Giotto, and their studios. So much philology enamored with "genius," hunting for "autographs"![6] But in fact, it was rather the Franciscan *community* that was at work there—within the very same profound contrasts that marked its existence. Different hands and different intentions converged into one *project*: to impose the face of a *proximate* figure of sanctity who, by moving closer to us, might dominate us with its energy—as opposed to eternally "watching over" us in contemplative prayer. A sanctity, then, representable only through its *stories*, where representation itself becomes a *testimony* to their veracity. Hence the necessity to arrange everything in a manner so similar to the original that, in Boccaccio's words, "had the appearance, not of a reproduction, but of the thing itself" (*Dec.* VI, 5).[7] The realism of representation must certify the reality of the event represented. The *what is* (*quid est*), object and question of the Oriental icon, gives way to the *who is* (*quis est*). Only within the finitude of the creature, within the shadows of its space-time, will light become visible. And, finally, we wonder: In this great workshop of the whole art of Europe, should we not also hearken to the word of Dante? Can the Francis of the double church of Assisi be understood *in analogy* with the Francis of Dante?

If Giotto was—as seems hard to dispute, beyond the troubled question of attribution—both the orchestra conductor and, at least, one of the main interpreters of the Franciscan *Stories* in the upper basilica, then the comparison should be between *the Two*: Dante and Giotto. Is such a comparison possible? Giotto: an artist cherished as much by the courts (especially the papal court, which commissioned him to paint the Triptych destined to glorify the tomb of the very same Apostle in Rome) as by the emerging financiers and bourgeois—that is, precisely by those "newcomers to the city" ("gente nuova") whose "quick gains" ("subiti guadagni") generate "excess and arrogance" ("orgoglio e dismisura," *Inf*. XVI, 73–74), and whose hypocrisy in terms of faith appears scandalous to the spiritual-minded. Dante: born in a very different social milieu, endowed with a political passion blended with a strong drive to knowledge (a drive always on the verge of being transfigured into mystical ascesis), nowhere at home but in his own grandiose, nostalgic, unrealizable projects, and everywhere at loggerheads with his era and its false gods. Their life events and personalities have little in common.[8] Yet, indubitable is the affinity of the *matrix language*—and of Francis as a profound, essential *analogue*, allowing us to understand what unites and separates them.

Dante himself is the first witness of this affinity of destinies. The confidence in one's worth and the "great . . . desire for eminence" ("per lo gran disio / de l'eccellenza," *Purg*. XI, 86–87) must certainly not lead to arrogance, even less in Dante's times, when glory so briefly "green endures upon the peak" ("com' poco verde in su la cima dura," *Purg*. XI, 92); and yet, the fame of the man who took the field from Cimabue (*Purg*. XI, 94–95) is by no means "empty glory" ("vana gloria," *Purg*. XI, 91). And equally not "empty" will be the glory of Dante, destined to "chase . . . out of the nest" ("l'uno e l'altro caccerà del nido," *Purg*. XI, 99) both Guido Guinizzelli, called *maximus* in *De vulgari eloquentia*, and Guido Cavalcanti, who, victorious over the former in the "glory of our tongue" ("la gloria de la lingua," *Purg*. XI, 97), perhaps "disdained" being *accompanied*—as Dante would be—on his ultimate adventure of language and intellect.⁹ Indeed, in this XI canto of *Purgatorio*, Dante appears to be fully cognizant of the historical complementarity of these two processes. One cannot understand the import of the first without relating it to the second. Did the poet directly know the painter's works? Judging from his rigorous assessment of them, it appears more than likely that he did. In his *Comment*, Benvenuto da Imola narrates that Dante had probably visited the masterpiece commissioned from Giotto by Enrico Scrovegni for his family tomb at Padua, perhaps overcoming the revulsion for that race of usurers, represented in the *Inferno* by Reginaldo, Enrico's father, caught in a gesture typical of the doomed in the great Judgment scenes: "At this he slewed his mouth, and then he stuck / his tongue out, like an ox that licks its nose" ("Qui distorse la bocca e di fuor trasse / la lingua, come bue che 'l naso lecchi," *Inf.* XVI, 73–74).¹⁰ Be that as it may, the mention of Cimabue immediately evokes the image of Assisi. That is where the passing of the baton occurs. That is where the young painter wrests "the glory of our tongue" from the affirmed master, whose lesson nonetheless he treasures, just as he treasures, perhaps to an even greater degree, the lesson of the Roman painters. (When we speak of "tongue," of course, we also mean it in a properly technical sense: indeed, Dante lets his competence in painting shine through in quite a few passages of his *Divine Comedy*.) And because it happens to be also the land of Francis, Assisi is clearly where the encounter must needs take place. Dante imagines his *not* "wild flight" ("folle volo," *Inf.* XXVI, 125) to take place in 1300, year of the Jubilee. In the imminence of the great event, Assisi was the home of Giotto's workshop—and the fame of the artist, and of his undertaking, must have been considerable, not only among contemporary painters. Is Dante already thinking of *his* Francis, exalting the artist who seems to him to operate at the same level of greatness as himself? In any case, the confrontation with Franciscan spirituality is certainly crucial both to the *Comedy*'s structural organization and to the formation of the language of the Assisi cycle. Indeed, it seems to me that the "novelty" of Dante's masterpiece (in particular, of the "theology" of the *Paradiso*) with respect to his other works lies precisely in the figure of Francis. By marking a departure from any philosophical presumption (though certainly not from philosophy!), Francis' humility shows Dante how the "divine way" is distant from the "school" he has followed ("quella scuola / ch'hai seguitata," *Purg.* XXXIII, 85–86). If there is any change between the *Monarchia* and the *Paradiso*—as indeed there is, at least in the overall tone—such change manifests itself under the sign of Francis.

Just as decisive is the saint's role in the formation of the idiom of the Assisi cycle. The "double portrait" of Giotto and Dante of which Giovanni Villani speaks, which Giotto himself is said to have painted on the wall of the Palazzo Pubblico, might well be a humanistic legend about the illustrious birth of Florence-Athens. Nonetheless, trying to figure out its meaning is the least a hermeneutics worthy of its name can do. It is neither a Dantean portrait of Giotto, nor vice versa. Rather, both Giotto and Dante find themselves mirrored in their own portrait of Francis. And precisely from their different interpretation the saint emerges who has been *traditus* ("delivered" but also "betrayed"), whose figure, inexorably and by intrinsic necessity, has been "delivered" to the history of its interpretations. By means of the same analogy (*per figuram*), we may venture this conclusion: in nothing is Francis more profoundly an *imitation* of Christ than in his being "betrayed."

II

Francis' iconography over the thirteenth century has been amply documented.[11] From the earliest effigy in Subiaco all the way to the great midcentury panels in Santa Croce, as well as the ones by Master of Lucca in Pistoia, a steady proliferation of images of the Saint accompany the "miraculous" development of the Order. Bonaventure's *Legenda maior* will then go on to define the iconographical canon, yet without altering its fundamental structure: the figure of the Friar Minor stands out as the axis of representation, and his *historiae* spring up around him. It is no longer the icon of the already transhumanized Model, whose life, even when remembered, is regarded as fully miraculous, but rather the icon of the Saint who narrates his own life: an image, therefore, that calls for maximum *proximity* to the *profane*. For Francis, to preach is no other than to *become* proximate. This goes for his image, too, which shatters any sacralizing aura to bear witness first and foremost to the *real life* of everything it represents. This includes the *stigmata*, the *last seal* that the Saint received *directly* from Christ—an "episode" that comes gradually almost to replace the more traditional depiction of the Saint standing in the act of blessing. The gift of the stigmata—culmination of evangelical perfection, of a perfect *imitation*—must look just as real and indubitable as the famous historical scenes (e.g., Francis giving up his possessions before the people of Assisi, meeting Pope Innocent III, or creating the nativity scene in Greccio), and concentrate in itself the whole significance of his life. No longer one event among many, however important, but rather *the* Event—as in the great Louvre panel, closely related to the Assisi fresco; the Event whereby the Lover transforms into the Beloved. Francis' wounds are *painted* by God, says Bonaventure.[12] But how is this divine representation being imagined by Giotto, and by Dante?

Dante's praise of Francis stands out in a tangle of cantos, in which the most extraordinary play of symmetries, similes, comparisons, metaphors, and analogies gives rise to a great *symphonic* form unparalleled, perhaps, even by the conclusive cantos of the *Commedia*. Here Dante paints the *summa* of his notion of catholicity as harmony of opposites, as community of *destiny* even more than of provenance, as harmony of difficult beauty between perfectly distinct limbs, each in its own grace (*charisma*), and for this reason united in Purpose. In perfect analogy with the notion of Empire, which can only have value if constituted out of the singular nations (*ex nationibus*)—as opposed to an authoritarian imposition on individual organisms—the choir of the wise Catholics expresses the polyphony which is the music of all Paradise, triumphant over the infernal clashing and shrieking (turning icy in the end), but also over the wistful troubadour notes Casella evokes on the shores of Purgatory.

Thus, we find Dante's apotheosis of Francis inserted within the formidable theological-historical-philosophical construct of the Heaven of the Sun, home of the wise spirits—a paradoxical location for the "unlearned" (*indoctus*), evangelical "beggar" (*ptochos*). Except that, here, it is not the ignorant who is exalted into wisdom, but rather the wise who "humiliate" themselves, upon recognizing Francis' *madness* as true, higher wisdom. The great Master of Paris himself, Thomas Aquinas, bows to the *madness of the cross* preached in Assisi. "In sorrow we see Paris, that has destroyed Assisi," wails Jacopone da Todi,[13] voicing once again the original, profound distrust of any form of *lust for knowledge*. But now Dante wants to illustrate the *movement*, one might almost say the *pilgrimage*, that the theo-*logical* discourse (the most arduous) can make—without betraying itself, but, on the contrary, revealing its intimate nature—toward the "East" that is Assisi. This is the essential narrative, the cornerstone of *Paradiso* X through XIII. The play of mirrors between Saint Thomas Aquinas and Bonaventure, between Dominican doctrine and Franciscan *caritas*, is asymmetrical. Indeed, in his praise of Dominic, which chivalrously responds to Thomas' previous praise of Francis (an "exchange" meant to signal the end of ponderous ancient disputes, and toward which both had striven, with dubious results), Bonaventure wishes, in his turn, to show that there is no contradiction between ardent faith and thirst for knowledge—between the *charismata* of the founding Fathers. Yet, the terms he technically employs to express the glory of Dominic indicate a precise hierarchical order whereby Francis is *first* among equals.

Francis' preeminence is made evident by the fact that it is Thomas himself who sings his praises. Thomas is unquestionably the first of the two guides of the crowns of blessed souls who, as festive women, greet the poet with singing and dancing. He is the one who opens and closes this grandiose episode. He is the one who answers Dante's queries. And that the crown he leads is the more excellent of the two is easily evinced by the presence of Salomon among its ranks. Appropriately, Thomas' introduction of his crown spans as many as forty-four lines, as opposed to the brief, almost insignificant mention, culminating in the apparition of Joachim de Fiore, which Bonaventure accords to the blessed souls escorting him. We shall see how the praise of Dominic will punctually follow that of Francis in such a manner as to suggest the excellence of the latter. There is no need to ascend all the way up to the Empyrean, where Francis is exalted alongside Saint Benedict and Saint Augustine (the three founders of Western monasticism) to understand how the authentic *novelty* of "modern" spirituality is represented, for Dante, by the *homo novus* Francis, and by what his Order appeared, at least, to promise. Thomas' words are evidence enough. Nor had the approval of the Dominican Order in 1216 raised as many tensions and preoccupations within the hierarchy (including the Pope) as those that marked the development of the Franciscan Rule. Thus, Dante discusses the latter with historical accuracy, while barely acknowledging the former. In sum, as the likes of Bruno Nardi, Alarico Bonaiuti, and Raoul Manselli have taught us to see, albeit from very different perspectives, the *Commedia* is thoroughly animated by Franciscan spirituality.

But it is a Franciscanism that cannot be confused with the Joachimite yearning for a new spiritual church (*ecclesia spiritualis*), nor separated from the other, Dominican form of preaching. A Franciscanism that, while still wearing the profound influence of Joachim's eschatology on its sleeve, is nonetheless foreign to any abstract symbolic-allegorical schematism. Dante's prophecy appears to me to stem from the realistic denunciation of the ills of the time, from the understanding of its remote causes and from the hope for remedies that may be historically-politically *possible*—

albeit only through Providence. Thus, Francis' preaching appears itself recalcitrant to any "utopianism" and firmly rooted in the exemplariness of the life of Christ. In other words, it is Joachim as (re)interpreted by Bonaventure, general of the Order, in an attempt at an almost impossible mediation with the spiritual faction—the Joachim also featuring in the *Legenda maior*.[14] It is this figure whom Bonaventure introduces to Thomas, so that the latter can accept him. The prophetic spirit must be welcomed, and Francis must be exalted as its maximum eschatological expression. This is ultimately what Dominicans must bring themselves to acknowledge, through the very words of Thomas, their most authoritative member: all the more so because the figure of Dominic, too, is eschatological. Indeed, this is also how Ubertino of Casale, in *Arbor vitae crucifixae Jesus*, had interpreted it, whom Dante condemns by the mouth of Bonaventure as the representative of the Spirituals' extremism. And does not the "story" narrate that Dominic had wished to make *one Order* out of the two flocks? Every enmity must cease between the prophetic spirit—sharply distinct from glossolalia, according to Saint Paul's teachings to the Corinthians—and theological knowledge.

But just as the authentic Franciscanism now welcomes the latter into its fold, so must theological knowledge recognize *the truth of syllogism*; that is, it must be able to defend the logical means of argumentation (which are *always* necessary) from their improper use, as when they are wielded against Revelation with the intent to contest it or even deny it. This explains the presence of Siger at the end of the first crown, as well as the rather enigmatic words with which Thomas, his great adversary in his lifetime, introduces him to Bonaventure—who was Siger's even fiercer enemy. Thomas rethinks Siger's rationalism and entreats Bonaventure to acknowledge him in that respect. Bonaventure does the same on behalf of Joachim, whose works were pure vanity in Thomas' eyes. Needless to say, here Siger and Joachim are Dante's versions of themselves, revisited in the context of an eschatological *pax catholica*. Together, Thomas and Bonaventure operate a *catharsis* of their respective stances and traditions, excluding none of their dangerous moments, but reconsidering them in light of a new beginning. Dante pressures both Thomas and Bonaventure into a dual "conversion"—something infinitely more arduous and complex than merely reminding Dominicans of their mendicancy and Franciscans of their preaching. On the one hand, they must welcome into their ranks the man who had been their most insidious internal foe and turn him from enemy (*hostis*) into guest (*hospes*)—and an outstanding guest at that, the last link of the crown, even though on the "left" side. On the other hand, they must acknowledge the value of the external foe as essential in the great salvific design of providence.

Such a "torsion"—stretching well beyond the teaching of Bonaventure himself—clearly turns Franciscanism into a new Dantean creation. But this is also true of the poet's Thomism. Here, too, what matters is the perspective from which the encounter occurs: a perspective that exalts the heart that listens and welcomes—without judging—the homily (*verbum abbreviatum*, "short Word," as in Bernard of Clairvaux) that strives "to humble itself in everything" (Saint Francis, *Earlier Rule* XVII[15]) and is inexhaustibly capable of forgiving. It is that very Rule, constituted by nothing else but the life and sayings of Francis "according to the pattern of the Holy Gospel" (*Testament* 14[16]) that Thomas is accessing. And because Thomas accesses it, the image of Francis as "illiterate idiot," as the most minor among minors, also undergoes a transformation. The dominating presence of Thomas in the encounter under the sign of the Sun (which revolves entirely around Francis' preeminence) signifies the essentialness of the study of all the "Queens" of the *Convivio*—the arts, philosophy, and theology—with which the mysticism of Assisi must needs engage if it wishes to be the opposite of any abstract separateness from the world, which is also the world of those Ladies (*Dominae*). Syllogizing on the Street of Straw[17] is also *Work*, that work which Francis forcefully recommends as cure for acedious sloth: as that work, too (the labor of philosophy as purely rational inquiring) may ultimately grant "eternal light."[18]

Francis expresses the essence of Dante's religious prophecy—an essence, however, inseparable from Dominic's. Francis is the East; he dialogues with the Seraphim, who is closest to God in the angelic court, as specified also in the *Convivio*. (Let us not forget that Cherubim can also be *black*—see *Inf*. XXVII, 113—just as the "cherubic light" of knowledge may become diabolical if it is not fused with love.) Francis is seraphic in ardor; he burns like the burning bush; he does not shine of reflected light or flame. Burning is a sign of true faith. Only by burning can we become coheirs with Christ (*Monarchia*, III, 3, 10).[19] Indeed, Beatrice appears "like ardent fire" ("colorata come foco," *Purg*. XXXIII, 9) (Angelus Silesius will write: "*On the tombstone of Saint Francis*. Here lies a Seraphim; I wonder how the stone, / with such a fiery blaze, could still remain a whole."[20]) The mark of the stigmata belongs exclusively to Francis. In no way could that ever be equaled.[21] But his mission can be carried on only side by side with Dominic. There are *two* men (*viri*), competing with each other in humility, as in the story of their encounter found in both Thomas of Celano and Bonaventure (and here, too, the Dominican is the first to speak!). The *reformation* to which a powerless Dante aspires (a necessary precondition for *renovation*) is conceivable only if the two "run" together ("and though he ran, he thought his pace too slow," "corse, e correndo, li parve esser tardo," *Par.* XI, 81), that is, if the two formidable mendicant Orders agree to fight as one to achieve it.

The power of Franciscan Poverty (*Paupertas*) is not enough to ensure historical-political affirmation. If he is to rescue the collapsing Church, Francis must wed the "other" prince, too. The dream of Pope Innocent III, which in the Assisi cycle precedes the central panel about the confirmation of the Rule, is also found in the life of Dominic. The courtly love of Francis and Poverty must represent the spirit of *reformation*, their "glad looks" ("lieti sembianti," *Par.* XI, 76) must outwardly express its eschatological significance, just like Beatrice's smile is *hilaritas paradisi*, heaven's merriment. True preaching is Francis' unarmed, soldierless preaching to the Sultan, which also intends to be testimony-martyrdom. Nonetheless, in order that Peter's prophecy to Dante may come true (*Par.* XXVII, 40–66), in order that the "high Providence," which once defended Rome with Scipio (and here Peter deems providential the dominance of the very city, "glory of the world," which had crucified him!), may now free it again from those "rapacious wolves" in shepherd's clothing who have made it into "a sewer of blood and stench" ("cloaca / del sangue e de la puzza," *Par.* XXVII, 25–26), the pure Franciscan mercy must ally itself to the impetus of that other, Western-born, champion—Dominic: "loving vassal / of Christian faith" yet "harsh to enemies," whom he strikes "like a torrent," with greatest force where they resist the most. The great doctor must also move "with both his learning and his zeal" so that the Church—to which, as such, reverence is always due—may be rid of the one who is usurping its seat (*Par.* XII, 55–102). (The imperative of due reverence to the Church is certainly what saves both Dante and Francis from heresy. "By reverence for those exalted keys" ("La reverenza de le somme chiavi"), as Dante puts it in *Inf.* XIX, 101, whereupon he immediately launches into one of his most fierce invectives against the avarice of church leaders . . .) But Francis must be praised first, and woe betide the doctrine that forgets that divine wisdom (*scientia divina*) surpasses any human knowledge and will. The moment Thomas recognizes, implicitly but with full clarity, that spiritual preeminence must belong to Francis, Bonaventure shows, in absolutely realistic tones, how Dominic's militant Church (*ecclesia militans*) is indispensable to those very reformist ends to which Francis, too, aspired.

But what sophisticated tonal difference between the two praises! It almost seems as if Bonaventure were taking special care to emphasize precisely those aspects of Dominic's work most at variance with Francis' preaching. Is it really possible to picture a Francis whose "impetus, with greatest force, / struck where the thickets of the heretics / offered the most resistance" ("e ne li sterpi eretici percosse / l'impeto suo, più vivamente quivi / dove le resistenze eran più grosse," *Par.* XII, 100–102)? No language could be more alien to the Franciscan lexicon. And yet, the monument Dante erects to the Saint is not a single portrait, readable in isolation. It is a *double* portrait, that of Francis *and* Dominic, as it could be painted by a lay prophet who, having survived the confrontation with radical Aristotelianism, as well as political strife and brutal disenchantment, finds renewed hope in the promise of religious eschatology. In Dante's genius, no mystical rapture can obfuscate the awareness of reality, of the personalities (*figurae*) who can operate decisively in reality, of the power relations that hold sway within it. Therefore, Dante sees the reformation of the two preaching Orders, their return to the founders, as the key weapon for the reformation of the entire Church—but only on condition that they proceed all the more united as they are aware of the strength of their difference and of the hierarchical order expressed in that very difference. Mysticism is needed, but it has to be of the Franciscan kind rooted in *doing* (*operari*), not the Joachimite kind that entrusts itself to the deterministic providentialism of the historical cycles and ages.[22] And, at the same time, one must be capable of *striking the enemies*, as Dominic did, so that charity and doctrine may be in accord. Bonaventure and Thomas must be able to speak to each other and understand each other. At the same time, each of them must amend the traditions and customs of his own flock—and for this, too, struggle (*agon*), and political skill are needed. Are the two men really the harbingers of things to come (*figurae futuri*)? And are there any real possibilities? Any realistic hopes? Or are they just two souls in heaven, with no more future on earth?

Dante's representation of Francis follows from the historical concreteness of this project. Francis is *also* the fulfillment of Joachimite eschatological expectations, Sun in the Heaven of the Sun, light from the East (*ex oriente lux*), Assisi being the new East ("Behold a man, the Orient is his name," Zechariah 6:12; see also Luke 1:78). That he is a true prophet is testified above all by his decision to sever himself from the world, by his falling "into war" with his worldly father to rush into a mystical marriage with Poverty. In Dante's idea everything revolves around these nuptials. They alone express the "war" that makes any return to the past impossible; they alone embody the honest, inflexible will to reform. Reformation means being indissolubly united to the Woman—Poverty— who *alone* "suffered with Christ upon the cross" (*Par.* XI, 72). It is not the event of the stigmata that determines Francis' preeminence—though it certainly confirms it. Francis is first and foremost the lover of Poverty; he alone is united perfectly with her. No one before him had dared as much: in fact, she had remained a widow and "had had no suitor" since the day of the Passion ("sanza invito," *Par.* XI, 66). Though we will need to look more closely at the significance that Poverty comes to assume in this context, it is safe to affirm that Dante's entire representation is centered upon it. Out of the lines devoted to the praise of Francis (equal in length to Bonaventure's praise of Dominic), as many as thirty celebrate the marriage of Francis to Poverty and its felicitous effects on the flowering of the Order. Dominic's portrait lacks a center of such potency. Dominic is merely a "servant of Christ," called by Christ to be "the worker in His garden" (*Par.* XII, 72–73), certainly not His "resurrection." Dominic's only wedding is to faith, through baptism, as for every Christian. Francis and Dominic may share the praise and the glory only as long as the hierarchy of the two *charismata* is made clear. Thomas and Bonaventure are hierarchical men in this respect, too, just as were their prophetic teachers.

Around the central image of the nuptials revolve, in Dante, the scene of the spoliation, that of the approval of the Rule, that of the preaching of Christ "within the presence of the haughty Sultan" ("ne la presenza del Soldan superba," *Par.* XI, 101), and lastly, that of the "final seal," followed by a *naked* death two years later. These last two images are no other than the fulfillment of the nuptials. The others are meant to express what for Dante is the core meaning of Francis' historical existence: the struggle for radical reform qua "simple" return to evangelical living, and to the form of its preaching.

Dante deemed both dimensions extra-ordinary. He sees the Rule as having been born of Francis' firm will, against the resistance and incomprehension of those who "usurp" the seat of Saint Peter. There is no direct polemic, as neither Innocent III nor Honorius III is "mistreated" by Dante—no doubt, thanks to their decisive role in winning over the hierarchy to the definitive approval of the Order, rather than out of sympathy for their theological-political stance. Let us not forget that Innocent III embodies the culmination of the medieval papacy's struggle to affirm the church's rule over the whole world—a power *erga et super omnes*, precisely in the direction of the bull *Unam sanctam* issued (in 1302) by the detested pope Boniface VIII.[23] But Dante's emphasis on how a first, purely oral "seal" given by Innocent had to be followed by the second, formal one, granted by Honorius, is clearly meant to signify that Francis' intention was not only "hard" in and of itself; that it was even harder for it to gain the acceptance of broad sectors of the College of Cardinals, of the secular clergy, as well as of many a bishop, especially in France and Germany; and that only the Order's miraculous growth ("And after many of the poor had followed . . . ," "Poi che la gente poverella crebbe," *Par.* XI, 94) had eventually allowed it to overcome such resistance. And how scrupulously Dante takes care to let us know that Francis' "sacred purpose" ("la santa voglia," *Par.* XI, 99) is crowned by the Holy Spirit *through* Honorius! This was decreed by Providence, not by the free will of cardinals and popes. The iron will of the new Saint, the bridegroom of Poverty, sanctioned by the Spirit: it is this energy that unfurls *regally* ("regalmente," *Par.* XI, 91) before the authority of the Church and forces it into consent. Francis, then, is also a leader; he is also a king, regally standing before the papal court. We will keep this "hard" image of Francis well in mind for later, when we visit the basilica.

The other scene is even more significant. The pilgrimage to the Holy Land occurs only "in his thirst for martyrdom" ("per la sete del martiro," *Par.* XI, 100), a thirst for bearing witness to the point of self-sacrifice. As in original Christianity, only martyrdom is proof of *good* faith beyond any doubt; only martyrdom *justifies*. Francis embodies here the notion of preaching the Word (*praedicare Verbum*); he is pure proclamation, humble and glad proclamation before the "haughty Sultan," who represents the arrogance of the world. Francis is humble, that is, devoid of the world's weapons. His journey appears completely foreign to the context of warfare and subjugation in which it unfolds. His approach is antipodal to that of the warrior monastic orders; it is the eschatological sign of a universal conversion by virtue of the Word alone. A conversion, however, that is still "unripe." Expectations have been disappointed, and it will take a while longer to get there—despite what figures like Francis may do to speed up the process. Judgment has been passed on history, but its powers are still active, also within the very Minors, where in the absence of Francis frictions have escalated.

The "unripeness" of the times forces the Saint to return; and the prize and seal of his very defeats will be the encounter with Christ "on the naked crag between the Arno and Tiber" ("nel crudo sasso intra Tevero e Arno," *Par.* XI, 106–107).

"At the feet" of the central icon—the stigmatization at La Verna—three fundamental scenes sum up, for Dante, Francis' *historiae*: the decision to marry Poverty, the dealings with the papacy for the approval of the Rule, and the preaching. Three scenes also form the *predella* to the Giotto panel in the Louvre: the dream of Innocent III, the confirmation of the Rule, and the preaching to the birds. Here we witness a dramatic shift in perspective. The Pope is *directly* inspired by Christ (just as Christ's signs "rain" down on Francis without any mediation) to recognize the Minor from Assisi as his champion. The subsequent approval of the Rule comes as a necessary consequence. But there are no dreams in Dante, nor any spontaneous, immediate approvals. (There are high stakes in this dream. While there is no trace of it in Thomas of Celano's *First Life*, it is strongly present in his *Second Life*, a book directly commissioned by the Pope. In it, though, Francis is described as a "small and contemptible religious man"; what difference from the "Atlas" of Assisi!) In Dante, the Holy Spirit breathes *univocally* into Francis; the popes, unknowing or unwilling as they may be, must follow "the Providence that rules the world" ("La provedenza, che governa il mondo," *Par.* XI, 28). There is nothing regal, instead, in Giotto's Francis kneeling before the papal court. The very scene Giotto and Dante have in common, then, is also the one that shows them at their greatest distance from each other. And the preaching? In Giotto, it is not one with the thirst for martyrdom, nor is it done in the place that has known the most outrageous profanation of the name of "crusade" (from the Spanish *cruzado*, "crossed"; for Francis, only the crucifix is "crossed"); Giotto's Francis preaches to the birds (*volucres caeli*). Thus, while in Dante's example Francis' preaching appears to be historical and incarnate, Giotto's representation makes it legendary—or rather, imbued with the vivacity of popular legend, in the service of a specific edifying project promoted by the Church.

III

Do the abovementioned considerations on Giotto's sponsors, as well as on the incomparable social and cultural conditions of the two *dictatores*, suffice to explain the differences in their approach to Francis? While those considerations, indeed, go a long way toward pertinently illuminating the literal content of many scenes (such as Innocent's dream, the confirmation of the Rule, and the preaching), the overall "flavor" of the representation should be ascribed in greater measure to factors inherent to the artistic intentionality of each author, to the peculiar character of their "will to art" (*Kunstwollen*). On one side is the painter, destined, like the poet, to become a myth for the new artistic era, whose imaginative power finds in the Francis cycle (and later in the Jesus cycle in the Scrovegni chapel in Padua) a reason to break with the old language; that is, the need to give mass, volume, and dramatic consistency to his figures, so that they may shed any connotation of contingency, of mere accidentality. On the other side is the great intellectual, who sees in Francis the incarnation of elements essential to his cultural, political, religious project, and thus wants the exemplary episodes of his life to speak on behalf of it. Giotto's representation necessarily stems from the story of the saint's life (which seems quite naturally to "offer itself" to being represented, even *painted*) *as told* by the community of Christians. Dante's representation of Francis' life, however, originates from the notion he has of it; consequently, only those episodes that may fit within the context of such notion will matter. In Giotto, reality, official story, and legend are intertwined; for him, even more real than reality is how this *homo novus* has been construed by his times, popular piety, *and* the Church. In Dante—an intellectual and a poet, a politician and a prophet—those two dimensions are distinctly separate: legend cannot have any significant role. Francis is valuable for what in him is an ascertainable symbol of the political-religious eschatology that Dante has been elaborating from different sources. Dante's Francis does not preach to flowers or birds: he preaches to this bestiary of men from his century, to those who should know and listen because that is the purpose of their nature, and instead remain worms, or turn into curs, dogs, hogs, foxes, and wolves, as happens to those who live along the course of the river Arno (*Purg.* XIV, 28–54).

However, the painter comes closest to the character of Francis by highlighting one of his most revolutionary traits—one to which Dante, straitjacketed by his own grandiose theological-political scheme, cannot really do justice. In fact, the preaching to the birds is not reducible to popular legend, nor to thaumaturgy. The episode evinces a precise symbolism of which no trace is left in Giotto—while it is explicit in Celano (*First Life*, ch. 21), wherein the birds are different, and by no means all images of meekness, of chaste, innocent souls.[24] (Celano's language is nothing like that of the *Little Flowers of Saint Francis*, although the latter, too, is foreign enough to vague spirituality to have appealed to Vasily Rozanov. We might recall that Paolo and Francesca, too, are described as "doves" in *Inferno* V. Here, however, we find even ravens and crows!) But above all, the preaching of the bird attests to the new idea of nature that expresses itself in Francis. And it is not just the preaching to the birds that is missing in Dante's representation: the whole spirit of Francis' *Canticle of the Sun* is missing. Dante the poet is deaf precisely to Francis the poet, the Francis who asks that one *sing* at times of greatest suffering, and who is heeded at once, if not by the friars, by the angels themselves. Francis' characteristic of *making himself proximate* to every being in creation is comprehended in Giotto's realism, not in Dante's. Real, for Dante, is the itinerary of our "being-there" (intended, no doubt, as synthesis of intelligence and sensitivity) toward the highest Reality. Nature, for him, is the "mighty sea of being" ("gran mar de l'essere," *Par.* I, 113), which depends entirely on the Being of the Maker, and leads us back to Him. When Dante looks down on earth from above, he sees it as "the little threshing floor that so incites our savagery" ("l'aiuola che ci fa tanto feroci," *Par.* XXII, 151), the place of "our tempest" ("la nostra procella," *Par.* XXXI, 30). His gaze is unable to linger on visible beauty as something of value *in itself*; it runs to "that point" ("quel punto") on which "depend the heavens and the whole of nature" ("depende il cielo e tutta la natura," *Par.* XXVIII, 41–42). In the *Commedia*, the most loving cadences toward terrestrial reality issue from the souls of the damned; for them, the air "that's gladdened by the sun" is "sweet" ("ne l'aere dolce che dal sol s'allegra," *Inf.* VII, 122); for them, "the life above" is "sunlit" ("là su di sopra, in la vita serena," *Inf.* XV, 49), "fair" ("bella," *Inf.* XV, 57), "happy" ("lieta," *Inf.* XIX, 102). Real, in Dante, is rather the struggle to *transhumanize*, fueled by an all-powerful nostalgia for the idea. Only within this struggle can the aesthetic-sensible reality be saved—and become the *divine aesthesis* that marks the rhythm of the basso continuo in the *Paradiso*. If there is a passage in the *Commedia* where Dante comes closest to Francis' sentiment for nature, it is in the marvelous tercets from Canto X that imagine the "ardent suns" ("ardenti soli," *Par.* X, 76) of the venerable wise souls whirling in celebration around the poet and Beatrice as women "not released from dancing" ("non da ballo sciolte," *Par.* X, 79–80).

The *Canticle*, however, is missing—or rather, the only canticle in Dante is the biblical one of Solomon, that great allegory of a nonadventitious relationship (Augustine's *relatio non adventitia*) between the lover and the Beloved. What is missing in Dante is the excitement for the very essentiality of every being that vibrates in Francis and makes him sing, turns him into a fool (*pazzus*) and a "jester." Indeed, there is in Dante a certain eroticism of the ideal typical of "saints of a transfigured, misunderstood sensuality" (Nietzsche),[25] but his emphasis falls entirely on the *ideal*, rather than on the "lovestruck, popular, poet."[26] Of course, even Francis' canticle should not be understood naturalistically. The love of Francis is, above all, love for the creature, *ordered* in every fiber of it. It is not a hymn to creatures unless in the sense of a *theology* of the hymn; it is not certainly a hymn to a creature's supposed autonomous beauty. Creatures are praised only to the extent that, through the praise of the perfect order that connects them all, the Lord praises himself. It is the Lord who, within that very Order, sings a hymn to himself. But just as indubitable is the further step that Francis takes. It is not only that our praise rises to Him through the *work*, as it were, of mediation that the vision of creation represents; it is also that we praise creation by virtue of the praise *that creation itself offers to its Lord*. Thus, we praise creation insofar as it appears to us to be itself *capable of praise*. Nor is this merely an image, or an analogy: for Francis, it is a real experience, just as real, for him, is the fact that a creature can *reciprocate* his love (see the episode of the fire that does not burn in Thomas of Celano, *Second Life*, ch. 125[27] and Bonaventure, *Legenda maior*, V).[28] He sings as he listens to the song of creatures. The *Canticle* is the measure of how far Franciscan spirituality is from the Cathar gnosis.

All nature appears to be, in Augustine's words, capable of God (*capax Dei*). We do not praise it merely because it was created "good" by God but also because we hear it sing its own hymn of praise. Even more than in the *Canticle*, this is manifest in *Exhortation to the Praise of God*: "Heaven and earth, praise Him. All you rivers, praise the Lord. . . . All you creatures, bless the Lord. All you birds of heaven, praise the Lord." And above all, let the "poor" among creatures praise Him: "children . . . young men, and virgins."[29] Although one should, no doubt, be able to discern the specific weight of each different *cum* (*with*) and *per* (*for*), over which many a philologist has labored, the end result is the same: we sing praise *together* with all creatures, given that man is also a creature; we praise God *with* his creatures—without losing sight of the difference and the *order* of the praise; we praise God *through* our praise of his creatures, as well as *because of* their beauty and their *usefulness*.[30] All these senses are inseparable from one another, their literal differences ultimately flowing into the one spirit of the Franciscan hymn. God has made his creatures "good" insofar as they all are, to varying degrees, capable of returning to Him, of offering their thanks and praise to Him. We, prideful animals, are not the only ones capable of praise: in fact, God is not praised for man but only for those who have obeyed and followed Him—for the disciples of the Sermon on the Mount.[31] There is no good fire and bad fire, nor good water and bad water. The Earth is all "good" and it produces good fruits. But there is the man who *for-gives*, and the man who will die "in mortal sin." Preaching is essential for the latter. One, however, does not preach to birds—but *with* them. It is a conversation, not real preaching—a silent conversation, the culmination of every breviloquence. Preaching is ultimately always obliged to proceed from mentor to pupil. And besides, true preaching takes place not in word but in deeds. In fact, the birds of the sky and the lilies of the field should rather preach to us humans! The authentically Franciscan hymn, then, is the one in which all creatures gather to comfort each other and preach to each other. Dante fails to hear and understand precisely this "tone" of preaching. Giotto, however, approaches it in his great work in Assisi—at least to the extent that he departs from the ideal grandiosity of the monument the poet erects to the Saint.

For both Dante and Giotto, though, the lines about praising God "through our sister bodily death" represent the cornerstone of the *Canticle*. Death is our neighbor par excellence, and therefore we cannot claim to love our neighbor unless we also love this "sister" of ours, unless we invite her, too—as Celano narrates—to praise the Lord. For if our neighbor is truly *loved*, then death will be merely "of the body"; death shall become "dying," and this is how "to die" (as *verbum*) resurrects from a merely mortal state. Is death our ultimate enemy? Indeed, and Francis' new and unheard-of command (*mandatus novus*) is precisely this: love thy enemy.

IV

The Basilica of Saint Francis in Assisi is a great papal church. Its construction took place entirely under the sign of Roman politics, first under Nicholas III, then Nicholas IV. A former general of the Order after Bonaventure, and the first Franciscan to be elected pope, Nicholas IV authorized the friars to use their alms for the purpose of building the church. The whole fresco cycle was probably carried out over the last decade of the thirteenth century, in light of the upcoming first Jubilee of 1300 (and perhaps somewhat hastily, which would explain certain lapses in the quality of the execution). Nicholas IV was a strong advocate for reaching an understanding with the other mendicant Order, as well as reconciliation between the different currents within his own. He collaborated fully with Matthew of Acquasparta but was also on good terms with the spiritual faction of the Franciscan Order. Unlike what we read in Dante's condemnations, Matthew does not "escape" the "sternness" of Francis' rule, nor does Ubertino of Casale simply make it "too strict" ("ch'uno la fugge e altro la coarta," *Par.* XII, 126). At the time of the great Assisi workshop, relations between the different souls of the brotherhood that Francis dreamed about had not yet exploded, as it would by the time Dante wrote the *Paradiso*, into a fratricidal war—a war that would end by the mid-fourteenth century with the nearly total destruction of the spiritual current. Ubertino certainly enjoyed a certain degree of influence in the planning of the frescos (the symbol of his book, *Arbor vitae crucifixae Jesu Christi, The Tree of the Crucified Life of Jesus*, is clearly visible in the allegory of Poverty in the lower basilica). The grand master of the spirituals, Provençal Peter John Olivi (like Matthew of Acquasparta, a former pupil of Bonaventure, and in 1287 a lector at Santa Croce in Florence, where Dante most likely had occasion to hear him), was very influential in the Order while also maintaining good relations with the Roman Curia and with Clement V, whose effigy celebrates the Triumph of Saint Thomas in Andrea di Bonaiuto's fresco at Santa Maria Novella.

The Franciscan cycle in Assisi intends to be the image of this accord between spiritual eschatology—though cleansed of the Joachim-inflected monastic tones, as well as of any "impatience" for the new epoch announced by the Franciscan event—and due reverence to papal authority and the ecclesiastical hierarchy. Such an image was to represent the solution to any tension between spiritual *fraternitas*, of whose idea the Minors wished to be the emblem, and real *ecclesia*, firmly governed by the spiritual-political authority of the pope. Certainly not the utopia of a spiritual *ecclesia*, but at least the acknowledgment of the irreplaceable role of the new Franciscan sanctity in sustaining a militant church (*ecclesia militans*) in its ever more arduous, almost desperate, struggle against heresies, Empire, and new large state entities. A weak accord, to be sure, which was bound to fall through shortly afterward during the pontificate of Boniface VIII, "prince of the new Pharisees" ("lo principe de' novi farisei," *Inf.* XXVII, 85), whom the spirituals accused of scheming to eliminate *pastor angelicus* Celestine V—an accusation essentially shared by Dante (*Inf.* XIX, 56), who, however, as is well known, also bears little sympathy for the man "who made, through cowardice, the great refusal" ("che fece per viltade il gran rifiuto," *Inf.* III, 60). Dante's condemnation of Celestine in *Inferno* III serves also as a reproof of the expectations that spirituals and pauperistic currents had harbored upon the election of the hermit of the Majella; in particular, a reproof of the form their eschatology had assumed after the banishment from the Order of Ubertino of Casale and Angelo of Clareno—the latter an extraordinary mix of missionary spirit, eremitical vocation, and unalloyed (*sine glossa*) fidelity to Francis' *Testament*.[32] It is well known that Peter John Olivi, too, had harshly criticized them both for their stance toward ecclesiastical authorities; which makes it highly significant that Dante should have singled out Ubertino alone for his criticism.

In sum, Dante's Francis is not the Francis of the spirituals. He stands providentially with Dominic, as both Thomas and Bonaventure (who would die in the same year) have had the great merit of understanding. Francis is exalted in a concert of voices as diverse as to comprise even Siger, the Aristotelian most loathed by the spirituals, and Joachim, the prophet most loathed by Dominican theologians! Would Dante, then, find himself reflected in the itinerary put forth in the Assisi cycle? Probably as little as in the choice Giotto made for the *predella* to the *Stigmatization* in the Louvre. Nonetheless, does it not seem obvious how the Assisi cycle corresponds in its program to Bonaventure's *Legenda maior*, the same *Life* that had condemned all other testimonies to the stake? Are the running captions under the Assisi frescos not culled from Bonaventure's text? And is not Bonaventure the voice of Franciscanism in the *Commedia*? Yes, except that, in the *Commedia*, we hear Dante's Bonaventure, whereas, on the Assisi walls, it is only his *Legenda* that speaks. But then again, to what extent is it the *Legenda* itself, and not rather its adaptation to those religious and political exigencies that had motivated the whole Assisi workshop? The affinities and contrasts may be understood only by analyzing the great cycle—a work perhaps just as culturally and theologically complex as *Paradiso* X–XIII.

The protagonist of the cycle is the *vir hierarchicus*, the seraph, the angel who bears the seal of the living God. At least three scenes—not counting the one at la Verna, the heart of them all—exalt Francis in the manner of Joachimite eschatology, as "the angel ascending from the rising sun" from John's Revelation 7:2. These scenes represent the Friars' view of Francis as the new Elijah; Brother Pacifico's vision of the heavenly throne that once belonged to the brightest angel, Lucifer, and now awaits Francis; the ecstasy of Francis, who, raised on a cloud and with his arms open in the shape of the cross, turns to embrace Christ, who is reaching down to bless him. All these scenes imply the perfect identification of Francis with his brothers, at the same time as they highlight the active role of the community of Minors. The Minors see and bear witness to all, always by the Saint's side at the most crucial moments. For the absolutely most crucial of all, it is Bonaventure himself who dictates the definitive iconography: Brother Leo is bearing witness to it, standing a short distance from Francis. (Jesus needs no witnesses for his "metamorphosis" in the garden of Gethsemane; humble Francis does. However, Francis will be alone again in Santa Croce, as he had been in the first pictorial representation of the Miracle, in the altarpiece by Bonaventure Berlinghieri in Pescia.) Francis does not tell his own story: in fact, he would like to remain silent, as in the event of the stigmatization. His brothers from the Order are the ones who see, touch, and narrate. The will to ground Francis in the community he has created, and thus in the Church that he has restored (and that he does not revolutionize, nor expect to fulfill itself in *ecclesia spiritualis*) is perhaps the dominant trait of the Assisi cycle. Here, there is no room for singularity. The absolute eminence of the saint is such insofar as it has been seen, witnessed, experienced, felt *by touch*, as in the scene of the "learned and prudent man," who, having been doubtful at first, becomes a faithful witness after touching "these palpable signs of the wounds of Christ" (*Legenda maior* XV).[33]

Here Dante's reading may appear essentially akin to that which orients the Assisi cycle. However, the difference soon becomes dramatic in what concerns the role of the papacy in Assisi—the very bone of contention over which the spirituals themselves voice their dissent, also with respect to Bonaventure's *Legenda*. The Francis dreamed by Pope Innocent III (at the foot of whose bed are two cubiculars, or counselors, who will return among the cardinals in the following scene, and then as simple onlookers at Santa Croce) in the act of supporting the tottering Lateran basilica is a beardless and not very ascetic-looking young man, according to an iconographic model that Giotto will make even more explicit in Santa Croce.[34] And, lo and behold! Pope Innocent, born Lotario dei Conti di Segni—once author of *De miseria humanae conditionis* (*On the*

Misery of the Human Condition) and now head of a church that draws its prosperity from human malice, and whose riches spring from the wells of Hell, as wrote a German chronicler of the times—rushes to approve the new Franciscan Rule! In fact, we know that things happened very differently from what we read both in Celano's *Lives* (especially the first) and in Bonaventure's *Legenda*, which in this particular case is obviously not the source of the Assisi cycle. (And this is not mentioning the more malevolent sources, such as Benedictine monk Matthew of Paris, who tells of a not exactly magnanimous reply that the aristocratic Pope gave to the Franciscan *pauperes*: "Listen, friend, go find a herd of swine . . . give them the Rule you compiled."[35])

This historical falsehood (barely corrected by the fact that the scroll Francis is handing to the Pope lacks an official seal) intends to signify that the Church acknowledged immediately the value of the Minors' preaching as its new foundation, and at once—being inspired by God—bore witness to the *event* represented, for all Christendom, by the Franciscan sun. All the struggles, tensions, confrontations—forgotten.[36] But what matters most is forgetting Francis' (and Clare's) desperate opposition to having an actual Rule in the first place! Whereas in the cycle, Francis has got the Rule ready just as quickly as the Pope confirms it! By all means, in the Assisi cycle, it is the Saint who must make the greatest sacrifice, the greatest renunciation. It is for him that the form of life (*forma vitae*) ought to have been worth *beyond* any form, just as the understanding and dialogue between brothers ought to have occurred beyond any verbal expression (as a seraph, Francis is able to see other people's thoughts; his love allows him to identify himself with the other, while remaining fully himself). His *Testament* is evidence of this: "And the brothers may not say: 'This is another rule.' Because this is a remembrance, admonition, exhortation, and my testament, which I, little brother Francis, make for you, my blessed brothers."[37] In Assisi, a Saint is glorified who aspires to *regulate* his life—upending the very meaning of the original message, which certainly consisted of resolving every law into evangelical *living*.[38]

We have seen the centrality that the theme of preaching assumes in Dante (a *magisterial* preaching, nonetheless, analogous in this respect to that of scholarly Dominic). On this point also, the dissonance with the Assisi cycle is jarring. In the cycle, the scene with the Sultan[39] loses all the polemical thrust it has in the poet (where preaching is, in its essence, like martyrdom; and in any case, a peaceful mission, never complicit with overpowering violence) to turn into a challenge between two thaumaturges—Francis' challenge to the Sultan's wizards, who can only helplessly recoil. The Francis of popular religiosity, the Francis of miracles—which over the course of the thirteenth century will carry more and more weight in the constitution of the legend—plays a fundamental role in the Assisi cycle, together with the figure of the *ecstatic*: the exorcist driving out the demons from Arezzo, the miracle of the fount, the series of miracles after death (*miracula post mortem*), which take up the whole last section of Bonaventure's *Legenda*. It is an aspect completely ignored by Dante, who would indeed subscribe fully to the words of Celano: "But we have not chosen to describe miracles—they do not make holiness but show it—but rather to describe the excellence of his life and the honest form of his manner of living."[40] In Assisi, too, Francis preaches through actions, but these actions are essentially *miracula* (from *mirari*, "to look with wonder at"). In the nativity scene in Greccio, when Francis almost spiritually resurrects Jesus (and on that occasion, too, it is other people who *see* the event, and have the "miraculous vision" [*mirabile visione*] of the child appearing in the manger), he has already left the pulpit—by the way, a wonderful piece of architecture, just like the baldachin over the manger, and in general, all the buildings represented in the cycle, all homages to Arnolfo di Cambio that foreshadow the work of Giotto himself as architect! Thus, in the scene of the chapter meeting in Arles, Saint Anthony is the preacher. Francis appears as a silent admonition, a crucified figure announcing the very next scene: the encounter with Christ in the guise of a Seraph (*sub specie Seraphi*) "on the naked crag." (It is Bonaventure who "decides" on the identification of the Seraph with Christ, or rather, makes the figure of the angel into the "harmonic mean" between Francis and Christ.)

The only panel depicting Francis in the act of preaching—besides, of course, the so-called preaching to the birds, which is not quite as such, however, as Francis does *not* preach, but rather invites the birds to join him in singing God's praise (*Legenda maior* VII, 9)—is that which illustrates the encounter with Pope Honorius III (as we have seen, the Rule is passed off as already "stamped"). Here Francis is standing before the Pope, seated amid his cardinals. Only the Pope is dressed as was Innocent III in the confirmation scene; the cardinals make a humble appearance, wrapped in monk's robes. Honorius is focused on Francis' words; everybody else is absorbed. Only one of them, seated to the right of the Pope, seems taken aback by Francis' speech, and looks at him in puzzlement: it is cardinal Hugolino of Ostia, the future Gregory IX, who will canonize Francis within a mere two years of his death. In his *First Life*, Celano recalls this preaching with great liveliness (overjoyed by his own inspired words, "he moved his feet as if dancing"[41]), an episode that returns both in the *Second Life* and in Bonaventure. But the Assisi panel is not so much about Francis' oration as it is about his request to the Pope for a cardinal protector of the Order, by then already shaken by harsh infighting. Francis prays for protection, pointing to himself with his right hand, and mentions Hugolino, who appears surprised by the request, while Honorius ponders it with the utmost seriousness. This is not, then, an edifying homily to the papal court, but rather a proof of humility (and political skill) given by that very Saint—that "champion"— whom Pope Innocent had seen holding up the tottering Lateran basilica. Also, in this case, the Assisi cycle appears to make a rather "free" use of Bonaventure's *Legenda*, with the unilateral purpose to envelop Francis both in his Order—as truly *order* in all senses of the word—and, as a perfectly *humble* man, in the universal order of the Church.

But it is in the combined scenes of the Stigmatization on mount La Verna and of Francis' death that the image of the Saint loses, in Assisi, his harshest tones. A decision is made in favor of an iconography of Francis that strips him of his most extraordinary, paradoxical traits and allows him to be subsumed into a "general" idea of sainthood. Not an easy thing to do on the basis of Bonaventure's account, which is, on the contrary, disturbingly realistic: right after the apparition of the Seraph, what Francis sees on his hands and feet are the nails themselves, not just their marks. "The heads of the nails [were] shewing in the palms of the hands, and upper side of the feet, and their points shewing on the other side; the heads of the nails were round and black in the hands and feet, while the points were long, bent, and as it were turned back, being formed of the flesh itself, and protruding therefrom" (*Legenda maior* XIII, 3).[42] Here the Seraph literally crucifies Francis, rather than blessing him with shafts of light within a context of pure contemplation, as seems to occur in the perfect balance of the Assisi panel.

In the Assisi cycle, we do not get to see the nails stuck in the flesh—an image that vividly recurs also in the account of Francis' passing (*Legenda maior* XV, 2), nor the naked body laid out on the naked ground, divested of the sackcloth so as to keep "faith with the Lady Poverty even to the end."[43] (Francis' inspiration is, of course, Jesus, who was stripped of his garments and placed naked on the cross.) In the corresponding scene in Assisi—pictorially static and relying on basic symmetries, far removed from the dramatics of its counterpart in the Bardi chapel—Francis appears composed and fully dressed in his habit, rather than lying on the naked ground as he had requested. It is a scene of grief, not of *struggle*, as it is, for instance, in Bonaventure's account: "When he had been brought thither [i.e., Saint Mary of the Little Portion]—that he might give an ensample of the truth that he had naught in common with the world—in that most severe weakness that followed after all his sickness, he prostrated himself in fervour of spirit all naked on the naked earth, that in that last hour, wherein the foe might still rise up against him, he might wrestle in his nakedness with that naked spirit."[44]

Francis' suffering, martyred body is missing from the Assisi cycle, and so are the nails in his flesh; and so is, in sum, the tragic *agon* of his existence *with and against* the Church, his own Order, and the world. The effort that an act of conversion requires is also missing; Francis appears haloed from the very first moment, as early as the scene of the "simple man"—the first of the twenty-eight scenes in the cycle—where the man spreads out a white cloth at Francis' feet, as if to invite him to write his own story on it. His prior life (when he "miserably wasted and squandered his time"[45]), the drama of the *turning point*, the sudden, precipitous return from Spoleto to heed the Lord's calling—all of that can be sensed only as a remote background in the scene of the suffering Christ (*Christus patiens*) who speaks to Francis in San Damiano. The first mark of Francis' conversion is also missing: the encounter with the leper, that is, the encounter with the authentic *neighbor*, he who at the beginning, upon surprising you unexpectedly along the way, fills you with *horror*, and who becomes a source of astonishment and joy only at the cost of your victory over yourself. And yet the decisive significance of that encounter is remembered at the very beginning of *Testament*: "And the Lord himself led me among them and I showed mercy to them."[46] Indeed, there is humility in Assisi, and even more obedience; there is the seal of *another Christ* (*alter Christus*), although the nails have been mercifully removed; there are the miracles. Forgotten, however, is the wounded, naked body on the ground, together with the brothers singing their farewell song (the same brothers who will betray him moments after his death, hastening to build sumptuous abodes over his naked body); forgotten are the leper, the care for the sick, and the moments of suffering, tears, despair, struggle, as described also by Bonaventure, in their paradoxical blending with the tones of merriment (Francis' *hilaritas*).

No one is more ravaged by illness and pain than he is, no one is more desirous to sing, to praise *with joy*, to *dance* while preaching. But things could not be otherwise, because the true, resounding absence in Assisi is precisely that of Poverty.

V

Herein lies the biggest difference also from the Dantean representation. Dante's symbolism can hardly harmonize with the living figure of Franciscan sanctity; and yet, as we have seen, Poverty constitutes the very character and destiny of Francis' legacy. In Giotto, too, poverty is either exalted as one virtue *among* others (in the lower basilica), or it is present merely as a kind of tacit presupposition (in the upper basilica). Only *oboedientia* and *humilitas* are triumphant. *Paupertas* does not stand out, does not impress. In fact, at times its image is openly contradicted. Whereas in Dante its profound relationship to merriment (*hilaritas*) and to the song of praise and joy is not explicitly represented, in some of the finest Assisi panels, where the hand of Giotto is also most evident, this song is indeed heard, but as if from faraway, as though it could overcome the rough (and yet happy) image of poverty. The Franciscan paradox, to which we will have to return, is missing—the vital tension between its constituents is broken. There is nothing "poor" about the figure of the knight to whom Francis gives his cloak. (Think, by way of contrast, of what is probably the highest and harshest representation of poverty in the history of painting, Masaccio's *The Distribution of Alms*, in the Brancacci Chapel!) There is nothing "poor" in Greccio. In fact, the last encounter with Saint Clare is rather "rich," with the women filing out of a marvelous Arnolfo-esque cathedral whose outline foreshadows Giotto's own architectural projects. They have abandoned the extremely poor area of San Damiano, just as Francis no longer lives in a "deserted hut" (*Legenda maior* IV, 3) with his brothers ("those most strenuous despisers of large and beautiful houses").[47] These are precise iconographic choices, carefully planned deviations from Bonaventure himself, and precisely with regard to the fundamental issue: the significance of Franciscan poverty—choices to which all the authors of the cycle adhere, most notably Giotto. The compromise between the Franciscan form of life and Roman political theology, between eschatological signs and popular religiosity, between Francis' "singularity" and the *order* protected by papal authority, constitutes the social background to the great artistic and architectural projects of the new era, such as the great Franciscan and Dominican churches that crop up everywhere, in competition with one another, over the twelfth and thirteenth centuries.

Francis' *historiae* are an essential component of the Franciscan spirit and Zeitgeist, but artists must be able to represent them on the walls of these churches without causing scandal; that is, with measure, *in perspective*. How could the harshest, most dissonant scenes—the leper, the nails in the flesh, the unalloyed and truly incarnate image of *Paupertas*—ever be expressed in the new illustrious vernacular that Dante theorizes, in *De vulgari eloquentia*, as "common to all yet owned by none"[48] and worthy of being spoken both in royal and ecclesiastical courts? Those scenes have no place in Dante, either. Yet in Dante—the exile from all courts, both royal and ecclesiastical—the conciliatory, hegemonic pretensions made by Innocent and Honorius (which will last through the tenure of Nicholas IV) are demystified through the words of Bonaventure, and the events of the Order of the Minors are by now contemplated from the perspective of the crisis that has been gripping it since Boniface VIII. It is also for these reasons that Dante applauds the return to the pure, original idea of Francis' poverty. And it is the tragedy of defeat that revives in the poet the idea of poverty, whereas in Giotto (both here and in Santa Croce) poverty can be articulated in the tones of comedy (*comedìa*), because his *historia* has a positive outcome—in fact, its happy ending stands at the very center of the representation. On the contrary, in the grandiose scene in the Heaven of the Sun, both Thomas and Bonaventure predict the failure of that concord for which, each in his own way, they had striven. Such concord is painted and "feigned" in Assisi, but at the cost of concealing the foundations on whose basis it had been loved and pursued: the essential meaning of poverty and compassion, and of their paradoxical yet necessary relationship to joy, gladness, merriment—a relationship that Dante, too, fails to appreciate in all its depth and exceptionality.

Thus, the question arises: *quid est paupertas*, what is poverty? Is it perhaps an allegory, representable as such? It certainly looks that way in the lower basilica, where we see a tall, gentle lady emerge from a thorn bush (but with the tree of life in the background) to offer her hand to a young, angelic Francis, as Christ gives his blessing. The sackcloth she is wearing is patched-up and tattered (unlike Francis' habit). Her appearance is austere, yet by no means young or glad. Here, detachment from the world spells renunciation and sacrifice. In Dante, that "joy" that is "everlasting" ("colà dove gioir s'insempra," *Par.* X, 148) just barely shines through in the nuptials between "the lovers" ("questi amanti") and in the image of the friars hurrying toward the bride, who "delights them so" ("piace," *Par.* XI, 74–84). But in the poet, too, the dominant tone is rather set by that "scorned, obscure" ("dispetta e scura") existence in which "she had had no suitor" ("sanza invito"), a state in which she had been abandoned, an inconsolable widow, for "eleven hundred years" ("millecent'anni," *Par.* XI, 64–66). Why does Francis desire her and love her? Looking at her portrait in both Giotto and Dante, we might venture: is it because she is beautiful? In the Saint's gladness (*laetitia*) we sense an energy that exceeds any allegorizing, as well as any theologically argued reason. We should not try to define the essence of poverty. Poverty exists in the figure of the lover. Here the true question should be: Who are you, Francis, *pauper*? Who are you, who find your *raison d'être* in wishing to be poor, so as to call yourself and make yourself into the lowest of all? Therein lies the Franciscan scandal. A scandal that we find theologically "resolved" in Thomas and Dante, and nearly removed in Assisi, in obvious polemic against the pauperistic currents.

Besides, Giotto's own artistic and cultural sympathy for such operation of removal is, so to speak, well on record. Suffice it to recall his *canzone*, edited for the first time by Karl Friedrich von Rumohr in 1827 and dating back to his mature period—that is, after Pope John XXII's bull against the spirituals—where he explicitly polemicizes against any exaltation of Lady Poverty's virtues. This, of course detracts nothing from our argument about the essential role Franciscan spirituality has had in the formation of the new artistic vernacular in all disciplines. After all, Giotto did name his children Francis and Clare! We are looking at two different, often antipodal, portraits of the same enigma, the same mysterious sign of the times—portraits that only in their dissonant harmony (*concordia discors*) can help us to approach the question: who are you, Francis, *pauper*?

VI

Poor is he who loves poverty as his own self. Thomas, a Dominican, knows the elementary meaning of poverty; but Dante's Bonaventure discloses another meaning, far deeper and more unsettling. Thomas only knows

Poverty alongside Chastity and Obedience, exactly like the Giotto of the lower basilica. He knows it not as having value in itself, but insofar as it is free from the impediments that shackle us in this world (*Contra gentiles*, III, 132–135).[49] This is also how he interprets the Sermon on the Mount: poverty is just the general term with which we designate the decision that Christ demands of all who intend to follow him: go and sell everything. Poverty insists on the dimension of renunciation, a necessary prerequisite to obedience. Profound as it may be, it is still a means through which we can follow Him. It is not the bride, the lover one loves for her "glad looks" ("lieto sembiante," *Par.* XI, 76), incomparably higher, more beautiful, and more beloved than any other virtue.

Not even the incessant invective against money and any kind of property can explain the profound reason why poverty should appear to be the highest glory, "that sublime height of most exalted poverty" (*Later Rule* VI),[50] and why only *in* poverty should we be able to call ourselves *heirs*, not just children or friends, but the very ones who are reborn with and from the Father. In and of itself, in Dante's era, marked by the establishment of the new urban financial and trading powers, the condemnation of the polluting, alienating, corrupting force of money is a recurring *topos* in every religious movement preaching a revival of apostolic life. Franciscanism's ties to those movements are obvious and well-known; but so should be the peculiar radicalness with which Francis revisits their central motif: poverty. The significance poverty assumes in Francis is purely contained in that "in spirit" (*pneumati*) from the first of Matthew's *Beatitudes*: "Blessed are the poor in spirit" (5:3), because they alone are the object of divine action, they alone stand in relationship with God through the spirit, and thus, they alone will inherit the Kingdom. The Kingdom belongs to the poor.

The principle therein expressed is incomparable to any "chivalrous" notion of defending or protecting the poor, of renouncing all deceptive worldly goods, and even more to any simple polemic against wealth, breeder of avarice and envy. The mysterious announcement contained in the Beatitudes, powerfully revisited by Francis, is precisely that of the election of the poor (*ptochos*): no longer the figure of someone who, owning nothing, lies curled up in a corner, at everyone's mercy (as the etymology of the Greek word *ptochos* suggests), but the heir to the Kingdom of Heaven (*basileia ton ouranon*). The social connotation of the term, though not lost, is completely transfigured. Poor is not the needy, he who lacks, but, on the contrary, the complete (*teleios*), the perfect one: he who perfectly imitates the Son. For Francis, in other words, the poor is the Christian. The Christian is either poor, or not Christian. The Christian is a mendicant, just as he is a foreigner and a stranger ("advena sum et peregrinus," Genesis 23:4), and finds his perfection or wholeness precisely in being such. Will his Kingdom be the place where poverty has been vanquished at last? Not at all. It will be the place where the poor have triumphed, showing the sublime height (*altissima celsitudo*) of their condition. This is also why Francis shows his "hard intention" *regally*: because it is the intention for the Kingdom. Poverty is the will to conquer the Kingdom. Poor is the violence of he who wants the Kingdom. Only the poor are truly *powerful*.

All this had a profound repercussion on the significance the figure of Francis came to assume in contemporary thought (even prior to the great stir caused by the publication of Paul Sabatier's *Life of Saint Francis of Assisi* in 1893). From Rilke's *Book of Hours*, whose third part articulates the notion of the *great Death* (*Der große Tod*, the one which we can call *ours, singular*), bridegroom of Poverty (that Poverty which is fullness of experience, freedom from the superfluous, not lack-of-ownership—or "mendicancy," as Adolph von Harnack seems to understand it in *The Essence of Christianity*), to young Lukács' autobiographical essay *On the Poverty of Spirit* (1912), all the way to the more "saturnine" Heidegger, caught at a time of great catastrophe, as he lectures on Hölderlin from the dungeon of a castle where his seminar has taken refuge. For all of them, we might say, poverty means opening up to a relationship with the *necessary*—freeing oneself from all that is not necessary, and therefore lacking nothing.[51]

But perhaps, at least when it comes to German literature, the fundamental inspiration for the development of this theme comes from no other than Nietzsche. After "the ugliest human being"—who despises himself, but loathes the idea of being pitied, and thus hails the death of God—that "most curious" God who *saw everything*—as a liberation—Zarathustra encounters the "voluntary beggar . . . from whose eyes goodness itself preached."[52] And he senses his proximity to this figure to be greatly dangerous to his mission. The voluntary beggar knows from his singular experience how much harder it is to give than to take, knows that "bestowing well is an *art* and the ultimate, craftiest master-art of kindness" (*Thus Spoke*, 218). Furthermore, he shares Zarathustra's revulsion for "lascivious greed, galling envy, aggrieved vengefulness, rabble pride." He knows that today the rich are the "convicts of wealth," and the poor are *rabble*. "Rabble above, rabble below! What do 'poor' and 'rich' mean anymore today!" (*Thus Spoke*, 219). Francis' *paupertas* remains unheard-of—and only in solitude, amid the animals, does he preach it. Yet Nietzsche's animals are different—they reject the meekness of Francis' animals. They are eagles and snakes. Herein lies his break from Francis; one, however, which clearly stems from an essential misunderstanding: Nietzsche reduces Francis to the level of the "pitying," failing to understand him as the very expression of that *great love* which surpasses both forgiveness (*Vergebung*) and pity (*Mitleiden*); that love which one offers one's *neighbors*, not to reassure them about themselves, console them, or "leave them in peace," but to transform them. It is the kind of love that demands the *conversion* of the beloved, that "wants to create the beloved" (*Thus Spoke*, 69). But this *beyond* love is profoundly akin to that which takes shape and voice in Francis' call to *poverty*. (One might notice here the same mix of extreme proximity and extreme distance, the same tangle of essential sympathy and radical misunderstanding, that is also manifest in Nietzsche's relationship with the figure of Jesus.)

But let us attempt a "reconstruction" of the Franciscan notion of poverty—not an easy task, as every theological reading of poverty always entails the risk of betraying the liveliness with which Francis *lives* it. Yet, it is a necessary task, in the face of the myriad misleading interpretations to which this notion has given rise. In an important passage from his *First Life*, Celano illustrates with how much violence Francis, even at the end of his strength, strove for even greater perfection, for perfect love (*teleia agape*). It seemed to him as though he always found himself still at the beginning of his itinerary, as though every day he ought to "make a beginning." Only a constant return to the origin, to the "former obedience," might make it possible to carry out the hard work (*improbus labor*) of tearing down every screen between oneself and Christ.[53] But what is the "former obedience"? Certainly, to give up everything; certainly, to obey the living Logos, to strip oneself of everything and follow Him, to the point of being able to say: "If anyone comes to me and does not hate father and mother, wife and children, brothers and sisters—yes, even their own life—such a person cannot be my disciple" (Luke 14:26)—precisely the evangelical passage that Francis "quotes" as he severs all ties with his earthly father, that is, with the principle that chains him to the ground, or rather, as we will see, to his *self*. But the expression seems to recall a deeper sense of poverty. Adam before the fall is perfectly obedient; he is perfectly poor, for he has everything in

God. Do we hear, in Francis' brand of poverty, this idea of restoration of the Edenic state? Is Francis originally more the other Adam (*alter Adam*) than the other Christ (*alter Christus*)?

In a work that I cannot imagine having been unknown to Dante, *The Sacred Bond of Saint Francis with Lady Poverty*,[54] Poverty begins to narrate her story precisely from the earthly Paradise, as she awaits the white knight who will restore her to her throne. To my mind, however, this is hardly an issue of fundamental importance. Neither in Francis, nor in Dante, nor in Giotto's pictorial power, is the notion of Paradise configured as nostalgia for the origin. In all three of them, future beatitude is represented in terms of radical *novelty* with respect to the Edenic state.

Central to the Franciscan mystique is, rather, the idea that links poverty to kenosis. *The Sacred Bond of Saint Francis* also proceeds along these lines. For love of poverty, the Lord has left the celestial orders to descend into the scum and mud, into the darkness and shade of death. And Poverty requites this mad, gratuitous love by never abandoning him, by following him all the way to the cross. To love poverty, then, means to retrace—with tenacious perseverance, overcoming the repugnance arising from our first encounter with the Lady's foul countenance—the path of the incarnation of Logos, until we arrive at the contemplation of the "eternal truths," which guard the secret of this path (Celano, *Second Life*, 50). To imitate Christ, in sum, entails imitating the kenotic dynamic that informs God-as-Relation (*Deus Relatio*). The renunciation of worldly goods stands in a relationship of attributive analogy (which here means measurable yet incomparable proportion) to divine kenosis.[55] This, indeed, appears to be its crucial theological significance. The only proper relationship that man is allowed to conceive between himself and God is founded on his indissoluble marriage to Poverty. Outside of this real relationship, there are only compassion, good deeds, allegories, or metaphors. It is because of the "historic" event whereby the divine Being made itself absolutely poor that human existence, its *historia*, can become His *true icon*.

But renunciation of what? A cloak? A few possessions? What do we stumble upon, between this immediate gesture of spoliation before the earthly powers (between the shedding of the burden that prevents us from "running" in Jesus' footprints) and this supreme imitation—to be poor on the model of the divine kenosis? We stumble upon the toughest *problem* (from the Greek *próblema*, "obstacle"): the emptying of *Self*. The highest Mount of poverty cannot be conquered unless we accomplish this crucial passage. The good that Jesus enjoins us to give up is our most cherished possession, the one we defend most stubbornly against everything and everybody—our soul (*psyché*). This is what we think of as our inalienable substance. This is what stands at the center of every other good or value. We may renounce everything *for our soul*, yet renouncing *our very soul* appears inconceivable to us. But this is precisely what Francis demands (without wishing to coerce anyone), in the radicality of his desire to return to the origin of the evangelical *Verbum*. As God emptied himself of his divine Self, so must you make exodus, to the point of hating every love of life (which we may call, following Carlo Michelstaedter, *phylopsychia*[56]) and shedding your very own self, which you had deemed your safest possession: "for he who is truly poor in spirit, hates himself and loves those who strike him on the cheek" (*Admonitions* XIV).[57]

One last step is adumbrated in Francis' journey of *kenosis* and *humilitas*—one that both Giotto and Dante are unable even to glimpse: it is expressed by Christ's great cry from the cross, the cry of he who has been *abandoned*. For radical poverty coincides with being-abandoned—*Gottlosigkeit*, the anguish at finding oneself *empty of God*. Only in such emptiness does one's love for Him attain a nontranscendable limit, thereby becoming truly infinite. Is this extreme height (*celsitudo*) of Poverty not precisely what Francis' whole life reaches toward? Indeed, it is a life that appears to unfold as an unstoppable representation of 1 Corinthians 4:12–13: "When we are cursed, we bless; when we are persecuted, we endure it; when we are slandered, we answer kindly. We have become the scum of the earth, the garbage of the world." The crucified Francis is unimaginable without the cry of the ninth hour.

Yet, the true poor, those who are *truly naked*, do not empty themselves of the *Self* merely to be able perfectly—by imitation—to welcome God. The kenotic dynamic is about welcoming the other, in all the faces with which he may come toward and against (*contra*) us. The shedding of all external impediments, all the way up to the shedding of one's Self, has value only if it happens *out of love*. One should not hate earthly goods for their vanity, for their fleetingness and inconsistency, as that would still be the attitude of the wise. By the same token, one should not renounce earthly goods for the peace of contemplation. To become poor means to free ourselves to be able to love perfectly; to exist solely in our relation to the other, in our exodus toward the other, with nothing holding us *in ourselves*. Poverty, then, becomes richness of experience, even curiosity—the opposite of every contempt of the world (*contemptus mundi*) and the indispensable condition for being able to welcome into ourselves every face, every encounter, every being *sub specie aeternitatis*. Through the path (i.e., the experience) of poverty, which once merely looked like abandonment, sacrifice, renunciation, the Self itself *is reborn*, but as a new event, equipped with a new gaze on reality, a gaze that conceives of any thread of existence in terms of a *neighbor* always as such, and therefore impossible to own.

Poverty is kenosis in a sense radically opposed to any will to annihilation.[58] It means divesting oneself of everything one has in order to be reborn with and for every being. Franciscan mysticism is not *de-creation*, but rather a love that *re-creates*—which, incidentally, makes it clear why it played such an immense role in the renewal of artistic languages. To really "have," and be able to represent, "our" world, we must lack (*de-habere*), divest ourselves of everything we do not "have" by the grace of pure love. One only "has" what one loves, but what one loves can never be a possession, reified in something that is owned. One cannot truly "have" unless in the lived experience of poverty. The sublime height of poverty cannot be attained, then, either through mere renunciation or by simply being a pilgrim (*peregrinus*). Poverty is acting energy, the force that goes to the beloved, discovering the new face of being as that which cannot be possessed or destroyed. Poverty is energy that envies nothing and wishes nothing to be available. Poor is not the needy, he who lacks, but he who "has" everything like brother and sister, that is, *without having*, he who enjoys everything, in the sense of enjoyment of God (*frui Deo*). For the only thing worthy of being loved is that which manifests its being as the incarnation of God's being. To experience one's poverty is tantamount to experiencing the divine essence of being, the fullest and richest experience granted to humankind. He who is wealthy in possessions, on the contrary, will be poor in experience. The decidedly cataphatic, affirmative character of Franciscan mysticism can be understood only within this context. For Francis, the names of God form a crown of really attributive analogies: God is love, charity, wisdom, humility, beauty, "our custodian and defender" (*Laudes Dei altissimi, Chartula fratri Leoni data*),[59] because God, in his kenosis, has given himself entirely to his creatures, thereby giving them the chance to be reborn in Him in the analogous form of poverty. Because these names are inexhaustible, naming will always be an approximation; however, they really do predicate the face of God that is turned to us, they do affirm the divine kenosis qua the energy and motion of love. By emptying himself of his own divine Self, God *has let the world be*. By the same token, the poor is he who, by loving, and because he loves, *lets be*. The poor wishes to *save* being—his neighbor—in himself, not to judge him. "Do not judge" is Francis' first commandment: but even "not judging" or "not condemning" will not suffice. One must be "careful not to be angry or disturbed at the sin of another" (*Later Rule* VII).⁶⁰ To retreat from the arrogance of judging is to show one's being-poor, in the image of the Father—and like His own, it is a gesture of *creative* mercy.

Now it is necessary to take a further step, which will be both the gladdest and the hardest. If poverty really means all of this—communion with the totality of beings, free from the chain of possession and dependency, and communion with God qua himself supreme humility and donative energy—then its image must coincide with that of the bride in the *Song of Solomon*, "spoliated" of every nostalgic tone. In other words, Poverty must appear completely "glad" (*hilaris*). He who performs works of mercy must do so in gladness ("en hilaroteti," Romans 12:8). But how is it possible to imagine simultaneously the theological smile of Beatrice (who certainly does not look "poor" in the *Paradiso*), the unspeakable sufferings of Francis, and the gladness of the minor, of the lowest, of the *pauper*? This is the most difficult imperative to follow. Yet Francis has no doubts about it. The minors *must* be glad. If their countenance does not express complete gladness, then they are not truly poor. "All the brothers . . . must rejoice," and especially when dwelling among "the sick and the lepers" (*Earlier Rule* IX).⁶¹ They must be careful not to wander around "sad and gloomy"; let them always appear, instead, as "joyful, cheerful and consistently gracious in the Lord" (*Earlier Rule* VII)—that is, as someone who is *capable of enjoying God*; and let them "lead people to the love of God in joy and gladness" (*Admonitions* XXI).⁶² Never let them forget that true Christians, if they are inhabited by Christ *today*, they *are* with him today in Heaven, and therefore their gladness must already show *here on earth*.

Yet what image could ever be able to "compose" the suffering God (*Deus patibilis*) of San Damiano, the ravaged body of Francis, with the gladness, the merriment that comes from being perfectly light, *free*, ready to welcome everything and to save everything in oneself? What creative force will ever be able to realize such a symbol?

No doubt Giotto would possess color, substance, and *body* enough to accomplish this task; but the program he is called upon to execute, the boundaries that have been dictated to him, and above all, his very cultural background, prevent him from doing so. In Assisi, humility and merriment do seem on the verge of conjoining over three consecutive panels: the Greccio nativity, the miracle of the fount, and the preaching to the birds. Here is a sainthood that quenches our thirst; here is the announcement of a rebirth, the song to the youth (*iuvenis*) who renovates the aging time; here are the stanzas from the *Canticle*! And yet, neither poverty nor Francis' suffering and illness are anywhere to be seen. The gladness from the announcement glitters in the smile of the Madonna enthroned in the Uffizi (as it certainly does not on the pale face of Poverty in the allegory from the lower basilica), but the gold that envelops her beclouds the passion experienced, and the resurrected body bears no trace of the crucified one. Perhaps only in Fra Angelico's *Annunciation*, in the convent of San Marco in Florence, does she retain the tones of perfect humility, of cognizant obedience to the destiny that awaits her, of the sovereign lightness that poverty vouchsafes, of serene gladness—whereas the Virgins of Mantegna and Bellini are rather marked by an air of tragedy, and they already seem to be carrying the Son in their womb as in a deposition from the cross.

Dante confers exceptional vigor to the figure of Poverty. There is nothing merely abstract about its loftiness (*celsitudo*), which on the contrary pulses through the story of the mendicant-preaching Saint in all its eschatological charge, with a force incomparable to any other virtue (e.g., chastity and obedience). But precisely the relationship to Dominic, and the setting of his praise in the heaven of the wise spirits—both necessary to Dante's representation of his theological-political prophecy—render imperceptible that very motif of merriment that really sounds as if it were Francis' last word. True, one must remember that neither Francis nor Dominic belong in this heaven; yet, "up above" ("più su," *Par*. III, 98), in the Mystic Rose, Francis appears, unlike Dominic, alongside the other two "persons" in the Trinity of saints, Peter and Benedict. It is the historical Trinity incarnate: Peter, the First; Benedict, the founder of Western Monasticism; Francis, the reborn Christ. This means that, for Dante, Francis and Dominic—no matter how much they may surpass the dimension of paradisiac existence (all equally blessed everywhere)—can be understood and preached only in this heaven, as wise spirits.

There is no doubt that Francis' love burns in Dante's heart: but it burns only *regally*. The tone of divestment or spoliation is more pronounced in Assisi, though it never quite attains the drama of kenosis.

In Dante, the energy of the preaching makes it impossible for us to hear forgiveness, or even the withholding of judgment. And the highest words in the Gospel, "do not resist evil" (Matthew 5:39) are perceived in Assisi only to the extent, precisely, that evil itself fails to appear with the realistic face with which Thomas of Celano and Bonaventure also describe it. In both grandiose portraits of Francis, then, the more profound and disquieting aspect of Franciscan mysticism—the one that conjoins in itself love, according to an impossible measure of giving and for-giving, and gladness, authentic gladness, also in the dancing body and in the singing voice—appears to be absent. It is the feminine, maternal aspect of this sainthood that Franciscan mysticism continually exalts. In his *Distinctiones*, Thomas of Pavia compares Francis to the terebinth from Isaiah 6:13 because of the tree's feminine nature.[63] And Ubertino of Casale himself says in his *Arbor vitae*: "Through Francis and Clare, Jesus was reborn in the female sex."[64] If an authentically analogical relationship links divine kenosis to poverty, even more intrinsic is the former's relationship to Woman's maternity. It is Woman who truly divests herself, hates her soul (*psyche*), and lets-be her Son, destined for His mission. She is the one who is banished. But she is also the one able to wear the smile of Beatrice, of the Madonna in the Uffizi, or the celestial serenity of the girl *seen* by Fra Angelico in the pure bareness of her cell in the Dominican convent of San Marco. The spirit of the Lord alights on those who perform the works of the Father, as "spouses, brothers and *mothers* of our Lord Jesus Christ"; we are the mothers of Christ himself when "when we carry Him in our heart and body . . . and give Him birth through a holy activity, which must shine before others by example" (Saint Francis, *Later Admonition and Exhortation to the Brothers*, second draft, 53).[65] Here Francis' language closely resembles that of the great female mystics such as Saint Clare, Saint Angela of Foligno, and Saint Catherine of Siena. Francis would like the Minors to *go around* like mothers, without the idol of rules, without the burden of written texts imposing upon the spirit and killing it. It is his last, desperate appeal: "Not to dare to ask any letter from the Roman Curia, either personally or through an intermediary, whether for a church or another place or under the pretext of preaching or the persecution of their bodies" (*Testament* 25).[66] If they are not welcome, let them leave after wishing for peace, as Francis did with the Sultan.

Indeed, Francis composes his *Canticle* at San Damiano, and dedicates it to Clare, and to women. Women are his true heirs, those who are really nourished by him. If there is a creature capable of reflecting herself perfectly in Christ's spotless (*sine macula*) mirror to recover in it her own *naked* face, it is Clare. Woman is an eschatological figure in the fullest sense; she puts an end to a church that is *potestas*, that is, *patria potestas*, the power of the *father*, the emblem of the overbearing predominance of the male figure and the violence inexorably associated with it. This is the formidable instance that Francis' religious reform carries within it, an instance that amounts to a true anthropological turn.[67]

In the Greccio nativity scene in Assisi (a scene missing in Santa Croce), this fundamental maternal facet of Francis is captured for an instant—albeit, as we already said, in a context that seems to bear no trace of Franciscan poverty. And in a way, one can also perceive its relationship to the gladness of the Minors' song. What has been completely lost, however, is the maternal aspect of suffering, the abandonment that it entails, and the solitude that produces the for-giving (*per-donare, de-mittere*). Both in Dante and in Giotto the victory that emerges from the mouth of misery, gladly announcing itself in defeat, is a paradox not capable of being represented. Yet, the image of a defeated Francis does find a place in Dante. In the story of Guido da Montefeltro, the Saint comes to claim his soul, "but one of the black cherubim / told him: 'Don't bear him off; do not cheat me. / He must come down among my menials'" ("un de' neri Cherubini / li disse: 'non portar; non mi far torto. / Venire se ne dee giù tra' miei meschini,'" *Inf.* XXVII, 113–115). Dante knows that any seraphic ardor can always be defeated by the distributive logic of a cherub's "justice" (no matter how "rebellious" the cherub might be). He also knows well the history of Franciscanism, marked by the tragic events that estranged Assisi from its being the new East, the coming light—a tragedy that Dante does not hide, unlike—inevitably—Giotto, in Assisi. Yet, he fails to see the Franciscan gladness erupt from desertion and banishment, the gladness that *here and now* we can derive from being the meek ones, the thirsty ones, the poor, those who suffer injustice.

In this sense, two scenes are missing both in Dante and in Giotto that exemplify this particular sainthood—one that is indeed fully incarnate yet conforming to that *over-human* measure that shines through in poverty qua imitation of the divine kenosis. The first scene is represented in Saint Francis' *Letter to a Certain Minister*, which greatly (and justly) impressed Auerbach.[68] Anything that might be a hindrance to you, even if the brothers were to strike you, you should reckon "as a favor" (*pro gratia*). You should "love those that do such things to thee," and not wish anything else from them than what they do unto you and wish "that they may be better Christians." And let there be no brother who, no matter how greatly he may have sinned, is not forgiven by you, if he were to seek your forgiveness. "And if he afterwards appears before thy face a thousand times, love him more than me" (122–123).[69] The second scene is narrated in the *Compilatio Florentina*, as an example of true gladness (*vera laetitia*): Francis is returning from Perugia at night, in the dead of winter. It is so cold that the bottom of his sackcloth has frozen into icicles, which are chafing against the saint's bare legs. Once he comes to the convent's gate, it is only after he has called and knocked on the door for a long time that a friar finally appears, and asks, "'Who are you?' 'Brother Francis,' I answer. 'Go away!' he says. 'This is not a decent hour to be wandering about! You may not come in!' When I insist, he replies: 'Go away! You are simple and stupid! Don't come back to us again! There are many of us here like you!'"[70] Abandoned *by his own*, alone before *the many*, suffering (*patiens*) the most perfect poverty, Francis finally experiences what true gladness (*vera laetitia*) is.

In Dante, Francis' patience consists in the tenacity with which he is at war with those powers that have transformed the Seat of Peter into Babylon. In Giotto, a peace is feigned both within Francis' Order and between Franciscanism and the real Church—one that Thomas, Bonaventure, and their most faithful disciples had certainly striven for, but that had no more hope of being realized in the imminence of the catastrophe marked by the tenure of Pope Boniface. The *historia* of Francis cannot be imagined without the portraits of our two great artists, Dante and Giotto, precisely because they are powerful and tendentious reconstructions, the expression of religious, theological, and political projects inherent to the real history that originates from the phenomenon of Francis, who lives within these projects as *figura futuri* while being in no way reducible to them. The singularity of Francis—that extraordinary, paradoxical singularity of someone who absolutely does not wish to be singular—lives on beyond these or any other images, in exactly the same way as Christ, his Model, endures beyond any Christianism.

Two

The "Sin" of Ulysses

I

The keenest and most erudite exegeses of Dante's great canto (*Inf.* XXVI) seem to have by now identified the sources on which Dante drew to shape the *irrepressible* character of his Ulysses.[1] In it are combined Virgil's inventor of crimes (*scelerus inventor*); Statius' fierce, dreadful hero (*acer, dirus*); Cicero's stoic (and Seneca's too, although in *The Trojan Women* we rather get to see the *ferocious* Ulysses of Euripides' *Hecuba*), the foe of all idleness (*otium*), and whose *virtus* aims to know from within (*inspicere*) the habits of man (*mores hominis*) as in Horace; but also a clear reference to Homer's Odysseus: clever in many ways (*polymetis*) and crafty (*kerdaleos*), prudent in words and deeds, who saw many cities and knew the mind (*noos*) of many men.

Of such *virtus* Dante exalts the literally indomitable character. The hero of trespassing erases all nostalgia "within himself." The Neoplatonic Ulysses of Homecoming (who knows how to transform exile into a strenuous, methodical ascent to his own divine "in himself" and, in spite of hardship, remains focused on this goal) is here completely forgotten, or rather, overwhelmed by the deceitful orator (Virgil's *fandi fictor*), who, using the potent weapon of speech, hatches disaster for those who are *won* over by it. There is no cunning (*calliditas*) in this hero. There may have been once in "the horse's fraud" ("l'agguato del caval," *Inf.* XXVI, 59)—which results in "providential misfortune," insofar as "Rome's noble seed" will escape from it ("de' Romani il gentil seme," *Inf.* XXVI, 60)—but certainly not in deciding on, and "arguing" for, the "wild flight" ("folle volo," *Inf.* XXVI, 125). Nor is it simply a matter of idle curiosity (*vana curiositas*). Rather, there is knowledge here (*sapientia*), yet a form of knowledge that is sinful and draws the ire of God (the ambivalence of the term *sapientia* was well-known in the Middle Ages).

To explain the sin and the ire suffice it to remember (as has also been explored at length by the keenest commentators) the condemnation, ubiquitous in patristic literature, of the irresistible longing (*concupiscentia irresistibilis*) for worldly knowledge: the knowledge of those who cultivate it is foolishness in God's sight (Saint Augustine calls them "the godless wise," *impii ingegnosi*). This "longing" ("ardore," *Inf.* XXVI, 97) is lustfulness (*luxuria*) analogous to that of Francesca. Inordinate love and immoderate intelligence form an indissoluble nexus. As the former leads the lovers to ruin, so the latter brings ruin to the false brethren (*falsi fratres*), the brotherhood led into the void (*in vacuum*) by Ulysses' oration.[2] Indeed, many clues indicate that their journey is headed into the void; they set sail in the morning but go West instead of East; and they turn left instead of right (*Inf.* XXVI, 124–126). And Virgil seems to know the outcome even before he hears it from Ulysses: "where, having gone *astray*, he found his death" ("dove, per lui, perduto a moriri gissi," *Inf.* XXVI, 84). "Gone astray" ("perduto"), not just "sea-tossed" (*iactatus*), as in Seneca.[3] In any case, the opposite of the "good death" to which Dante aspires.

Thus, Ulysses' sin would seem to consist in his decision to sail past the Pillars of Hercules of the human intellect, in wishing to reach *all by himself* toward what remains inaccessible to it. Hell opens up *on earth*, and so will the great mount of Purgatory rise up from the earth, but no simply earthly journey can lead to, or cross, either realm. We are dealing here with an extraordinary reality, one that is both unquestionably *real*, yet *inaccessible* to anyone who is not accompanied and enlightened by *gratia*—a grace that is truly "added on" (*superaddita*) when this occurs in one's lifetime.

But is it really from this perspective, as advanced by Romano Guardini, that we should regard Ulysses' journey?[4] On what evidence can we affirm that Ulysses has the *inaccessible* in his sights, and for this reason he falls into the error of pursuing it through philosophical teachings (*per philosophica documenta*)? If that were the case, his oration would not merely be a "brief address" ("orazion picciola," *Inf.* XXVI, 122), but rather a speech purporting to present as true things that are radically untrue. It is the bad rhetoric abhorred by Gregorius Magnus, which prescribes ruinous advice and inflames the souls, deceiving them on the nature of true Purpose—to which Dante is probably alluding with the flames in which Ulysses and Diomedes are "suffering" ("si martira," *Inf.* XXVI, 55). According to this theory, then, we would have a Ulysses-Siren, a Ulysses who, embodying the *hubris* of a human intellect that refuses to acknowledge its finitude, *deceives* his companions and, like a false preacher, surpassing even the ultimate Argonautic crime (*nefas*), buries them in the deepest sea ("Veni in altitudinem maris: et tempestas demersit me," Psalms 68:3).

On this view, Ulysses' journey would mirror point by point Dante's own journey, which in turn is the reflection ("modest" only in appearance) of those of Saint Paul and Aeneas. Indeed, Dante extols the nature of his journey with words than leave no room for doubt: his quest is certainly no less audacious, his undertaking certainly no less scandalously new than that of his Ulysses. In fact, the poet surpasses the Argonautic crime even more drastically than the hero. While through his actions Ulysses expresses his own virtue, Dante is called upon to go even further and *surmount* it if he wants to conclude his mission.

Being guided does not lessen in any way the *protagonism* of someone who ventures to confront truths never pursued before. To ascend entails an even more immoderate effort (*improbus labor*) than to navigate the ocean's immense plains. Dante is the heir, but an "heir to divine things," who takes all from his father (Virgil) and then surpasses him as he returns to the First Maker. The *reality* of Dante's journey—in its concrete occurrences, in its being a lived experience that overwhelms every symbol by translating it into itself—shows how Dante's mind is as far from every negligent or reassuring faith as that of Ulysses, "inventor of crimes." Dante's mind, too, is *all-questioning, all-daring* ("lo troppo dimandar," *Purg.* XVIII, 6).

However, do we not fall into a curious anachronism when we use the Fathers of the Church to explain Ulysses' sin? Why on earth should pagan Ulysses have sought the things of God through the restraint of obedience? He can know nothing of Aeneas' *right path* (*rectum iter*), because the nature of that path can be grasped only by someone schooled in the Virgilian poem, which for Dante has prophetic value. Was Ulysses aiming for transcendence by natural means (*per naturalia*), attempting to "pass beyond the human" ("trasumanar," *Par.* I, 70) by his own strength alone? This is nowhere attested. True, he is shipwrecked before Mount Purgatory, which may not be accessed by force of intellect, but that mount is not where he was headed. In fact, he had turned his prow to *nothing* definable in advance. The fact that he indicates an inaccessible destination should not deceive us, as the ports he passes on his voyage are all marked on the maps, and after all, even that last crossing into the uninhabited hemisphere (which mirrors Ulysses' own solitude) takes place *on earth*, it is indeed a *possible* terrestrial journey.

Besides, could Dante have felt such profound *sympathy* for the hero (only comparable to his feelings for Francesca) had Ulysses' sin merely consisted in having misrepresented the power of human intellect? Dante certainly mirrors himself in Ulysses, as he does in Francesca, as well as in Cavalcanti, in the canto he dedicates, through interposed figures, to the great friend from his youth. Besides, when has Dante ever ignored the distinction (however it may have been construed by the Fathers and Doctors of the Church) between truth of reason and truth of faith? How could Ulysses be blamed for not caring enough about it, for not having limited himself to the mere fact (*quia*) of God's mysteries (*mysteria Dei*)? His speech has only one meaning, unequivocally set in stone: the essence of man, unique among all animals, consists in his being endowed with *logos*, and *logos* demonstrates all its virtue or potency in pursuing and incessantly trying to enhance knowledge, which can be done only through experience. How can such a speech be called fraudulent? Extracted from its context, it might fittingly resound within the walls of the castle hosting the great souls in Limbo. It is pure Aristotelianism, or rather, it is its *letter*. Might its *spirit* perhaps be missing? Might Ulysses perhaps be *deceiving* himself and others as to such spirit?

Either Ulysses' sin consists in Virgil's initial declaration, so that the story of his journey has no essential relationship to it and (as proposed, among others, by Fubini[5]) serves only the purpose of solemnly cautioning against braving the high sea unequipped with any safe hopes and faiths, or else it is in his very speech that we must seek the reasons for his sin of being a fraudulent counselor—a sin of which the story of the horse represents merely the ancient memory. If, however, the nature of his sin lies in his self-aggrandizement, in the presumption of his *virtus*, what is he doing in this circle? Besides, what *hubris* does ever show through his words? Far from sounding assertive, his words seem to us rather heartfelt, imbued with the melancholic tone of that "brief waking time that still is left / unto your senses" ("a questa tanto picciola vigilia / d'i nostri sensi ch'è del rimanente," *Inf.*, XXVI, 114–115). Uttered by someone "old and slow" ("vecchi e tardi," *Inf.* XXVI, 107), they are mature, sensible, stripped of any titanism. They do, however, arouse a sudden rush of excitement—and therein lies the mark of fraudulence: in the attempt to eliminate that very restraint of patience and reflection to which Dante refers at the beginning of the canto: "and more than usual, I curb my talent" ("e più lo 'ngegno afreno ch'i' non soglio," *Inf.* XXVI, 21). But what is its essence? One would be hard-pressed to find it in the Aristotelian principle that Ulysses makes his own. Perhaps, rather, in the Aristotelianism of which Ulysses is the emblem (*figura*), in Aristotelianism as it comes to be *embodied* by Ulysses, the very one Dante had encountered and almost succumbed to, and whose tragic greatness he nonetheless continues to acknowledge, if not admire.

Ulysses' presumption cannot consist in steering his intellect "deep in the abyss / of the Eternal Ordinance" ("ne lo abisso / de l'etterno statuto," *Par.* XXI, 94–95) without a guide ("senza duce"); nor can the symbology of the Pillars of Hercules have any relevance to his adventure. As a pagan, he could never have been the figure of the mind that "on earth is dulled and smoky" ("in terra fumma," *Par.* XXI, 100), and yet he presumes to "enwomb" himself ("m'inventro," *Par.* XXI, 84) in the mysteries that we can believe only *gratia*, through grace. Even the oft-noted parallel between Ulysses' *libido* and the *steadfastness* in the service of God that characterizes the contemplative spirits threatens to lead us astray. How could Ulysses have attained "contentment," how could he ever have been "content within [his] contemplative thoughts," as is Pier Damiani ("contento ne' pensier contemplativi," *Par.* XXI, 117)? Perhaps a more fitting parallel can be made to Aeneas' quest, aiming to find "homes, where we'll settle in peace" ("sedes quietas") for the Penates of Troy (*Aen.* I, 205).[6] Ulysses does not deceive as to the relationship between reason and faith, he is not a harbinger (*figura futuri*) of the drama that roils Scholasticism. Nor can he be perceived as a forewarning of the pridefulness before Revelation exhibited by the Averroist philosophers, which Dante himself had experienced very well.[7] Ulysses' deception or fraud, if there is any, should rather be sought in his *rationalism*. And the comparison with Aeneas serves to clarify the negative consequences of such form of rationalism on the level of praxis, of *political* action.

It is within the very boundaries of reason that Ulysses must not have *reasoned* very well. In fact, he deceives others because he has already deceived himself *within these boundaries*, not because he wished to overcome them. His shipwreck occurs in conformity with those very same principles of intellect—thus prompting a correction of intellect (*emendatio intellectus*) as such: a task Dante presents as utterly crucial insofar as the evolution of his own navigation, which aims well beyond the Pillars of Hercules, rests entirely on the foundation of that correction. You cannot sail any sea if your intellect is ill. Ulysses cites his philosophical teachings (*philosophica documenta*) without really comprehending their meaning. He does *not* sin because he is ignorant of the "peace" of the last heaven, the Empyrean, or because he does not love its "dove," divine knowledge. He sins because he betrays the spirit of all sciences (all of them *Queens*), and whose common motto lies precisely in the words of his "brief address" (*Inf.* XXVI, 121), a formidable dictum conceived in clear antithesis to those with which the poet holds tightly—as if in a fist—the essence of Christian dogma: "Eternal Light, You only dwell within / Yourself" ("O luce etterna che sola in te sidi," *Par.* XXXIII, 124).

In Greek parlance, we could say: Ulysses does not sin, he *misses the target*. His is not sin but Greek *hamartia* ("error"). He does not orient himself by the reason and purpose of knowledge; in fact, he misses knowledge's goal by misconceiving its foundation. Even the meaning to be attributed to Ulysses' unstoppable longing should be carefully understood. It is not a commandment enjoining moderation and temperance, but rather the necessity to keep the ship of inquiry (Dante's is a ship, Ulysses' only a *bark*) well oriented and well steered. Inevitably, then, the error of intellect produces a catastrophe on the plane of ethics and of religious conscience.

The most pertinent reference is to *Convivio* III, 15. After reiterating that our intellect cannot *look at* (in the sense of *in-tuere*—our intellect is not, in other words, *archetypal*) the essence of "things . . . that display some of the pleasures of Paradise" (*Conv.* III, 15, 2),[8] Dante rejects at once the notion that this inability might signify lack of perfection or entail the infinite unappeasability of human questioning. If that were the case, God would have endowed us with a *natural* desire for beatitude, impossible to attain through human knowledge (the Socratic *anthropine sophia*). Thus, the field of science would be that of *always desiring*; but desire is "defective and lacking" (*Conv.* III, 15, 3), and only if it is "brought to its proper end" (*Conv.* III, 15, 4) will our *being-there* be at peace, "contented." Does the intellect lack *perfection*? Why, then, should one proclaim the sciences its *queens*? And is it perhaps not true that everything desires its own perfection, strives to complete (*perficere*) its essence, to be *energeia*? And, from an Aristotelian perspective, everything *can* achieve this goal. Should this goal be denied, of all sciences, to Lady

Philosophy (*Donna Filosofia*)? Not at all: in each and every thing, *natural* desire is *commensurate* to the possibilities of the *desirer*, or else it would follow that nature produced such desire "in vain" (*Conv.* III, 15, 8), or worse, with the intent to make us unhappy.

This passage is crucial to understand Dante's thought: philosophy-science is not the servant (*ancilla*) of any other queen; it has clearly determined, and *perfectly* attainable ends, which make it *content in itself*. If this were not the case, "desiring its perfection, it would desire its imperfection: it would desire always to desire without ever realizing its desire" (*Conv.* III, 15, 9). But philosophy-science cannot "look at" (*in-tuere*) the mysteries of God; this is not its end. It cannot be "unhappy" about something that is not commensurate to its nature: "and so human desire is proportioned in this life to the knowledge which we can have here" (*Conv.* III, 15, 9). However, we might add, the scientific-philosophic investigation is constantly making new developments, appears to always begin again, keeps asking new questions while confusing answers that seemed certain. Is its image ever "contented"? Undoubtedly so, Dante answers insofar as it is perfectly content within the answer it has found *now* to *this* specific question. Indeed, Philosophy is always developing, but from port to port. It *stays on* (the meaning of *episteme*) the achieved result and is content within it. A new adventure detracts nothing from that result and from the contentment it ensured. This entails having a clear idea of the goal one is aiming to achieve; and before that, having accurately formulated the query that motivates one's search. And one should "begin again" only if it proves necessary, after a new question and a different goal have been scientifically formulated. There is no conflict between this beatitude and the joys of Heaven (*gaudium Paradisii*). Both possible perfections have been granted to us, and to deny this attribute to the former would almost be tantamount to denigrating the goodness of God's creation.[9]

Thus, Dante reads "the master of the men who know" ("'l maestro di color che sanno," *Inf.* IV, 131). Man has been created to pursue knowledge ("canoscenza," *Inf.* XXVI, 120), but "the desire for knowledge is not always one, but is many—when one is completed, another comes along" (*Conv.* IV, 13, 1). Desire renews itself not because I may have failed to satisfy its first expression but, on the contrary, precisely because I managed to "complete" it, so that I can now leap *beyond*, set myself new goals. This is an *other* desire, one that bears witness to the port already reached, and is predicated on the previous journey having been completed. Not a mark of imperfection, but rather of greater perfection: the occurrence of a new desire "does nothing to take away the perfection to which the other desire led me; and this expansion is not a cause of imperfection, but of greater perfection or completeness" (*Conv.* IV, 13, 2).

The "opponent" (*Conv.* IV, 13, 3) of this notion of science, then, is clearly he who affirms that, on the strength of his intellect alone, man will never attain *the ultimate goal*, that the achievements of science, however important one may judge them to be, and however far they may expand, remain constitutively *im*-perfect. "Here again the answer is that the opposing argument—that the final desire is never attained—is untrue" (*Conv.* IV, 13, 7): nature organizes our desires in such a way that they have specific ends, so that once they reach those ends, they may find their peace in them. That this peace may not be definitive, that it may not be the beatitude of the Blessed, detracts nothing from the contentment it bestows. The labor of intellect "expands" from contentment to contentment, as long as it proceeds in a well-ordered manner. The fact that "few, because they mistake the way, complete the journey" (*Conv.* IV, 13, 7) does nothing to disprove this principle—just as the existence of a sinner does nothing to disprove the joy of Heaven. The desire for knowledge "achieves perfection," and since knowledge "is a noble perfection . . . its perfection is not lost through the desire for it" (*Conv.* IV, 13, 9), if not through ignorance of the rules for the direction of the mind (*regulae ad directionem ingenii*) that the Master (Aristotle) taught, or from a radical misunderstanding of the relationship that must hold between the natural ends of intellect and the hyperessential (*yperousios*) End in which, *through faith*, we hope.

Clearly, Ulysses' sin cannot consist in such misunderstanding, even less in confusing the perfection of science with "cursed riches" (*Conv.* IV, 13, 9), as if his acquisition were comparable to the conquest of material, ephemeral possessions. Ulysses wants to learn, not to conquer, and his adventure is the harbinger (*figura futuri*) of anything but an "imperialistic" expedition. If his errancy has anything to do with the infernal location Dante has assigned to him (and it is entirely inconceivable that there might be less than an essential relationship between the two), it can be understood only as a radical errancy from the scientific method expounded in the *Convivio*, errancy from which derives the ill, fraudulent counsel (*consilia*) by which Ulysses spurs and guides his crew. His words may be Aristotelian, but he has not understood them in the sense that Dante explains, which for Dante is undoubtedly the only true sense. With those words, Ulysses crafts *a new Trojan horse*. Indeed, the horse with which he had *won* over the Trojans to their own ruin was a real construction. And it is with the real words of Aristotle that he penetrates the heart of his companions ("you were not made to live your lives as brutes," "fatti non foste a viver come bruti," *Inf.* XXVI, 119), making them *wild*, incapable of seeing and understanding, just like the Trojans, intoxicated by the mirage of victory. The difference seems to consist in this: with the invention of the horse Ulysses knew he was deceiving others, whereas here he is, first of all, deceiving himself. While the Ulysses of the great myth led others to destruction (only to atone for his "crime" in the *Odyssey*, where he takes on the traits of the suffering hero par excellence), Dante's Ulysses is the victim of his own deception—almost a contrapasso. Or, rather, it is Dante's profound comprehension of a kind of ontological foundation of fraud, almost as if the ultimate reason for deception lay not in a free will directed to that end but in an innate disposition to errancy that overwhelms others as well as oneself. It is precisely this irresistible "letting oneself be overwhelmed" by one's own unintentional error (a *necessary* mistake, worthy of a hero of Attic tragedy, of an Aeschylean character, as Bruno Nardi once observed) that makes the Dante's Ulysses a figure of extraordinary greatness.[10]

II

It should have become clear by now in what this error consists. Ulysses conceives the path of knowledge as a desiring that is never fulfilled. He braves the high seas without asking himself exactly what goal he wishes to achieve. He wishes to "gain experience of the world" ("divenir del mondo esperto," *Inf.* XXVI, 98) without trying to determine from time to time what his end will be. He "touches" several places only to abandon them at once. He leaves behind what he encounters without really getting to know it. His is the path of *dissatisfaction*. He does not acquire any experience, but *longs* to experiment; he does not finish anything, until he sets the *unfinishable* itself as his goal. How could it ever be possible for anyone to gain experience "of the vices and the worth of men" ("de li vizi umani e del valore," *Inf.* XXVI, 99) by sailing "beyond the sun" to "the world that is unpeopled" ("di retro al sol, del mondo sanza gente," *Inf.* XXVI, 117)? Ulysses is shipwrecked not because he goes beyond the port of philosophy-science but because he never reaches it. The port, or rather ports, of philosophy have each perfect perfection in themselves. The journey only increases that perfection. But Ulysses does not *stay* in any one place, he leaves them all, not because his intellect might be formulating new questions or new problems, but because of his irrepressible unfulfillment. He leaves because he cannot stay. The *result* he achieves, and from which he moves, is the nostalgia of impotence, rather than the one that issues from knowledge. This hero seems to burst out of everything that is "finite," yet science-philosophy proceeds by definitions and determinations, or else it would dissolve into the formless ocean of differences. Then it would no longer be *queen*, it would turn into an *escape without end*. It would no longer discover true things (*vera*) but invent ills (*scelera*).

Within the frame of these principles, we must include the other elements of Ulysses' errancy from the Aristotelianism that Dante deems authentic. First of all, the contradiction that a priori "ruins" him. Ulysses' desperate quest unfolds from being to being, from finite to finite, entirely on the plane of the horizon. How could he possibly achieve an *infinite* satisfaction? And yet the hero appears to be aiming precisely for that. Inevitably, every port is abandoned almost even before it is sighted, because *in-finite* is the end the hero has set himself and, nonetheless, such an end can be pursued only by *moving across* from finite to finite. In a different way, the same contradiction shines through in the supreme moment when Ulysses resolves on undertaking his last journey: he knows that only the briefest "waking-time" is left to his "senses" (*Inf.* XXVI, 114–115), and that no authentic experience can be had without their testimony. And yet, precisely in that moment, he presumes to achieve the ultimate experience, even the experience of something that seems to exceed the very senses. Only the contemplating blessed can hear inaudible music, yet Ulysses wishes to transcend the humanly sensible even as he arrives at the eve of the senses' demise. We could say, in the words of Simone Weil, that his appears to be *an absolute physics*.

Such contradictions derive from having "missed" the heart of Lady Philosophy. Her *smile* (precisely a symbol of joy, *laetitia*) means that the unfolding of the quest is not adventurous, but rather founded on principles that are by no means the mere product of sensible experience in its occasional, contingent aspect. Those very same contradictions show that Ulysses, in his nostalgia, violates the ironclad principles on which every authentic experience must be founded. To follow knowledge (*canoscenza*) does not mean to accumulate encounters, but to proceed according to the principles of knowledge with a view to forming an *accomplished* experience. The knowledge Ulysses talks about, then, is not that of Philosophy, as it incites one to a journey without method (*methodos*). By the same token, *virtue* does not mean audacity, but *staying* with the method, complying with its rules, not going on ad *infinitum*. Virtue is the courage of one's steadfast fidelity to principles, not the reckless daring that presumes to venture as far as the ultrasensible armed merely with the power of the senses. Again: words like Trojan horses.

Among these principles, there is one that for Dante is certainly superior to all others, although not of a strictly logical nature. No truth can be accessed unless the first movement manifests itself as a return of the person to himself. No theory, no experience can exclude the *self-re-flecting* of the questioner himself, the *converting* of the researcher into himself—in other words, the firm will to know oneself. Here Dante's Augustinianism compounds his clear, confident affirmation of the autonomous, *perfect* value of science. If, on the one hand, Ulysses deceives himself and others about Aristotle, on the other, he is simply ignorant of Augustine—not, of course, the Augustine of Grace and Christian doctrine, but the Augustine as Plato's pupil, the philosopher of the care of the soul. Because the soul may no doubt know everything, but only on condition that one keep its mirror clean, clearing it on a daily basis from vain curiosity and superfluous appetites. Ulysses runs away from every place he encounters, as he runs away from himself. In fact, what he is running away from is precisely self-exploration. This, more than the (self-evident) moral-ethical one, seem to be the essential meaning of his first act: the irresistible longing (*concupiscientia irresistibilis*) that prevents him from returning to his homeland represents his impotence to return to himself (*redire in se ipsum*). And just as he cannot make Penelope happy, so he will never be able to reach happiness—the happiness that comes from achieved knowledge—for himself. If one does not wish to lose one's path moving from desire to desire "by going in the wrong direction, just as we do on earthly roads" (*Conv.* IV, 12, 18), one must be able to halt before the abyss of the Self, descend into it and shine a light. Is this not the decision Dante himself makes "midway upon the journey of his life"? But Ulysses proceeds without ever feeling "astray"; he wants to experience foreign things (*aliena*), but nothing outside of us is really knowable if we do not know ourselves, and within ourselves, the forms and limitations of our knowing. This is the *spiritual thirst* that must sustain and nourish all will to know, which forces the soul out of every vain *curiositas* and makes it strain toward its very principle.

This last aspect, too, is characteristic of the "philosophical teachings" Ulysses fails to welcome into his heart. If in the abyss of the self where we dare descend lives the truth that summoned us and that we were seeking, in a very different yet not incomparable sense, for Dante, the metaphysical principles on which the enterprise of knowledge rests must *by their own principles* open themselves to the *theological* dimension. No pure research into the essence of beings and, concurrently, into the forms of their scientific "predicability" (i.e., what can be predicated of them in a scientific proposition) can exist unless it entails an interrogation of the immutable, eternal Being. Physical knowledge, in fact, demands to explain the cause of the motility of beings, and such an explanation can be arrived at only if—through the definition of the different *ousiai*, namely, of the ontological differences between the distinct categories of beings—one comprehends the essence of the Supreme Being: eternally present, supersensible, unmoving, and moving all things by attracting them to itself.

The starry heaven of metaphysics, which is the science of being qua being, is followed by the *theo-logical* heaven of the Primum Mobile. Physical inquiry, metaphysical theory, and theology form one powerful architecture. Ulysses, on the contrary, embodies an Aristotelianism that is purely *physical*, and thus deceptive, fraudulent, *astray* from the very beginning. Ulysses does not wonder about Being as such, nor about its Cause. Indeed, he could have found perfect satisfaction in each and every one of the ports he achieved, had he based himself on that question and oriented himself toward that End. Indeed, Dante senses a mortal danger in the affirmation of a type of experience that is carried out at the cost of forgetting oneself, of suspending radically (*radicitus*) the question of being and of its general predicability, even of rejecting the reasonableness of an inquiry into the ultimate End of the knowing soul and the totality of the knowable beings. It is an experience that *prides itself* on its autonomy as it runs from state to state of things, from fact to fact, ever unfulfilled, yet always at same time proud of its ability to abandon every *terra firma*, deluding-deceiving itself as to its freedom—which is no other than infinite longing and infinite repetition of the finite.

Philosophy taught Dante that this is not Aristotelianism. Nevertheless, Dante had most likely already encountered this particular version of it and had most likely sensed the power of its courageous reliance on experience, without predetermined dogmas, in the service of no one; he had already encountered the power of this opening toward things, unafraid to venture down any path without acknowledging any authority besides the evidence provided by intellect. It was the birth of a secular, radical *intelligentsia*. Dante's new guides (Virgil, Beatrice) may show its errors but cannot erase its *heroic* dimension. In fact, it is precisely here, in the moment of its necessary shipwreck, that Dante chooses to represent it most intensely: a shipwreck that the hero, unable to stay in one place, pursues with indomitable resolve. A merely physical (*physicus*) Aristotle is not Aristotle, but the betrayal is magnificent, and without confronting the challenge it represents, Dante could never have defined science as *queen*, nor every stage of its journey as *perfect*. The error is not simply abolished, but rather subsumed into the achieved truth. The true notion of science—the true Aristotle—is ultimately grasped also through the lesson of Ulysses' deception.

A physical Aristotle must of necessity also be an atheist. At most, in such an Aristotelianism, the spiritual-religious dimension will be confined to the field of beliefs, of traditions, of customs, of *religio civilis*, the preservation of which will perhaps be deemed opportune, giving rise to a covert atheism (*atheismus larvatus*). For Dante, on the contrary, even the highest mystical flight is wedded to the knowledge of God as Supreme Being, and thus, ultimate result of every metaphysical inquiry. Dante ascends; yet, as we have seen, he does so from the very *heart* of Ulysses' experience. Ulysses denies the value of precisely that *ascent-ascesis*. Here, then, a comparative reading of this canto with that of the missed encounter with Cavalcanti is absolutely in order. Farinata's atheism must be condemned as such for being a conscious rejection of Revelation (a rejection that may be arrived at also through an erroneous conception of the powers and limitations of reason itself, in its relationship—constitutive, as we will see—with love), whereas Ulysses' atheism may present itself as a philosophical error.

Why is Dante's great friend, and indeed mentor of the "New Life," not standing beside his father and the Ghibelline hero? Why does the poet pretend he is still living? Is it just for utterly external reasons, imposed by the fictional dating of his journey? Or rather because he still cannot bring himself to judge Guido's fate as definitive? Was Guido's Averroist Aristotelianism, too, destined for an *atheistic* resolution? Or did he perhaps only disdain Aristotle the theologian, that subordination of intellect (and thus also of metaphysics as properly understood) to Revelation preached, in very different forms, by Scholasticism? Clearly, he could not have loved Dante's Beatrice. But Beatrice as the last (or rather second-to-last) guide to the Empyrean, or Beatrice the Philosopher? Perhaps Dante does not have a sure answer, perhaps the shadow of the great Guido continues restlessly to linger between *Inferno* X and XXVI. Did his naturalism really go so far as to postulate the mortality of the individual soul? True, his concept of love is opposed to that of the *Convivio*, it cannot turn into intellectual love (*amor intellectualis*); but does this necessarily imply that for him physics is the prime science, as it certainly would be for Ulysses? I believe Dante's judgment remains suspended. *Perhaps* Cavalcanti's Aristotelianism can "expand" enough to meet the one that Dante conceives in the *Convivio*—and thus, in a certain sense, it still *lives*—whereas on that of Ulysses the sea must close forever.

Nevertheless, in another, decisive sense, it is very likely that Dante was remembering his friend Guido as he told of Ulysses' *hubris*—an aspect in which both "betrayed" Aristotle. To understand this, we must once more return to the *Convivio*. While the starry Heaven symbolizes the nexus between physics and metaphysics (the study of the different *ousiai*, that is, of the essence of the very beings that physics investigates), it is the Primum Mobile or crystalline heaven, beyond and above, which "arranges the daily revolution of all the others" (*Conv.* II, 14, 15), teleologically directed toward allowing procreation and life. Without this ninth heaven, "all the universe would be disordered, and the movement of the other heavens would be in vain" (*Conv.* II, 14, 17). To it, Dante compares "moral philosophy" (*Conv.* II, 14 18), which commands that the sciences not be abandoned, but rather learned and taught. Dante interprets Aristotle's *Ethics* in light of this notion of the primacy of moral philosophy. We might explain it so: without the *order* that Justice imparts (a sort of supreme and original *orexis*, that is, an overbearing *desire* for every particular science), no scientific *movement* is conceivable, no research could ever be set in *motion*. Yet, as Étienne Gilson aptly observed,[11] this is true only *for us*: ontologically, *first* is the highest *Ousia*, pure Act toward which all the others strive. We, however, can only move toward its contemplation (*theoria*) by virtue of that *ethos*, that fundamental disposition of our nature whereby we wish to know.

Could we not, then, apply this moral primacy to Ulysses, too? Perhaps so, if the Aristotelian argument, rehearsed by Dante, stopped at this point. But the question of the *Ethics* pertains to the Good and the Best (*to agathon kai to ariston*),[12] the Good itself, at least to the extent that it constitutes a necessary object of inquiry, and thus of science. And the science (*episteme*) that the Good pursues, which the Good attempts to define by teaching its *methodos*, is the most *constructive* and *architectural* of all: the science of Politics. Politics revolves around "the spheres of what is noble and what is just" (*kala kai dikaia*),[13] it is geared toward the building in the *polis* of relations inspired by justice and stability (*kala*: to be whole, to keep "in shape"). On the one hand, then, for Dante, who is commenting on the Master, there could be no order in the heaven of sciences, be they physical or metaphysical, without a moral impulse. On the other hand, that impulse must of necessity unfold within a practical-political praxis whose end is the common Good of the city. The sciences themselves must acknowledge this primacy inasmuch as they belong to political life and their own enterprise strives toward "things fine and just."

In Dante's view, a will to know abstracted from this political dimension would inevitably betray the essential meaning of Aristotle's teachings. Science may be *queen*, but then all queens go on to form one great choir. No one is subordinate to another, but each is subordinate to the End of the Good, which Politics is called upon to achieve within the scope of the *polis*. There cannot exist, in Dante's architecture—nor, essentially, in the classical notion of *episteme*—any abstract autonomy of the distinct spheres of knowledge. Herein lies the radical difference from the figure of Ulysses. Ulysses' inquiry *moves itself*, is completely self-referential. The idea of knowledge that the hero represents closes in upon itself in its own exclusive identity. It is not an impulse to knowledge aiming at "things noble and just." Its theoretical error, on which we have dwelled, becomes then ethical errancy, in the declared absence of any political *interest* (from *inter-esse*, "to be between"). According to Dante, the essence of Aristotelianism is forgotten if knowledge, too, is not directed to human happiness, if it does not affirm the supreme *evidence* that happiness constitutes the ultimate purpose of our nature. We might say that Ulysses' knowledge is utterly "unpolitical," has no regard for its usefulness (*utilitas*); the opposite of the Aristotle of Dante's *Monarchia*.

The famous lines 94–97 of *Inf.* XXVI ("neither my fondness for my son nor pity," "né dolcezza di figlio, né la pieta") are read too reductively when they are taken to signify merely Ulysses' lack of *pietas*. In reality, they already clarify the crucial fact: the hero does not comprehend the true significance of Aristotle's teachings, despite proclaiming them in such lofty rhetoric. Ulysses does not know that theory and praxis are indivisible. He does not know that the animal endowed with *logos* that we call man, precisely because he is endowed with *logos*, asserts, reasons, practices science and philosophy, and for this very reason is also a "political animal" (*zoon politikon*). It is his very ability to speak that makes him so, because to speak is also to dialogue, with others or with oneself, in any case with the language that lives within us and *speaks to us*. Dante's own political passion could not have failed to notice Ulysses' "sin" here: abandoning home and country—abandoning them before attempting to return—is tantamount to fleeing from the most constructive and necessary of all arts: the art of making *polis*. This is the "owed" love that should have "gladdened" Penelope ("'l debito amore / lo qual dovea Penelopè far lieta," *Inf.* XXVI, 95–96). Ulysses should have understood that the sense of his search for knowledge and virtue required—as his people rightly required—not so much a domestic sentiment, or the longing for a serene household, but rather love for the realization of justice and harmony in one's own *home*. At the antipodes from Ulysses, then, stands Aeneas: suffering, like Ulysses, yet oriented toward a goal that he pursues with all his strength, even "reluctantly" (*invitus*; whereas Ulysses always obeys his demon—his own pleasure—without having been able to recognize it in its true nature, and thus to purify it), a goal that he, Aeneas, pursues with steadfast *pietas* toward his home, toward his *oikos*—but an *oikos* that has value only within the project of building the common Good of the *polis*.

Ulysses loves only his journey. But that means not understanding the "owed love" that binds together Love and Philosophy. If love dies out, it becomes impossible to philosophize (*Conv.* III, 13–14). Already in the *Vita nuova*, Dante's notion of Love marks a sharp break from Cavalcanti's Averroism, by assuming clear Platonic inflections. Philosophy is "the name of the lover" (*nomen amantis*); love *reasons* in the mind. This is the form in which the divine virtue descends into the mind, and the will to speculate is created from their union. The fact that Ulysses has extinguished this love within himself is already enough to lead him down the path of a fraudulent, false philosophy, which is really a nonphilosophy. Because he fails to acknowledge the primacy of moral philosophy, he must strain from coast to coast, from port to port, from being to being—without love. He does not see the love that descended into his intelligence to enlighten it, nor is the gaze he directs onto things a gaze of love. In fact, his gaze seems rather to consume things in themselves. Since it is light reflected from the angelic intelligences who are first enlightened, love manifests itself "in the face of Wisdom" (*Conv.* III, 13, 11), rendering it of admirable beauty, and at same time it produces in the soul the will and the energy to "be like" the Principle (*Conv.* III, 14, 3). If philosophy does not ascend to the Principle, if it is not first effort (*conatus*), then methodical search for truth, it will inexorably wither away. If it does not love, a radical error will debilitate it and kill it. Lack of love, then, sums up all the forms of Ulysses' errancy: metaphysical, ethical, and political. And the face of a loveless philosophy will never be able to express the gladness or contentment that an inquiry that has reached its end can ultimately grant us. It will rather bear the solitary (unpolitical), cloudy (*nebulosus*), disdainful look of Cavalcanti as described in Boccaccio and in the *Chronicles* of Dino Compagni.

If Ulysses represents the tremendous danger incurred by an Aristotelianism that has turned into mere desire to know (*libido sciendi*), thus betraying the very spirit of the Master's system by radically misunderstanding the limits and purposes of intellect, that does not mean, in my view, that his position may be entirely assimilable to Averroism. Quite a few traits of radical Averroism are well visible in Dante himself, especially in *Monarchia*. And that Dante is very far from condemning it *tout court* is demonstrated, with "heretical" evidence, by the eminent position he assigns to the figure of Sigier of Brabant, side by side with Saint Thomas in the first crown of the twelve wise souls in *Paradiso* X. If Ulysses were really assimilable to Sigier, how to explain the opposite judgments? Ruedi Imbach's argument seems to me to miss the mark: Ulysses' adventure, as we have seen, by no means embodies an only natural intellectual happiness, nor does it represent the natural desire for knowledge in the form that this must assume in order to achieve its end.[14] Ulysses clashes as much with the Aristotle of *Convivio* as with the Averroist one of Sigier. Ulysses does *not* syllogize; he *enchants* by abusing philosophic formulas. Or, at the very least, he passes off false things as true. On the contrary, Sigier syllogizes true things (*vera*). Syllogism, the argument that founds itself on its form, is necessary and leads to solid conclusions. It is an essential factor of *queen* Philosophy. Thus, the reason why Dante placed the Averroist Sigier in Heaven should be found in the conviction that the weapon of syllogism had been used by the Parisian master not *against* Revelation, nor arrogantly to try to explain its mystery, but in full awareness of its limitation—limitation that, as we have seen, detracts nothing from its happiness (*felicitas*). Sigier's arguments would have been "deceiving syllogistic reasonings" ("difettivi sillogismi"), the symptom of the "senseless cares of mortals" ("insensata cura de' mortali," *Par.* XI, 1–2), had they served to prevent Dante's soul from being "delivered" ("sciolto," *Par.* XI, 10) with Beatrice until the last vision. On the contrary, those syllogisms "earned him envy" ("sillogizzò invidïosi veri," *Par.* X, 138) for the power with which they reason about physics, mathematics, and the ninth Heaven—evidently a heaven that Dante deemed "open" to the next ascension also for Sigier. For both, the joys of the intellect did not contradict the hope to complete the journey "where joy is everlasting" ("dove gioir s'insempra," *Par.* XI, 148).

Thus, Dante seems to be considering three fundamental variants of Averroism. The first, represented by Ulysses, cannot even be called that, insofar as it lacks, at bottom, the spirit of Aristotelianism; yet, precisely herein consists its heroic, grandiosely heretical power, its embodying almost a time of ultimate destruction (*apopleia*), to which a journey without a beginning or an end must lead. The second is that of Cavalcanti, who is *expected* by those who believe the individual soul dies with the body, and thus syllogize against the truths of faith (those syllogisms are ultimately *vain* because, unaware of their limitations, they presume to go beyond the Pillars of Hercules of a *sane* intellect); from the womb of this second option issues the formidable movement of Western thought that will culminate in Spinoza. The third variant is that of Sigier, who is recognized as a *pure philosopher* without this being at odds with Dante's itinerary.[15] Sigier, in his life, might not have seen Beatrice's smile, but he never rebelled at the notion of it, unlike Cavalcanti, a true "rebel against the light" (Job 24, 13, KJV). He merely syllogized, but he did it *perfectly*, and thus he may well have achieved an earthly happiness, though a much-envied one, and now be enjoying full beatitude with all the other wise souls. Since Sigier was able to proceed with method, he must not be numbered among the fools who "without distinguishing" ("sanza distinzione") affirm and deny about things both human and divine (*Par.* XIII, 112–142). He may not have produced any harmony between two opposite stances ("passo" in the original, *Par.* XIII, 117), but at least he did not confuse them. And his great merit, in the eyes of Dante in the *Convivio* and *Monarchia*, consists in not having slavishly subordinated the reasons of intellect to the truths of faith. It would suffice to read this passage from *Par.* XIII along with that from *Par.* X where Sigier is introduced by his enemy "on earth" Saint Thomas, and compare them to Ulysses' "longing," to understand how between Sigier's exploration and Ulysses' adventure there lies an unbridgeable abyss.

Dante has had lived experience of all three avenues. He has freed himself from the first through an effort expressed in the most dramatic way by the silence with which he receives the words of the ancient hero, a silence nearly equivalent to his falling "as a dead body falls" after Francesca's story ("come corpo morto cade," *Inf.* V, 142). To Guido's "high intellect" ("altezza d'ingegno," *Inf.* X, 58), he pays explicit homage. Only an exercise of humility that passes through an authentic meditation on death (*meditatio mortis*), and the discovery of Philosophy as a name of *modesty*, have allowed the poet to find the guide who would render the intellect *perfect*, and at the same time open it to its last ascension. Sigier's is the way of syllogism, of logical rigor, of the exact distinction, envied on earth by those who ignore the virtue of Lady Philosophy, those whose theology is as *vain* as the *curiositas* that overwhelms Ulysses' lust for knowledge (*libido sciendi*).

Indeed, Dante does not stop at Sigier, yet the ladder-cross on which he ascends encounters a crucial turning point in the figure of the "accursed" philosopher. However, this could not be fully understood unless on the backdrop of those other moments of truly tragic stature: the one where the possible abyss of a pagan Aristotelianism, atheistic and unpolitical, stands agape; and the one that, on the strength of its own syllogistic weapon, would wish to counter the truths of faith, either by denying them or by arrogantly presuming to own the key to them, to make them into a "concept." If he had not found himself at loggerheads with these figures, if he had not suffered them within himself, Dante could not have "approached" the grace of his two guides. Thus, these figures, too, must be deemed a decisive factor in his journey to God (*itinerarium in Deum*).

Addendum

Here it would be opportune to review the different exegeses of *Inferno* X, specifically with respect to the very troubled question (*vexatissima quaestio*) about the meaning of the words Dante addresses to the shade of old Cavalcante. Who is the person whom "perhaps . . . your Guido did disdain" ("forse cui Guido vostro ebbe a disdegno," *Inf.* X, 64)? (I do not think the term here should be taken as an equivalent of pure "contempt," but rather as a refusal to acknowledge that *dignity*—in the Latin sense—that Dante evidently attributes to the person he is referring to.)

It seems to me that, essentially, there are two main theses that confront each other, each finding its most exhaustive formulation, respectively, in Antonino Pagliaro and Enrico Malato.[16] On the understanding that "he who awaits me there" ("colui ch'attende là," *Inf.* X, 62) is Virgil, should the *cui* of the next verse ("forse cui Guido vostro ebbe a disdegno," *Inf.* X, 63) be read as *quem* (whom), as *ad eum quem* (to him whom), or rather as *ad eam quam* (to her whom)? In the first case, it could refer only to that very same Virgil. In the second case, *ad eum quem* could refer only to God himself, or to the Highest Good to which Dante is *freely brought*. But, really, could such a "perfect" atheism be attributed to Guido? Not to mention that Virgil is not Dante's guide all the way up to God. Thus, we are left with two options: either Virgil (as maintained by Malato) or Beatrice (as argued by Pagliaro). Is it conceivable that Cavalcanti did not acknowledge the "dignity" of Virgil in general? It seems evident to me that it is not. Cavalcanti is no irrationalist. One should then be obliged to understand that Guido disdains—that is, rejects as not "worthy" ("degno") of his high intellect—the possibility that Virgil might be his guide. Indeed, the arrogant and solitary poet-philosopher has always presumed to make the journey *relying solely on his own strengths*.

However, the disagreement between Dante and Guido does not essentially pertain to the figure of Virgil, but rather to the conception of love, and it is a disagreement already obvious in the *Vita nuova*. That is why, in my view, we must also detect, in that *cui*, the presence of Beatrice, since it is precisely over the significance of Lady Beatrice that their friendship came to an end. Of course, in this notion of love, a whole philosophy (and, tied to it, a whole theology) was at stake. Virgil clarifies the issue in *Purgatorio* XVIII, but his word is not meant to be the last on the issue. For a definitive solution to the vexing conundrum Dante poses to him, Virgil hints at the words Beatrice will pronounce in heaven about the meaning of *innate freedom*, the supreme gift that God infuses directly into the soul. Now Virgil is guiding the pilgrim, but he can guide him only up to that doctrine of free will that is the natural faculty, innate to us humans, to "keep the threshold" of our "assent" ("e de l'assenso de' tener la soglia," *Purg.* XVIII, 63), and therefore to vanquish love-passion—a faculty that Cavalcanti seems to deny in *Donna me prega*, his great *canzone*. In fact, Guido is steadfast in denying any scientific foundation to that doctrine of free will; he disputes that it may have any cognitive dignity ("*ebbe* a disdegno" has a clear *aoristic* value). But such is the doctrine that Dante "harmonizes" between the figures of Virgil and Beatrice. Is it, then, really so necessary to choose one or the other, with regard to the *cui*? The extremely delicate problem here is that, without the ultimate reference to Beatrice ("What reason can see here / I can impart; past that, for truth of faith, / it is Beatrice alone you must await," "Quanto ragion qui vede, / dirti poss'io; da indi in là t'aspetta / pur a Beatrice, ch'è opra di fede," *Purg.* XVIII, 46–48), Dante remains stuck in an aporia that he dramatically perceives ("that has filled me with still greater doubt," "ciò m'ha fatto di dubbiar più pregno," *Purg.* XVIII, 42), and which Gennaro Sasso has masterfully clarified.[17]

If the origin of amorous passion is utterly accidental, if the soul *created for love* gravitates naturally toward what it likes, irresistibly drawn by its image, and "just as flames ascend" ("como 'l foco movesi in altura," *Purg.* XVIII, 28) continues to grow, "never resting / till the beloved thing has made it joyous" ("e mai non posa / fin che la cosa amata il fa gioire," *Purg.* XVIII, 32–33), how could one really think of defeating Guido's counterdoctrine, disdainful of Lady Philosophy? Is not the origin of anything always its most powerful part (*potissima pars*)? And from the natural doctrine of love, conveyed by Virgil, how is one to build a (just as rational) bridge to the notion of an *innate freedom*? No, Virgil cannot lead to it; his reasoning must not be considered "worthy." He does not teach the essence of love, but how to overcome it, how love must cease to be such, so it can turn into "ethics." Guido does not disdain Virgil's rationality. On the contrary, he disdains the fact that, on this decisive point, Virgil should fail to carry out his argument consistently, and be forced to abdicate to Beatrice—an abdication that should be even more thoroughly rejected. In conclusion, if we wish to understand the full significance of Dante's words, we cannot separate, in them, his two guides. Besides, are we really so certain that he meant to refer to only either one of them? That the ambiguity might not be intended? What if the ambiguity issued precisely from Dante's own uncertainty ("perhaps . . . ," "forse . . . ," *Inf.* X, 64) as to the central kernel of Guido's error? And does the error consist in a defective Aristotelianism, or rather in the rejection of Beatrice qua Christian faith? If any interpretation succeeds in conferring on the scene the vividness of a lived experience—in making it the present memory of a profound friendship and of its crisis, in *incarnating* the figures and symbols that confront each other—it must certainly be the interpretation that puts Guido in a dramatic relationship with Beatrice, toward whose *smile* Dante strains, and hopes to be led by "he who awaits."

Three

Dante's Divine Perception
(*Aesthesis Theia*)

It is now a critical commonplace to note that the extraordinary character of Dante's experience—authentic bearing witness (*experiri*), arduous "opening the way"—transcends every allegorism to constitute itself as full experience (*Erlebnis*), thus coming to represent a foundational *myth* of European culture. At the same time, however, such experience appears to be an inexhaustible well of motivations and problems, inasmuch as it draws on diverse philosophical and theological sources that are at times in contradiction with each other, and whose ongoing exegesis is still far from reaching conclusion. Every "doctrinal" theme assumes here the character of this individuality on the road (*in itinere*), of this singular being-there. It is Dante himself who must *transhumanize*, who is called upon to overcome every one of his faculties, to rise "beyond the power that was mine" ("me sormontar di sopr'a mia virtute," *Par.* XXX, 57) in order to "last-in-the-future" (*infuturarsi*; see *Par.* XVII, 98), to "unite-with-God" (*indiarsi*; see *Par.* IV, 28), to "penetrate-in-Him" (*inluiarsi*; see *Par.* IX, 73), to "rise-to-heaven" (*incielarsi*; see *Par.* III, 97), as conveyed by his many parasynthetic verbal inventions, up to the most astonishing and violent of them all: to "settle-in-the-womb" of God (*inventrarsi*; see *Par.* XXI, 84), here dramatically grasped in his *maternal aspect*. Through its very sound, language identifies "physically" with the idea. Every concept incarnates itself in the image, which is almost immediately expressed through the word's timbre, a fact that the great twentieth century writers, such as Mandelstam, Joyce, and Pound, understood very well.

The pilgrimage that, through free will (*per arbitrii libertatem*), the soul undertakes from a state of misery to a state of happiness incarnates itself in the concrete hopes of this unheard-of Argonaut, in the faces of the people whom he loves or hates, in the passions that animate him to the point of threatening to crush him, in the effort he makes to understand them. In this sense, the tragic ethos of learning from suffering (*pathei mathos*) seems profoundly adequate to Dante's *Comedy*.

The scope of this transformation (*conversio*) exceeds in every way that of pure *metanoia*. It is not just the mind, intelligence, or the intellect (*nous*), that must be transfigured, but the whole being-there, in all its faculties. Thus, the future citizen (*civis futurus*, the Augustinian idea that dominates the entire third *Cantica*) continues to portray himself as *civis*, as fully belonging to the *civitas* until the very end (wherein precisely lies the profound difference from Augustine's political theology). The nostalgia for reaching the End contains fully in itself the passion and the struggle to achieve Paradise on Earth. Not only Dante but also Beatrice, and Saint Peter are citizens. They are the ones who remind the pilgrim that his mission will continue to be *political*, since he must eventually return to "the little threshing floor / that so incites our savagery" ("l'aiuola che ci fa tanto feroci," *Par.* XXII, 151). The journey, and its experience, do not end triumphally at the vision's summit, but rather down below, back at the bottom of the cave. Only "down here" will the pilgrim be able to prove that he is a *prophet*. To unite-with-God (*indiarsi*; see *Par.* IV, 28) and to become incarnate are indissoluble expressions. We might say that one unites-with-God only to re-incarnate oneself once more! Dante's mystique is only conceivable from this absolutely *Christocentric* perspective.

The whole ascent is a conflict (*polemos*) between the energy of the pilgrim's eye and that of Light itself. The metaphysics of Light of Neoplatonic origin, which in different ways runs through medieval theology, becomes here a dramatics of seeing—of the *acting* eye of the one who ascends. Every step of the way calls for greater concentration; no negligence is allowed. We must *lift* the gaze, *fly* with the eyes. And it is precisely the bodily eyes that we must *fix* (*ficcare*; see *Par.* VII, 94: XXI, 16, and XXXIII, 83) to the extent permitted to us humans, "on the profundity / of the Eternal Counsel" ("per entro l'abisso / de l'etterno consiglio," *Par.* VII, 94–95). In this extreme navigation of the gaze we must manage to see that which lies within the invisible itself, in the "summit," the abysmally high point that not even the Seraph can envision with perfect clarity: "that Seraph with his eye most set on

God, / could not provide the why, not satisfy / what you have asked; for deep in the abyss / of the Eternal Ordinance, it is / cut off from all created beings' vision" ("quel Serafin che 'n Dio più l'occhio ha fisso, / a la dimanda tua non satisfara, / però che sì s'innoltra ne lo abisso / de l'etterno statuto quel che chiedi, che da ogne creata vista è scisso," *Par.* XXI, 92–96).

Seeing, here, carries all its *eschatological* meaning, while at the same time retaining intact the value, the energy of the *experience* of he who is straining in every fiber of his being to see *further and further beyond*, to transcend himself by seeing. Imagination and language may fail him, but not seeing, which seems to keep on flying until it merges into infinite Goodness: "until / my vision reached the Infinite Goodness" ("tanto ch'i' giunsi / l'aspetto mio col valore infinito," *Par.* XXXIII, 80–81). Dante is a truthful witness because he sees and has seen what he represents; because he is *histor*, precisely in the etymological significance ("witness") of the Greek word. It is the mind that must follow vision: "Let your mind follow where your eyes have led, / and let your eyes be mirrors for the figure / that will appear to you within this mirror" ("Ficca di retro a li occhi tuoi la mente, / e fa di quelli specchi a la figura / che 'n questo specchio ti sarà parvente," *Par.* XXI, 16–18). The eye must be able to reflect perfectly the image that the celestial mirrors reflect back to it. Only if the eye is translucid will the mind be able, in turn, to *reflect* on the image that sight has transmitted to it. Only if the mirror of our gaze can reflect without deforming, will the intellect be able to comprehend the form it has seen. What an extraordinary amalgam of mysticism and Aristotelian gnoseology!

The different degrees through which the gaze travels in order to *fix* on the abyss correspond to those that Light itself crosses as it is gradually revealed. Light grows brighter to the extent that the eye perceiving it grows stronger, in a formidable dialogue between *luminous energies*. Just like music, light is always changing. And it is always *colored*, a Light that *wants* to be perceived, to be of value as a *phainomenon*. Even the glow from the supreme Light appears colored to the poet: "In the deep and bright / essence of that exalted Light, three circles / appeared to me; they had three different colors / but all of them were of the same dimension" ("Ne la profonda e chiara sussistenza / de l'alto lume parvermi tre giri / di tre colori e d'una contenenza," *Par.* XXXIII, 115–117). Light is never pure intelligible Light (*Lux intelligibilis*), nor is the multiplicity of its colors-timbres ever effaced in the unity of the highest Light. We could say: trinitary is the very light that expresses the divine. The difference of the colors in their relation is essential to its essence. This way the human eye, which perceives only colored light, can *reach* the Light. The Light is always also *radius*: it radiates through the different lights (*lumina*), making radiant—*chromatically* radiant—the bodies that reflect it. Though Dante's Light is certainly increate, it is always clearly perceptible by an eye that has acquired sufficient spiritual power. As writes a great Byzantine theologian to whom we will return, it is a Light that, while certainly inaccessible and ineffable, immaterial and uncreated, is nonetheless also sensible, even as it remains beyond any normal perception (*aesthesis*), or aesthetical dimension. It is a Light that *deifies* the very sensible powers of the soul.

The eye begins by perceiving a figure's *radiance*: "And even as each shade approached, one saw, / because of the bright radiance it sent forth, / the joyousness with which that shade was filled" ("E sì come ciascuno a noi venìa, / vedeasi l'ombra piena di letizia / nel folgór chiaro che di lei uscia," *Par.* V, 106–108). It is true that the face of the shade is not visible, yet the shade is by no means a kind of evanescent, dim corporeality: on the contrary, it is radiant, it responds to the Light by shining. In the same way radiates the gladness of Carlo Martello, safeguarding, rather than concealing, his face (*Par.* VIII, 53). And as the eyes acquire virtue, they penetrate beyond the ray-radiance into the river of Light—into the light from the Light (*lumen de Lumine*), issued directly (*immediate*) from the highest Light—until they finally fix into the eternal radiance that dwells only within itself: "and only You know You; Self-knowing, / Self-known, You love and smile upon Yourself!" ("sola t'intendi, e da te intelletta / e intendente te ami e arridi," *Par.* XXXIII, 125–126). From the dimension of the *radii*, the eye manages to see as far as the Place of Light.

And now, in the same way that the God-Trinity appeared in all its colors, the vision captures our very effigy, immersed in the abyss of the Good it has found, and it is filled by it. At the height of ecstasy, at the extremes of the power of seeing and of Light, at the very center of that circulation from rainbow to rainbow in which the divine mystery expresses itself, it is *our* image that appears. Now the Light is no longer concealing but revealing; it reveals the perfect merging of divine and human in the figure of the Son, thereby turning into a perfectly deifying Light. Here imagination—the ability to put things into images, *to paint* them in any way—fails, but the *event of seeing* has taken place and the happiness it bestows on the pilgrim is complete. Both supreme intuition and supreme *aesthesis*.

All the lights that Dante encounters along the way are "saved" in the last vision. All exist as authentic *preface* to the Light, albeit a shady one (*umbrifera praefatio*). No merely metaphysical light can extinguish them. No supra-essential One can render them ultimately superfluous. They stand in the Greatest Light in the same way as our effigy does. The Blessed Kingdom is an immense play of Light and shade: no shade could exist without the different timbres that the Light radiates, just as no Light would be visible without such timbres or without shade—not a deceitful shade but a true one, veridical preface to the reality of the Kingdom. The most peculiar sign-symbol of this is Beatrice's smile. It is her smile that always *harmonizes* Dante's eye with its object. It is as if Dante were always seeing through his Woman's eyes. "The eyes of Beatrice were all intent / on the eternal circles; from the sun, / I turned aside; I set my eyes on her" ("Beatrice tutta ne l'etterne rote / fissa con li occhi stava; e io in lei / le luci fissi, di là sù rimote," *Par*. I, 64–66); "Beatrice gazed upward. I watched her" ("Beatrice in suso, e io in lei guardava," *Par*. II, 22). In the end, Dante's eye will indeed be able, by itself, to penetrate into the Light: but it never could have been without the prior *experience* of *loving* the face, the smile, the gaze of Beatrice. As the *radii* reflect the Light, so Dante's gaze reflects itself in the Woman's gaze.

Full experience turns into *symbol*. If "symbol" means that the name of a thing becomes one with the thing it designates, then no figure is more symbol than Beatrice. Her smile signals the very merriment (*hilaritas*) of the divine Light trinitarily conceived, that is, the Light of God-as-Relation (*Deus Relatio*), of God-as-Love (*Theos Agape*). As the energy of the Light and the power of the gaze increase, Beatrice's smile grows merrier (*hilaros*) and more enchanting at every "turn of heaven" until it *surpasses itself* into "beauty beyond beauty"—the *hyperkallos* of Dionysius the Aeropagite: "The loveliness I saw surpassed not only / our human measure—and I think that surely, / only its Maker can enjoy it fully" ("La bellezza ch'io vidi si trasmoda / non pur di là da noi, ma certo io credo / che solo il suo fattor tutta la goda," *Par*. XXX, 19–21). But whereas in Dionysius's mysticism the result seems to annul in itself the value of the journey that has led there, here every step, every figure *stands*, captured *sub specie aeternitatis*.

Thus, Beatrice's smile, which leads to the eternal, from the human to the divine (the true divine, which is divine-humanity), is still the smile on the face of Beatrice, the woman whom Dante loved. Woman-*citizen* up to her very last words, a true invective; just as her knight is a citizen, by vocation, even more confirmed in his political being-there by his journey through Paradise.

Like Dante, Beatrice is a passionate participant in the suffering of the world, leading a strenuous battle against its sins. When, in Dante's ascent-ecstasy, we cross the river Lethe, it is not in order to forget life, but rather so that we may remember it all in its truth. Dante's Lethe is not oblivion but, on the contrary, repentance and conversion. We see our whole life reflected in it, in all its omission, negligence, and faults, and we regret not having lived it according to truth, that is to say *with* Beatrice.

The vision contains in itself all the powers of the soul, excluding every dualism. The divine is an object of *full enjoyment*, not just of mere contemplation. The Augustinian enjoyment (*frui*) relives in Dante in all the paradoxical power of its significance. Intellectual love must be able to unite perfectly with sensible enjoyment. Dante's Paradise is precisely this *marriage*. The figures of the third *Cantica* are all images and shades of it. They, too, then, must be understood in light of the fundamental category of the harbinger or *figura futuri* ("figure of things to come"). Dante's *Paradiso has a future*, it is a Paradise that *awaits*, even more essentially and dramatically so than *Purgatorio*. (In Dante's theology, the *Inferno* cannot know this dimension of expectancy—and this deficiency renders its "movement," apparently so much richer and more realistic, less *necessary*, as it were, less an expression of an ontological yearning connoting the different figures.) Disregarding this aspect of Dante's idea of Paradise leads to misunderstanding the very nature of his mysticism and prophecy. Paradise awaits, and it awaits precisely the *essential*, that is the reunion of the soul, which now Dante still sees, with a body that will become, it too, *eternal*. Only then will it be Paradise, the joy of Paradise (*gaudium Paradisii*). Only then will the vision also be *touching God*. In the state of misery (*in statu miseriae*), Dante can experience that joy only through its signs. Even the radiance of the blessed is not yet the perfect clarity that will triumph upon resurrection, on the day of the Lord. Of such clarity, the Paradise—through which the poet journeys—is the certain promise. But though it grounds our hope, it is still not yet (*nondum*) the perfect fruition—body-and-soul—of the divine. *Paradiso* XIV is therefore crucial to our understanding, both theological and poetic, of Dante's universe.

It is Solomon, the wisest one, who clarifies Dante's doubt: the eternal light of the blessed does not just follow from the ardor of love (*caritas*), and the latter from the vision, and the vision itself from Grace, which always bestows its gifts on us beyond our merit and worth. The light of the blessed grows infinitely more intense when it is dressed in the flesh "glorified and sanctified" ("glorïosa e santa," *Par.* XIV, 43). Only then will the power of the vision and the ardor of love have reached perfection; only then will they be *in act*. The light by which they now shine is *figura futuri* of that which they will acquire by finally reuniting with "reborn flesh, which earth now covers up. / Nor will we tire when faced with such bright light, / for then the body's organs will have force / enough for all in which we can delight" ("da la carne / che tutto dì la terra ricoperchia; / né potrà tanta luce affaticarne: / ché li organi del corpo saran forti / a tutto ciò che potrà dilettarne," *Par.* XIV, 56–60). *Figura futuri* of such *organs* is our current sight. Our body *here-and-now* foreshadows the glorified flesh that will have "force enough" to bear the eternal *joy*, not measurable in duration, not subject to time (*Chronos*), but eternal Now (*Nunc aeternum*), pure Instant. In sum, the flesh, too, is called upon to be "capable of God" (*capax Dei*).

The source is of course Paul: the whole creation "will be liberated from its bondage to decay (*pthora*)"; now, it groans as it awaits "the redemption of our bodies" (Romans 8:21–23); and our lowly bodies will be transformed and be "like his glorious body" (Philippians 3:21). The "glory of the body" (*doxa tou somatos*) concludes the mystic itinerary. The metamorphosis of Light, its rainbows, Beatrice's smile, are all figures of that face-to-face vision of God (*visio facialis*) that, in order be perfect, must reveal itself through the perfection of all the energies of the soul, in the unsurpassable perfection of the body that, far from being the soul's opposite, expresses it by incarnating it. Because this is the Purpose, the eyes *fix themselves* on the abyss, the blessed *show* themselves, Beatrice reveals her *beauty*. The Purpose is not the overcoming, or even less the negation, of perception (*aesthesis*), but rather its exaltation, its divinization. The climax of ecstasy and of the journey that leads to the Vision expresses itself in a *divine perception* (*theia aesthesis*), in perfect analogy with our effigy, which Dante sees painted at the center, in the heart of the divine mystery.

"What we hold here by faith, shall there be seen" ("Lì si vedrà ciò che tenem per fede," *Par.* II, 43) but already now, on the road (*in itinere*) we *see*, and the nexus between this seeing and the eschatological one is stronger than any theological-philosophical analogy of being (*analogia entis*): it is lived experience. Human and divine nature are *already now* conjoined, in the image of the incarnate Logos, in the power of the poet's *eye*, in the energy of his representation, in the audacity of his journey.

The signs and figures in the third *Cantica* are *figura futuri* of the eschatological faculty to *enjoy* divinely and eternally. Not vague images, not pale similes, but *true signs*. Our very organs are *signs*; chief among them is the sense of sight, but also the sense of hearing, which perceives and comprehends the extraordinary musical polyphony accompanying the pilgrim, and the sense of touch, which so often compels the pilgrim to hold and embrace the "seen object" ("veduta forma," Cavalcanti, *Donna me prega*, 21).[1] Our corporeal constitution can transfigure itself into the veridical sign of the "glory of the body" (*doxa tou somatos*) and evolve into a perfect perception (*aesthesis*) that is theologically analogous to perfect love (*teleia agape*). It is precisely this nexus between the two dimensions that constitutes the essential content of the *singing* of poets, *elected* by God—the singing of poets-seers-prophets, capable of a biblical language. Speech itself cannot but transform into song, in which one must strive to say the unsayable and to imitate the inimitable. The Vision follows from the ardor of love (*agape*), and the word, for as much as it can, follows from the Vision, surpassing itself into song and prayer, without ever forgetting that the word ought to be prophetic to those who listen to it and wait; that the word, weighed down with the burden and labor of experience, must be able *to return* to the city from which it has been driven, to its cares and passions; it must be able to communicate and *act* here and now.

Now the power of the soul, body, and mind does not permit oneness (*henosis*) with the divine, but it does deification (*theosis*)—that is, a transhumanizing that is not yet an *understanding* (*intelligere*) of that "deep and bright essence" ("profonda e chiara sussistenza," *Par.* XXXIII, 115), the common essence (*ousia*) of a Person, but is nevertheless the *intuition* of it. The entire journey seeks to be the veridical testimony that while we are already on the way (*in statu viatoris*) we are allowed to be conjoined with the highest Light, that the mind can really be struck by its Light ("fulgore," *Par.* XXXIII, 141) and be perfectly satisfied in this Purpose, although it is unable to reduce it to a representation or concept. The deifying grace, of which Beatrice is the symbol, opens the way to an entirely viable pilgrimage between the essence of God, in itself "unpartakeable" [*impartecipabile*], and the soul, which freely aspires to partake of it.

But how can such a miracle be explained theologically? What if this is nothing but delirious arrogance on the part of the poet-seer? Or just a piece of fanciful fiction? The divine essence is not a fixed, immobile Being. It must be understood as a beam of infinite energy. Such Source shapes the human soul in different forms and with varying intensity. And it is the divine essence itself, *in itself*, that signals its presence through the manifestation of its energy *in the soul*. The blessed whom Dante meets are nothing but the signs of such essence. "They showed themselves to you here not because / this is their sphere, but as a sign for you / that in the Empyrean their place is lowest ("Qui si mostraro, non perché sortita / sia questa spera lor, ma per far segno / de la celestïal c'ha men salita," *Par*. IV, 37–39). Platonically, Light is the first Energy, that which makes possible the connection between seer and seen, and in whose unveiling every intuition and every word take place. A light that is perfectly sensible, and at the same time transcending every limitation. The Taboric light is also perfectly sensible. And all our lights arrange themselves according to this one Light, lights from the Light (*lumina de Lumine*), they are coordinated with the Light, just like the Light is coordinated with the Father whom it reveals and whom, however, no one ever saw.

It seems to me that a similar theology of divine energies presides over the structure of the *Paradiso*. It is on its basis that we can affirm that the soul, in the entirety of its faculties, is capable of entering into a real relation with the divine essence—and that therefore the figures we experience constitute a symphony of *figurae futuri*, veridical signs of the *gaudium Paradisii*, not in the sense that the Old Testament figures were said to be pre-figurations of the Christ to come, but in the most radical eschatological sense: they are figures of absolute novelty (*figurae de novissimis*). The most grandiose development of such a theology is not to be found in the Latin West but in the last great representative of Byzantine theology, Gregory Palamas. I think his greatest work, the *Triads for The Defense of Those Who Practice Sacred Quietude*, written in polemic against Barlaam of Calabria (Petrarch's ineffective Greek teacher), could be a formidable support to the exegesis of the peculiar mysticism that dominates the third *Cantica*.[2] It is, of course, what Nietzsche would call a "stellar friendship." A whole world separates Dante from Palamas, even though, technically, they are a mere generation apart. The Byzantine master is completely foreign to Dante's civil and political *pathos*, just as Byzantium is completely foreign to the society of Florence. Palamas tends to devalue secular intelligence and is even farther away from any literary or poetic interest. And yet the affinity between the two—who both maintain that the energies-radii of the divine essence are its authentic expression, its true Logos, so that in partaking of them we actually partake of the divine mystery itself—is extraordinary.

Extraordinary is the energy of their Vision—which Barlaam condemned in Palamas as "deluded fancy and unrestrained imagination"[3] (who knows what he might have said about the *Commedia*!)—a Vision, that is, of the glory of the body (*doxa tou somatos*), whereby the culmination of the mystical ecstasy is conceived as a full recovery of the very sensible-corporeal power. (However, Dante's vision still bears traces that I would characterize as "Sienese," especially in its notion of Light. In some parts of the *Paradiso*, we can still hear the symphonies of the *Maestà* of Duccio and Simone Martini. Dante's realism is not yet that of Giotto.)

The mysticism of the divine energies upends any abstract spiritualism. At the end of the itinerary, in the act of *theosis*, everything is gained back, everything returns. Nothing of the soul's powers is lost; in fact, they all acquire that force and light that now the earth may enshroud but could never destroy. If the old seed dies, the plant will grow more luxuriant and fertile than ever before. Such eschatological fullness also awaits the very Paradise that Dante experiences. Even in the heavenly Rose there vibrates the sound of expectancy: that the human figure may finally "unite-with-God" (*indiarsi*; see *Par*. IV, 28) as the Son with the Father, that the human being-there may reach its divine fulfillment. But what is extraordinary about Dante's poetry (and Palamas' theology) is that it already *sees* here on earth the Time of fulfillment, in the concrete signs and living testimonies of the human capacity to transcend itself, to deify itself. The creature can do the impossible, such as flying and conquering gravity: "You should—if I am right— / not feel more marvel at your climbing than / you would were you considering a stream / that from a mountain's height falls to its base" ("Non dei più ammirar, se bene stimo, / lo tuo salir, se non come d'un rivo / se d'alto monte scende giuso ad imo," *Par*. I, 136–138). The essential trait of the human being-there is not to "fall to its base," but to *rise*. For Dante, the deifying Grace may grant that this rising become natural to us, like a habit, just like going downstream. The miracle of the man of flesh and bone in the heart of the Rose is the very expression, and the greatest energy, of this Grace.

Four

The Concrete Ineffable
The Last Cantos of the *Commedia*

The inexhaustibility of the last cantos of the *Paradiso*, as attested by the relentless challenge they have posed to hosts of interpreters, perhaps will justify one further attempt to highlight their speculatively more arduous and paradoxical traits. I am talking of the dialectic that is established in those Cantos between hearing, seeing, and speech—between the different ways in which each of these dimensions is articulated, and between the different forms in which these different ways interweave with each other. In the *symphony* that this play of relations creates, no element must be viewed as a *state*, because each of them is constantly moving toward the other. The seeing stirs within itself and stretches out toward speech. Speech, in turn, opens itself to seeing; there is no seeing or speech that does not presuppose hearing, that is not accompanied by it. Every part *exists* in its going out of itself toward the other. The energy of hearing—the hearing (*aesthesis*) that here becomes its being in act, thus turning into *divine perception* (*theia aesthesis*)—expresses the fulfillment of the potentialities of all its organs. Each organ of hearing here becomes *energeia* insofar as it conjoins with the others and *goes beyond* its own specific individual being. This is the paradisiacal condition of hearing, the only one capable of giving perfect Joy. But that, too, cannot be viewed as a *state*; even the highest pleasure must be considered within the potent *theo-drama* represented in the third *Cantica* as a whole.

Dante prepares for the ultimate vision as early as his passage from the heavens of the planets to the foot of Jacob's ladder, which Benedict points out to him, and which will lead him to the Empyrean. The "stars of glory" ("gloriose stelle," *Par.* XXII, 112) that Dante contemplates here, however, still belong to our heaven, are the well-known ones under whose influence we live. They seem to be there to illuminate the human scene, rather than to "transhumanize" us. Benedict's gaze is turned to the decadence both of his own Order and of the entire Church, in which "no one now would lift his feet from earth" ("mo nessun diparte / da terra i piedi," *Par.* XXII, 73–74). Let Dante understand this well and take the prophecy to earth: God's "help" will come and will be less "wonderful" than when the Jordan reversed its course, and the waters of the sea were "in flight" ("fuggir") before Moses (*Par.* XXII, 94–96). Even Beatrice, at the same time as she warns him that he is "near the final blessedness" ("sì presso a l'ultima salute"), knows that before he can "enter farther" into it ("prima che tu più t'inlei"), he will have to "look *downward*" once more ("rimira in giù," *Par.* XXII, 124–128). One does not enter the last heaven without carrying *the earth into it*, without making sure one has *seen* this visible globe, at whose center appear "the little threshing floor / that so incites our savagery" in its entirety ("l'aiuola che ci fa tanto feroci," *Par.* XXII, 150–151). Benedict's ladder foreshadows the Empyrean, throwing open Dante's gaze onto this "little threshing floor." The *contemplator* does not flee history not even for a moment. Instead, he teaches us that only *from on high* can history be comprehended in its wholeness. History reveals its sense and purpose only to those who are able to *transcend* its appearance of a simple becoming. This is also Beatrice's teaching: "do look downward, see / what I have set beneath your feet" ("rimira in giù, e vedi quanto mondo / sotto li piedi già esser ti fei," *Par.* XXII, 127–128). The gaze is trained to grasp the highest vision by measuring the glorious visible stars, the cosmos, admirable in its orderliness, and which, however, hosts the terrifying spectacle of that of which man is capable. Dante must never forget this. He must return to the world that his mind has "transcended" and *preach the Word in it*: this is what Peter's fiery, heated words remind him in Canto XXVII, words that cause even Beatrice to "change in appearance" ("trasmutò sembianza") and her smile to be painfully eclipsed (*Par.* XXVII, 34). The purpose of Peter's invective—so expressly theological-political that it sets a perfect correspondence between the liberation of the Church from those who turn it into a sewer and Rome's salvation by the Scipios!—is to wrest Dante, on the very eve of his last flight, from the highest enthusiasm, for the sake of the reforming mission to which he is destined: "and you, my son, who through your mortal weight / will yet return below, speak plainly there" ("e tu, figliol, che per lo mortal pondo / ancor giù tornerai, apri la bocca," *Par.* XXVII, 64–65).

Here everything is clear, nothing is hidden, everything can and must be said in plain words. Dante himself will gain Heaven if he proves able to adequately "speak plainly," if he proves able to communicate to the "people of the future" ("la futura gente") at least "one gleam" ("una favilla") of the Glory that he has been allowed to see by grace (*Par.* XXXIII, 71–72). For this reason, he will make sure "his sentiments preserve their perseverance" ("conservi sani . . . li affetti suoi"), he must "curb his mortal passion" ("vinca tua guardia i movimenti umani," *Par.* XXXIII, 35–37). Nothing is assured and there is no guaranteed happy ending. The struggle continues, God's protection and help are still needed. Herein, however, a problem arises: the theological-political prophecy is unmistakable and can be perfectly communicated. And so inextricable is its relationship to the vision of the "heaven of pure light" ("al ciel ch'è pura luce," *Par.* XXX, 39), of the "noble triumph of the true realm" ("l'alto triünfo del regno verace," *ibid.* 98), that this canto ends with the invocation for the "noble Henry" ("l'alto Arrigo") to come "set right your Italy" ("drizzar Italia") and with the invective against the "blind greediness" ("cieca cupidigia") that rejected his rule, his stewardship, his authority (*Par.* XXX, 136–139). How can these two perspectives be espoused at the same time? There is an evident dissymmetry between them, but it is also clear that for Dante, at this point in his journey, the epochal import of his discourse acquires sense and value only *from the height* that he has reached. In other words: while the prophecy appears to be perfectly expressible, it is only so by virtue of what exceeds the power of the *logos*, that is, the order of discourse with which we designate things. It seems pertinent, at this point, to draw a parallel to the great Platonic myth: only he who has reached the supreme vision of the Good (*Agathon*), having surpassed every natural virtue, could possess the strength to return to the bottom of the threshing ground to try and convince of the goodness of what he saw and enjoyed the infant (*infans*) incapable of *logos* who insists on holding on to his chains. But how to express the *Agathon*? Does the imperative to "speak plainly" also apply to its vision? And can the eyes stay open, can the Truth of this vision be "depicted" on the "eye-lights" ("e come ambo le luci mi dipinse," *Par.* XXIII, 91)? And how can the mind picture that which is being *divinely depicted* on it?[1]

All of Canto XXIII resounds with the foreshadowing of the conclusive rapture; the spirit "awaits the sun with warm affection" ("e con ardente affetto il sole aspetta," *Par.* XXIII, 8), the gaze anticipates the break of dawn. But the emotional intensity of these verses cannot hide the problematic of seeing that has arisen here. After contemplating the "gladness" ("letizia") of Beatrice, Dante sees "a sun" ("un sol") kindling "a thousand lamps" ("migliaia di lucerne"), just as our sun "kindles the sights above us here on earth" ("come fa 'l nostro le viste superne," *Par.* XXIII, 23–30). And yet the image that forms in his mind is not that of a sun, but that of the moon! The sun that Dante sees illuminates with moonlight, "like Trivia—at the full moon in clear skies" ("Quale ne' plenilunïi sereni / Trivïa ride," *Par.* XXIII, 25–26). Dante sees the sun of the triumphant Christ behind a smiling moon, almost still in shade (*per umbras*). In fact, his eyes are not yet strong enough to sustain its "living light" ("viva luce") *face to face*. Or rather: his gaze cannot yet set into the "glowing substance" ("lucente sustanza") of the light that he was nonetheless able to grasp (*Par.* XXIII, 31–32)—a substance that will be unveiled only at the very end of the ascent. His faculty of vision is overcome by the redeeming power "that opened roads between the earth and Heaven" ("ch'aprì le strade tra 'l cielo e la terra," *Par.* XXIII, 38); this power is both revealed and re-*veiled* by the light that Dante admires. What Dante truly sees in all its reality is only Beatrice, the lady's *smile*: "'Open your eyes and see what I now am'" ("Apre li occhi e riguarda qual son io," *Par.* XXIII, 46). It is this vision that the faithful lover can finally sustain, a vision that acts as a middle ground (*metaxy*) between the first triumph and that of Mary. Perfectly in love with Beatrice's countenance, Dante can rise to contemplate the Rose "in which the Word of God became / flesh" ("in che 'l verbo divino / carne si fece," *Par.* XXIII, 73–74). And yet the light is still that of a full moon, and "the battle of my feeble brows" ("la battaglia de' debili cigli") is far from over. Dante does see, but as if from a place covered in shade (*Par.* XXIII, 79–81). After thousands of lights revealed/re-*veiled* the substance of the power of Christ, now "troops of splendors" ("turbe di splendori"), the apparition of the Archangel, the "deep affection" ("alto affetto," *Par.* XXIII, 125) that all sing for the "Lady of Heaven" ("donna del ciel," *Par.* XXIII, 106), are the sign of Mary's triumph, which the eye cannot track to its very end—that is, the "wedding" of the Mother to her "Son" in the Empyrean. At this point, only the name of the Virgin is heard in a melody of incomparable sweetness. The faculty of hearing, of *listening*, has by now reached perfection. Not so that of seeing. The seeing "follows" the voices of the great choir in order to reach, through their beauty, the figure that is being sung by them. Music assumes a decisive role in the relationship between visible and invisible. There is no luminous epiphany in the *Paradiso* that is not expressed musically.

In love with Beatrice, with the melody, with the thousands of lights and troops of splendors that cannot be but lights from the Light—only lights (*lumina*) themselves, not the Light—and that in turn propagate radiantly (according to a "luminology" that in different forms pervades the whole medieval Neoplatonic thought), Dante experiences the first stage of rapture (*excessus mentis*). A stage of paradoxical complexity: the mind "expanded" by the manifestation of that "Power / against which nothing can defend itself" ("virtù da cui nulla si ripara," *Par.* XXIII, 36) does not spread its wings and fly after it, but "down to earth, descends" as "lightning breaking from a cloud" ("come foco di nube si diserra / per dilatarsi sì che non vi cape, / e fuor di sua natura in giù s'atterra," *Par.* XXIII, 40–42). Lightning breaks from the cloud "against its nature" ("fuor di sua natura"), as, indeed, the nature of fire is rather to reach upward! Paul fallen off his horse: this is the first, necessary stage of *ecstasy*: humility, perceiving one's impotence, the deficiency of one's virtue in the face of the Wisdom-and-Power revealing itself. The fallen mind does not know, right after the blow, how to remember the experience it has suffered and enjoyed, but the words ("open your eyes") spoken by Beatrice act as an awakening. Dante "wakes" from that vision and "tries in vain to bring / that vision back into his memory" ("io era come quei che si risente / di visïone oblita e che s'ingegna indarno / di ridurlasi a la mente," *Par.* XXIII, 49–51). He strives to remember it, for he knows it had not been a dream. Beatrice's "offer" is proof of it. If you "bear the power of my smile" ("se' fatto a sostener lo riso mio," *Par.* XXIII, 48), she says, which is undoubtedly all real, and could never be erased from your memory, then you will find in it the measure that will allow you to picture Paradise down to its ultimate mystery, and picture also what exceeds memory and speech in spite of being the object of your truthful seeing. Just as she had been his guide in the anguish of conversion and repentance at the end of the *Purgatorio*, in the same way Beatrice now leads Dante through the first stage of rapture toward the supreme vision—toward the Point that her beauty and wisdom will no longer be enough for him to be able to "touch."

The second stage of rapture opens with the entrance to the Empyrean. This stage is a metamorphosis of the first, and there is no break between the two, but rather a difficult harmony. The Point that encloses all within itself appears to Dante, yet his sight is still not fully "ingathered" ("s'interna," *Par.* XXXIII, 85) in it. The eyes glimpse it, but the mind does not intuit it, cannot even gaze at it "intent, / steadfast, and motionless" ("fissa, immobile e attenta," *ibid.* 97–98). The organ of seeing, the sensible sight, is unfolding perfectly. The sight of the soul, however, still needs to be educated. The pilgrim is no longer simply blinded by the lights, as was he who strove to gain freedom from servitude at the exit of Plato's cave. His sight "fades gradually" ("al mio veder si stinse," *Par.* XXX, 13) before the Sun of the sun, the Point that encloses the visible sun within itself. "Seeing nothing else" ("nulla vedere," *Par.* XXX, 14) means here to have one's sight fixed only on the Light that exceeds every finite being, every particular light (*lumen*). Now it is necessary for Dante to return to Beatrice—to the contemplation of her beauty, which only now appears in its perfection—as if in order to get a running start for the last "leap." Dante sees this beauty, even though he believes that only its Maker can fully enjoy it. Eyes and mind have reached the end of the Way of Beauty (*via pulchritudinis*) that coincides with knowledge (*Scientia*): the beauty of his Lady, the same he loved "in this life," and the solidity of the knowledge he obtained from her form the same whole.[2] This beauty would also be sayable in itself, as that knowledge is expressible through discourse. But, at this point, both have value also for what they indicate beyond themselves, insofar as they are grasped in the instant of their self-transcending. And no singing could keep up with this beyond. Indeed, Beatrice's beauty is the highest "lure" ("pasture," *Par.* XXVII, 92) to induce the mind to the contemplation of the "light of the intellect" ("luce intellettual," *Par.* XXX, 40), beyond the crystalline heaven itself, "matter's largest sphere" ("fore del maggior corpo," *Par.* XXX, 38–39). But her beauty does not suffice for the last ascent, for the completion of ecstasy. It remains on the threshold between, on one side, the visible and the *act* of the faculty of seeing, and, on the other, a "new vision" ("novella vista," *Par.* XXX, 58); between "the sun of my eyes" ("il sol de li occhi miei," *Par.* XXX, 75) that has hitherto illuminated the pilgrim, and "the yellow of the eternal Rose" ("nel giallo della rosa sempiterna," *Par.* XXX, 124), whose vision exceeds every natural faculty. And yet, Dante affirms three times that he can *see*.

Looking into the eyes of Beatrice, he caught the marvelous figure of the "light that took a river's form" ("lume in forma di rivera," *Par.* XXX, 61); his gaze was enough for the "shadowy / prefaces" ("umbriferi prefazi," *Par.* XXX, 78) of Truth. The "Sights" he had gained with Beatrice, though, were "not yet that sublime" ("non hai viste ancor tnato superbe," *ibid.* 81), were not yet able to cause the image of "the noble triumph of the true realm" ("l'alto trïunfo del regno verace," *Par.* XXX, 98) to be created in the *mind*. Instead, now he truly *sees*; he sees the Light that makes God himself visible to "the creature / whose only peace lies in his seeing Him" ("a quella creatura / che solo in lui vedere ha la sua pace," *Par.* XXX, 101–102). Up until now his eye had obeyed "the laws of nature"; only now "within that breadth and height" does he not find his "vision gone astray" ("la vista mia ne l'ampio e ne l'altezza / non si smarriva," *Par.* XXX, 118–119), only now does he contemplate in its reality "this council of white robes" ("'l convento de le bianche stole," *Par.* XXX, 129), Paul's Heavenly City (*politeuma en ouranois*), and its seats—the few of them awaiting (as Judgment Day is nigh) those who will be worthy of sitting in them. "By now my gaze had taken in the whole / of Paradise—its form in general" ("La forma general di paradiso / già tutta mïo sguardo avea compresa," *Par.* XXXI, 52–53). The moment Dante expresses this thought, Beatrice *flies away*. But it is not an infinite distance. To Dante's eye, nothing is near or far anymore; such earthly metrics have been left behind. Simply put, he sees now with superhuman clarity. However, how can one *express* that which, at last, one sees more clearly than daylight (*luce meridiana clarius*)? Dante prays that he may be able to: "give / to me the power to speak of what I saw!" ("dammi virtù a dir com'ïo il vidi!" *Par.* XXX, 99). Beatrice's beauty, as well as the end of the experience that Dante had fulfilled under her guide, were already, in a certain way, ineffable. How can one imagine expressing what transcends that beauty and the joy that arose from its contemplation? A double order of the ineffable now must correspond to the double order of the seeing.

Dante sees, and what he sees are no longer "shadowy prefaces." Truth "depicts" on his sight images that the mind recognizes as corresponding to the thing seen. We cannot call such a vision incomplete,[3] nor can we still call "weak" the imagination that corresponds to it (the mind's ability to translate into images). It is speech that is not as "rich" as the imagination ("e s'io avessi in dir tanta divizia / quanta ad imaginar," *Par.* XXXI, 136–137). By now sight has spread its wings (*Par.* XXXI, 97, 118), free from any "servitude," from any spirit of gravity, and Dante can say a prayer of thanks to his Lady—who responds with a smile sealing their eternal proximity—for having led him to such goal. To what extents of contemplation Bernard is now going to lead him, as soon as he is certain of the poet's "burning fervor" to "gaze," is now explicitly stated: "to see Him" ("a veder Cristo," *Par.* XXXII, 87), to see Him through "the face that is most like / the face of Christ" ("ne la faccia che a Cristo / più si somiglia," *Par.* XXXII, 85–86), and around which gather—in the most majestic of polyptychs[4]—"the great patricians / of this most just and merciful empire" ("i gran patrici / di questo imperio giustissimo e pio," *Par.* XXXII, 116–117). Dante can see them all, all the way up to Lucia, *nomen-omen*; his gaze seems to penetrate that Light, which is anything but an undifferentiated One: it is a Light teeming with figures, histories, and destinies. Figures that have distinct names, which Dante distinctly expresses. Then, even here memory has value. He remembers the words of Bernard and those of Beatrice and has indelible memory of the Order of the Blessed. He sees and will always remember "the eyes that are revered and loved by God" ("li occhi da Dio diletti e venerati," *Par.* XXXIII, 40), which gaze upon Bernard after he has uttered his sublime prayer.[5] Which form could the *topos* of the ineffable assume at this point? How to hearken back, in the realism of this theo-drama, to a mysticism inspired by Dionysius Aeropagite?

"Seeing nothing" can in no way constitute the conclusion of the itinerary into God. This, at most, is characterized by the most extraordinary enhancement of the organ of sight. The eyes "fix" themselves "on the profundity" ("ficca mo l'occhio per entro l'abisso," *Par.* VII, 94), deep into the mystery. Scarcity (*inopia*) affects only speech (*eloquium*). The problem is: in relation to what dimension of reality does speech *fail*? Resorting to the simple *topos* of the ineffable does nothing to answer this question. This *topos* can be expressed with regard to the beauty of Beatrice, or to paradisiacal splendor, but when Dante utters his triple "I saw," once he acquires the "new vision," in the heart of the heavenly Rose, he prays to that very splendor that it may accord him the faculty to speak of what he saw (*Par.* XXX, 99). Dante sees, recognizes, and describes: the intellectual light that "enwombs" him ("in ch'io m'inventro," *Par.* XXI, 84) is such precisely because it allows him to understand (*intelligere*) fully, to discern the Order of the Heavenly City and name its faces. He sees the face of Mary, notices its likeness to Christ, and, through Bernard's oration, he expresses the essence of its figure. Only "from that point on" ("da quinci innanzi," *Par.* XXXIII, 55) do the motifs of an apophatic mystique seem to assert themselves. The seeing acquires more and more power, until it conjoins with the "Infinite Goodness" ("valore infinito"), allowing the pilgrim to presume to "set" his eyes "on the Eternal Light" ("ficcar lo viso per la luce etterna," *Par.* XXXIII, 81–83), whereas "the minds of mortals" can no longer match the energy of the vision. And yet the emphasis here is not on the scarcity (*inopia*) but on the extraordinary undertaking that consists in inventing a "tongue so powerful" as to be able to represent "one / gleam of the glory that is Yours" ("e fa la lingua mia tanto possente / ch'una favilla sol de la tua gloria / possa lasciare a la futura gente," *Par.* XXXIII, 70–72). It is necessary to try to say what is not sayable.[6]

This is the task, the labor of the poet-seer. He does not merely say the ineffability of that Light with which he unites ("s'india," *Par.* IV, 28), nor does he merely say that he has seen it. Rather, he explains its "universal shape" ("forma universal," *Par.* XXXIII, 91), how substances, accidents, and their reciprocal relations are interwoven within it. And thus, he also explains the nature of the Point he has striven to reach during the last leg of his ascent: *coincidentia oppositorum*. Dante knows this: the totality of being can truly be known only *sub specie aeternitatis*, that is, only in God. And this he *says* with the greatest precision. Just as, with equally concise clarity, he expresses the mystery by definition, through the Joachimite image of the "three circles" of "three different colors" and "the same dimension" ("tre giri / di tre colori e d'una contenenza," *Par.* XXXIII, 116–117). Sight grows stronger until it penetrates the "Living Light" ("vivo lume," *Par.* XXXIII, 110), grasping its substance; and here certainly sight is followed by "concept": that eternal Light can be comprehended only trinitarily, because Light cannot but be effusive of itself, the creator of its own effusion, which loves what it illuminates-creates even as it brings it back into itself. The eyes grasp this circle *in every aspect*, and inside, in its deepest point, see how it is "painted with our effigy" ("pinta de la nostra effige," *Par.* XXXIII, 131), that is, the effigy of the *human-divine*, a necessary conclusion of the God-as-Relation or Trinitarian God, which the *intellectual intuition* had first conceived.

True, Mary's beauty, unlike Beatrice's, cannot be said in any way, and Dante's speech, even now that it has been drawn "out from slavery into freedom" ("di servo tratto a libertate," *Par.* XXXI, 85), is not worthy of pronouncing the oration. The humble pilgrim listens to it, and gratefully obeys his guide. The woman's gaze does not even turn to him; it remains "fixed upon the supplicant" ("fissi ne l'orator," *Par.* XXXIII, 41). Nor does he see Christ qua Logos in the beginning (*en arche*), but only in our effigy, Logos incarnate, supreme mediator-conciliator of the human and the divine. Nonetheless, he sees all this, and his speech is powerful enough to show at least "one gleam" of it. This means that speaking is really *light from Light*, that speaking stands in essential relation to Light itself. Does this entail a contemptible degradation of the primordial power of divine Splendor? A fall that desecrates the Invisible and Ineffable, that tumbles from Perfection down into the Imperfect? Not at all, and quite the contrary. The light is all-pervading. One same light emanates from the perfectly intellectual Good to the visible Sun, all the way to the end of the cave, where not even the shadows and reflections would be visible if the Light did not reach there. And is not the same true for Dante's *Inferno*? One same light that always gives itself without ever running out, exactly like "the Love that moves the sun and the other stars" ("l'amore che move il sole e l'altre stelle," *Par*. XXXIII, 145), "because the light of God so penetrates / the universe according to the worth / of every part, that no thing can impede it" ("che la luce divina è penetrante / per l'universo secondo ch'è degno, / sì che nulla le puote essere ostante," *Par*. XXXI, 22–24). A light both intellectual and *absolutely real*. The Way of Beauty finds its fulfillment in the image of the Light's supreme beauty, the highest sign (*vestigium*) of divine Goodness. By his grace we see and are seen, by his being always in act (*energheiai*), every being has life and constitutes himself in the bond that harmonizes the totality of beings, where each preserves its own figure *sub specie aeternitatis*. Which dimension of this experience, of this extraordinary journey of body, mind, and soul, then, proves truly, *radically* unsayable? Which one of its instants will we never be able to put-into-image?

In the dynamic of this height of rapture (*excessus mentis*), I believe we should distinguish two moments. First of all, memory seems incapable of holding on to the image of the lived experience; it is just as when we awake, and of our dream only the "passion that has been imprinted stays" ("la passione impressa / rimane," *Par*. XXXIII, 59–60), and the things that we dreamed melt away like snow in the sun or blow away in the wind like the leaves that bore the Sybil's prophecies. But no simile, here, can do justice to the idea. What Dante experienced was not a dream! It is not in a dream that he focuses all his attention (the mystical *prosoche*); he does not entrust all his being on that Point! Memory bears a precise trace of this experience. However, no rational *demonstration* can be built on the basis of such memory. The language that illustrates it cannot be that of argumentation or demonstration. That experience *gave itself, gives itself*, shows itself in the speech of the Canto. It is a saying that is an indicating, a signaling. It is the saying of the mind-that-imagines. This saying is the only one consistent with the experience Dante has undergone. Here the ineffable concerns the very *evidence* that what his new vision allowed him to contemplate takes on. It is the evidence of vision that surpasses any predicative-demonstrative language. And it is a highly *singular* evidence: how to conceive of a "discourse" around something that appears absolutely irreducible to the common parameters of human experience? The symbol of the human-divine with which the *Commedia* ends is ineffable precisely because it cannot be figured, in the same way that the squaring of the circle cannot be figured; in other words, its ineffability essentially coincides with its rational indemonstrability. The same goes for the "abysses" of faith, as in the case of predestination (*Par.* XXI, 94); here, too, it would be improper to call it ineffable; dogma is indemonstrable, not unsayable.

Memory holds a trace of the rapture on which an "obedient," contemplating, in-*dicating* and pre-*dicting* form of speech can be predicated. What, on the contrary, is not even memory, in that it has become one with the pilgrim's being—what is not even rememberable, since remembrance entails a stretch of time (*distensio temporis*), a before and an after, whereas here everything occurs in the immediacy of the instant—is *pleasure*, the *highest pleasure*, which is the true sign of the conjoining of the vision "with the Infinite Goodness" ("col valore infinito," *Par.* XXXIII, 81). The *enjoyment* of that intuition of the nexus that harmonizes the dimensions of Being, the enjoyment that puts an end to desire itself operates as both the testament of the reality of the vision—though in its absolute singularity—and the index of the truly, irreducibly Ineffable. The instant in which human and divine unite, the instant (*exaiphnes*) that breaks the continuum of *Chronos* and that is signaled by an ineffable pleasure: this is the "light that flashed" ("fulgore," *Par.* XXXIII, 140[7]) in which the mind "received what it had asked" ("in che sua voglia venne," *Par.* XXXIII, 140–141), and that not even one's "high fantasy" ("alta fantasia," *Par.* XXXIII, 142) could express. The highest pleasure that the ultimate vision produces is not visible. The ultimate vision itself is still, in some way, sayable-imaginable, but the enjoyment that accompanies it is an unspeakable instant. This pleasure is the Light's twin. Just as Light allows one to see but in itself is not visible, although it is sayable in and by the lights (*lumina*) and rays (*radii*) through which it gives itself (or sacrifices itself) and by which it is expressed, so Joy, the Gladness upon "touching" God, attests to the reality of the accomplished journey and of the experienced visions, remaining, as such, ineffable. Its ineffability does in no way detract from the contentment it gives; pleasure *shows* that the will has fulfilled all its desires, and that will and desires rotate in unison with the will of God. The term "Ineffable"—in its proper literal, not metaphorical, sense—only befits this Joy, the sign of the Eternal Now (*Nunc aeternum*), the opposite of duration.

Five

Dante's *Intellectual Love*

Can we say in what consists, in essence, the extraordinary experience that Dante—*homo viator*, body and soul, Dante as *figura*, as Auerbach would have it—accomplishes in the *Paradiso*? What knowledge does he attain through his *real* experience of it? It is, we might say, what the world "cannot / discern of God's own grace" ("veder non può de la divina grazia," *Par*. XX, 71). The "deepest site" ("il fondo," *Par*. XX, 72) of this knowledge must remain hidden *in hoc saeculo*, on this earth, to every finite gaze. Yet now divine grace manifests itself in all its extraordinary, pardoxical power: who "in the erring world below" ("giù nel mondo errante," *Par*. XX, 67) would believe it capable of such mercy?

Gathered in the Eagle's eyebrow are examples of the highest justice: not only the humble (*humilis*) Roman emperor Trajan but also Ripheus the Trojan, most just (*iustissimus*) because he fell defending his city on its fatal night. Two pagans have been elevated into the heavenly Rome. "Can such things be?" ("Che cose son queste?," *Par*. XX, 82). Love accomplishes the miracle. Love surpasses every measure of judgment and will, overcomes every doctrine and norm by making Trajan and Ripheus contemporary with Christ in spirit, upsetting the "order of Time," because it has loved the perfect justice that was in them.

Love can conquer Heaven's will ("vince la divina volontate," *Par*. XX, 96). However much the universe and its order may hang on God's will, it is ultimately Love that has the last word as to His deeds. *Theos Agape*. God loves His creature more than His own will or the parameters of His own justice—to which, in theory, there should be no exception. "Ardent love" must needs be accompanied by "living hope" ("da caldo amore e da viva speranza," *Par.* XX, 95), insofar as loving someone is tantamount to desiring their salvation. Does hope itself, then, live in the heart of God's grace? Here is the supreme paradox: God acts *hoping* for our salvation, and in order that we are saved he lets himself be conquered by Love.

Does he *let* himself be conquered, or is he really conquered? There can be no doubt: God's will *wants* to be won, and by being won, "it wins through benevolence" ("vinta, vince con sua beninanza," *Par.* XX, 99). The perfect divine will wants the *good* of its creature, and it only truly wins once that good is accomplished—even though it means defying the *letter* of the law. At the center of God's will, precisely because it is perfectly *good*, stands supreme Justice: that is, the supreme possibility to *exceed* even the apparently most stable Norm wherever the spirit of Love breathes.

However, our human will, too, can ultimately be conquered only if it allows itself to be: "for will, if it resists, is never spent" ("che volontà, se non vuol, non s'ammorza," *Par.* IV, 76); in fact, it becomes all the more inflamed the more it is "compelled" ("vïolenza il torza," *Par.* IV, 77–78), as the Christian Lawrence and the Roman soldier Mucius Scaevola demonstrate, *both of them martyrs*. The former overcomes his will to live thanks to his love of Christ, the latter out of patriotic virtue. And Dante makes them into one symbol! Mirroring divine mercy, then, we are also accorded the ability to win by excess of love any hard law (*dura lex*), the absolute first of which is, of course, the natural will tied to the defense, preservation, and interest of our individual existence.

The divine will is conquered only because it wants to be, whereas the human will can do as much only through God's grace. What counts, however, is the audacity of the break, of the leap. Between the parameters of Justice and the Love that saves—the love that exists only to save and not to judge—every dialectical agreement is merely apparent. The language of mysticism expresses it: the Kingdom of Heaven *suffers*, but it *suffers* only from the violence of the *loving* spirits. The Lord may love all His creatures yet will *suffer violence* only from those who love—from those who, with all the violence of their "ardent love and living hope," wish to *conquer* the Kingdom.

It is the violence of love (*caritatis violentia*)—discussed by Saint Bernard (the pilgrim's last guide), Hugh and Richard of Saint Victor—that determines an *excessus mentis*. While *mens* entails measuring, comparing, calculating, *caritatis violentia* overwhelms all difference in its aim to become-God (*indiarsi*; see *Par.* IV, 28), to be-contained-in-Him (*inluiarsi*; see *Par.* IX, 73), to be enwombed (*inventrarsi*; see *Par.* XXI, 84) in divine Love (Dante's neologisms always attest to his inexhaustible quest to express the unsayable).

This is the fundamental theme of the *Paradiso*: how the mind surpasses itself (*si trasmodi*; see *Par.* XXX, 19) and how such supreme metamorphosis is conceivable only through the *violence* of love, which holds in itself the letter of the law and, precisely for this reason, at the same time surpasses it. Here are, then, the hopes harbored by the *homo viator*: that his love may *vanquish* divine justice (if the latter were invincible, there would be no hope); that the love with which he attempts to surpass himself (unless he tries to *superhumanize* himself, his hope will be vain) might conquer God's will; in sum, that in God may live a hope for our salvation so powerful, so *violent*, that He himself might wish to be vanquished by it. The conclusive image of Mary encompasses this great theme: her prayer to the Son is infinitely more than a mere intercession. It is a prayer that needs no words since *it already speaks from within the Logos-Verbum itself*. Its figure expresses, at the very center of the divine *economy*, the *ultimate* possibility, the *eschatological* Possible—and that is, that the *violence* of Love may win in God, that God in the end *may wish to be vanquished* by his Love, and that his own justice be transfigured in light of this "passion."

Is it legitimate to conceive that this divine self-overcoming goes, eschatologically, for everyone? Dante would disagree. The *Inferno* shows mercilessly that this is just not the case. And yet, one cannot help feeling that, in the *Paradiso*, such a question and such a doubt become unstoppable. Throughout the *Commedia* runs a powerful, distant echo that contradicts the injunction to "abandon every hope, who enter here," thereby making the whole of Dante's theology dramatic. Between Love, Will, and Justice, nothing is "arranged" once and for all. Love tends to "descend" toward every miserable lost soul in the woods—the Women are its image and its messengers. Yet, Will must resist its impetus and follow the reasons that Justice puts forth. No certain or safe rule could establish a priori which force should prevail. Why did Love prevail for Dante? We can only make conjectures. Is it really necessary that we feel infinite anguish over our condition for the Women to come to our rescue? Does it suffice to answer the call of our own free will (*sponte*)? What seems certain is that, in the *Paradiso*, Love is declared to be the *substance* of God, and that for this reason its energy can achieve the *excessus* and win it all.

But how is this Love expressed? What is its Word, which we are called upon to understand so that we may set out to follow it? God is the highest Cause, loving Cause, both final and efficient, unconditional Love, and thus free from all necessity, uncaused Cause. A Cause that flows out into the totality of its effects, without its power ever diminishing. *Effusivum sui*: the perfect Gift, or rather, *For-Givenness*. Could we ever achieve this on earth? No, but we can *love* it. We can manage to love this Love that is the perfect gratuity of giving. In fact, as soon as we intuit its substance, it is impossible for us not to love it. For not to love it would mean not to love an unconditional, perfectly free Being; it would mean not to wish ourselves, too, to be Cause in its image. If we manage to understand (*intelligere*) the substance of divine Love, then our very *mind* is obliged to love it.

The *action* of His Love is always *actu*, in *act*, such as ours could never be. And yet, if we *love* after having understood it—if our love is, in this sense, *intellectualis*—then we, too, shall become truly *agents*, sharing in that unconditional and free Action—in that being pure Cause, which coincides with divine Love. We shall be agents insofar as we are moved by the purpose of achieving its power—an endless journey, indeed; yet one during which our love shall grow, and the intellection of its substance—as well as the will to express it—shall become clearer and clearer, however finite. The love *in itinere* is therefore always stronger than the love of the blessed, who have at last "conquered" Paradise.

Beatrice explains to Dante the superessential nature of this Love, how it unfolded before time and outside of all time when she narrates the creation of the Angel. God did not create "to acquire new goodness for Himself" ("per avere a sé di bene acquisto," *Par.* XXIX, 13); the Cause lacks nothing, nor does its *splendor*, which outshines every *lumen* insofar as the eternal is "outside of time"; what encompasses all within itself cannot have any border ("comprender," *Par.* XXIX, 17). The Cause *subsists*, as the only true substance; and yet, precisely in its eternal subsisting, in its *nunc stans*, it *opens up* and flows out, freely, by its own will (or rather, by the will that is won over by Love), and bestows life on *new loves*, on new loving spirits.

The Substance is not "jealous" of its being-eternal; its very eternity *subsists by opening up*; it reveals its splendor by illuminating, it reveals its freedom by freeing. Does this extraordinary image pertain merely to angels? Perhaps it pertains less to the Angel than to any other creature. The Angel has "decided" once and for all with respect to the revelation of the act of God's love. For man, the drama of decision is destined to repeat itself until the end of time. It is man who is called upon to match the free will he was given (according to the doctrine that underpins the architecture of the *Commedia*) with the Love of that Substance that opens up into new loves—an intuited-imagined Substance in the act of ever *renewing itself* through their manifestation.

You cannot truly love unless you give in the form of perfect gratuity—but even that is not enough: you cannot understand the substance of this Love unless by *creating* new loves. One does not merely *subsist* in the act of love, nor does love exist merely in an act of giving and *for-giving* that leaves the beloved's condition unchanged. Love demands that more loves be born, and that those who receive the gift be themselves transformed by freely turning into lovers. I would stress that this is the exact opposite of the "Love that releases no beloved from loving" ("Amor, ch'a nullo amato amar perdona," *Inf.* V, 103): on the contrary, this Love *demands* that the beloved's freedom be left intact. It *demands* that other loves as unconditional as its own be created.

The loving Cause that, forced by no necessity, has wished to flow out by shining, longs to open up into other *agents-lovers* made in its image. If it attempted to determine them, it would betray its nature. The Cause has expressed itself, has spoken, has conceded to this man the grace of being able to understand it, supporting him through exceptional guides. Has the *viator* really understood this Cause? Has he finally attained the true *intelligence of love*? Because, indeed, this is an intellectual matter, as no immediate intuition can procure knowledge of the Cause. The *viator* has had to sink into the most hidden substance of his being-there, has had to run the risk of getting lost again on his arduous journey, so that he could drink at last from the source of its light. Now he understands that being *agents* is tantamount to being lovers, that to love is to give, and that to give is to open oneself up to new loves, to let them freely express themselves, outside any logic of exchange or reciprocity. Now he finally understands that to love means simply to wish for the beloved's perfect health-salvation (*salus*), to wish to be like a *grace* for him or her.

Of necessity, the new loves will always be infinitely distant from the first Love. To understand its substance does not mean to want to be His equal. But again, this has nothing to do with statically measuring a distance: the difference between the perfect gratuity of God's gift and the measure of the love of which we are capable is commensurate with the distance that always stands between any love that truly opens up to *new* loves, and the latter. He who loves is destined to remain at a distance from the beloved if the beloved is to be a new loving subject. Love assimilates nothing, incorporates nothing into itself: in fact, it rejects the very notion of "unification" (*enosis*) with the beloved. Love conceives of the latter only as someone who loves in himself and by himself, someone whose spirit blows wherever it wants. Just as Dante's effusive splendor illuminates all beings and is mirrored by them—yet without resolving itself into its effects, but rather remaining infinitely distant from them even as it gives itself and gives us life—so is our love an interminable *approximation* to the beloved-lover—an approximation that grows closer the farther away it moves. And the deeper we feel the distance, the more unbreakable the bond becomes. Every "logic of identity" is overcome from the start (*ab origine*) by that Love that opens itself up into new loves. It is a love *sub specie aeternitatis*—and yet, if we manage to understand it, we are given the ability to reflect its substance, in a manner commensurate with our freedom.

The inseparability of nearness and farness that the *intelligence of Love* requires is expressed with sublime *pathos* in that crucial moment in the *Commedia* where Beatrice is suddenly spirited away from Dante and Saint Bernard, "an elder" ("un sene," *Par.* XXXI, 59), appears in her place to take the pilgrim the rest of the way, so that all his "longings may be satisfied" ("a terminar lo tuo disiro," *Par.* XXXI, 65)—but notice that, once more, it is the Women who "urge" Dante's guides: "Beatrice urged me from my place" ("mosse Beatrice me del loco mio," *Par.* XXXI, 66). "Where is she? / I asked him instantly" ("Ov'è ella?, subito diss'io," *Par.* XXXI, 64)—the question he intended to ask his beloved choked in his throat. Beatrice has flown an incommensurable distance away, a distance greater than that between "that region where the highest thunder forms," and a mortal eye "plunged into deep seas" ("Da quella regïon che più sù tona / occhio mortale alcun tanto non dista, / qualunque in mare più giù s'abbandona," *Par.* XXXI, 73–75).

High up, *at an extreme distance*, Dante sees "that round her now a crown took shape / as she reflected the eternal rays" ("che si facea corona / reflettendo da sé li etterni rai, *Par.* XXXI, 71–72). Yet this distance, real as it may be, "was no hindrance" ("nulla mi facea"); though it is not erased, it accords with an equally real nearness that allows for spiritual communication: "for her semblance / reached me undimmed by anything between" ("ché süa effige / non discendëa a me per mezzo mista," *Par.* XXXI, 77–78). Beatrice has now separated from the pilgrim, who is destined, beyond the vision that awaits him, to return to his "family of humans" ("umana famiglia," *Par.* XXVII, 141) and preach the Word (*praedicare Verbum*). But it is a separation *of love*: Dante the lover eternalizes in his memory the beauty of his woman, a beauty that surpasses itself ("si trasmoda," *Par.* XXX, 19) the very moment it leaves him, and in this distance, he is closer to her than ever before.

She has drawn him out of slavery to freedom ("Tu m'hai di servo tratto a libertate," *Par.* XXXI, 85); indeed, this is what Love accomplishes. Love frees new loves, turns us into agents-lovers, people who love others *to make them free*, who love the hope of freedom that constitutes everyone's soul and substance of being. This is the grace that Beatrice reveals fully to Dante, *now that she has flown up into her heaven*—now that she is *far away*. From this stellar farness, her smile is near to Dante's soul, which she has healed ("sì che l'anima mia che fatt'hai sana," *Par.* XXXI, 89); *inseparably* near: "So did I pray. And she, however far / away she seemed, smiled, and she looked at me" ("Così orai; e quella, sì lontana / come parea, sorrise e riguardommi," *Par.* XXXI, 91–92).

Dante re-lives, *re-members*, his whole life in this Smile, together with the mission still awaiting him. He is now ready to encounter the Woman, Mary, who expresses the same Love of God. Beatrice has made him free and loving. She will remain in the deepest reaches of his soul, a dramatic *symphony* of extreme nearness and farness.

Six

Latin and Vernacular in the *De vulgari eloquentia*

It is appropriate to begin by mentioning the extraordinary edition of the *De vulgari eloquentia* by Enrico Fenzi, which inaugurates the new commented edition of Dante's *oeuvre* sponsored by the Centro Pio Rajna.[1] From this very first volume, the project appears to be a truly monumental undertaking. Not only is the *De vulgari* commented on, particularly on the strength of Pier Vincenzo Mengaldo's fundamental research, with unprecedented erudition and critical acumen, but also the volume comes accompanied by Francesco Bruni's crucial essay on Dante's *geography* elucidating the linguistic areas considered in the treatise, and by a vast appendix containing all the French, Provençal, and Italian poetry that Dante quotes, as well as the first Italian translation of the *De vulgari* by Gian Giorgio Trissino, whose publication in Vicenza in 1529 rescued the treatise from a centuries-long oblivion.

To my mind, the *De vulgari* is a work so revolutionary that it should no longer remain the exclusive preserve of historical-philological erudition. In it, too, Dante confronts truths never before addressed. No one before him had discussed the common speech, which is nonetheless "necessary" for everyone (including women and children!). With perhaps even more urgency than in the *Convivio*, here the poet feels duty-bound to dispense the highest good of knowledge to everyone. Here, too, in other words, he is a "prophet." And the first, fundamental truth he reveals is that only humans speak. No other animal does, nor do angels. Animals use signs, make signs, but only sensory ones, "guided only by their natural instinct" (*De vulg.* I, 2, 5).[2] Nor are they able to communicate across species. There is no, as it were, friendship (*amicitia*) between signs from different species, unlike human languages, which are translatable, albeit within the limits inherent in the notion of translation. However, angels communicate immediately by reflecting themselves in the infinite mirror of the superessential Divine. But language is both sensible and rational, it conjoins both spirit and nature. Indeed, this is what constitutes its intact nobility, "symbolic" in the richest meaning of the term.

Instinct, moreover, is the same for all animal species. Not even the angelic species can be differentiated, if not for the place they occupy in the celestial Hierarchy. They speak one and the same language, so as not to give rise to any misunderstanding in their communication. Instead, in humans, "reason takes diverse forms in individuals" (*De vulg.* I, 3, 1) and manifests itself differently in each person. It is almost as though we each exhibit our own unique individual reason, in the same way as we each have our own unique, individual soul. Every person "enjoys the existence of a unique species" (*De vulg.* I, 3, 1). This is not a "bad" thing—quite the contrary, in fact: we "enjoy" it. But we must also understand the difficulties and responsibilities that arise from such an *extra*ordinary condition. Communication between humans will always run the risk of *mis*understanding. We must be aware of that, and therefore strive to elaborate a skillful eloquence, a language as orderly as possible and capable of expressing our ideas with the utmost rigor, since, in order to be voiced, all ideas must inevitably be embodied in sensible signs. Hence the imperious necessity to "construct" an illustrious vernacular, with which we may express ourselves in the academia and in the courts, in the tribunals and in great politics. A vernacular, that is, that may be the cornerstone of our political being-there, of that essence of the human animal that is living in a community. A vernacular that may rise above municipal miseries, those that seek to weigh in even on the matter of linguistic preeminence. Not because Dante has stopped loving Florence; quite the contrary, he loves it even more as an exile. But precisely as an exile, he has learned that cities can live only if they are "universal," that is, if their language is powerful enough to "communicate" with the whole world.

Although this is not the place for a thorough analysis of this first "philosophy of language" that we find represented in Dante's work, it is nonetheless well worth making a brief list of its fundamental, most innovative elements.

1. The idea of a "sign" that connects in itself both the sensible and the rational.
2. The notion that language did not originate in Adam's naming of things (*nominatio rerum*)—the conventional-arbitrary sense of origin. Rather, it originated in an exclamation, thus, in a "sign" that is fully sensible, even though it was addressed to the supreme Maker! The very human language begins with a sound and, in some measure, a gesture. Herein Dante inaugurates a path that will lead to Vico!
3. The notion of the "becoming" of languages—the essential image of the not *fixed*, *incurabilis* nature of humans (a becoming that in the *Commedia* will also be affirmed about Hebrew: there is no "sacred" language!).
4. But the most innovative element of Dante's philosophy of language is most likely the idea of the "form of language" (*forma locutionis*), that is, of a structure perhaps "innate" to humankind that allows each individual to learn no matter what particular language from the "matrix." "That man should speak at all is nature's act" ("Opera naturale è ch'uom favella," *Par*. XXVI, 130), but the multiplicity of idioms is a function of change (*vicissitudo*) and human will. Almost a foreshadowing of Chomskyan linguistics?[3]

There are no perfect nor sacred languages. All languages are in flux. No grammar can inhibit their life. The nobility of the vernacular lies precisely in this: all languages are born vernaculars. Vernacular is the first language. But a language does not merely "become" in the sense that it transforms once it is thrown into universal change. A language becomes also in the sense that it "constructs itself" ever more powerfully and harmoniously over time, and it comes to "represent" the thing with ever more consistency and precision. A language becomes also on the strength of its "wordsmiths," those "builders" that mold it so as to make it truly analogous to the soul of the speaking animal. Indeed, just as the soul is capable in potency of representing all things (as wax on which every image leaves its imprint), so must be its language. Thus, we understand the nobility of Latin or *grammatica* (as the Latin language was referred to in the Middle Ages), by no means in contradiction with that of the vernacular.

Not only is Latin not "dead," the vernaculars spoken in *Romania*[4] being nothing but its current life, but also, Latin must not die, unless we want the vernaculars to sink into an episodic, contingent, municipal existence lacking universality and power. Latin is not merely their memory, or their supporting past: it is what constitutes their "project." The vernaculars must be able to "construct" themselves as Latin did, if they wish to gain the same kind of power. We are not talking here about pedantic imitation, or preservation through memory. The "game" that must be played is rather one of emulation and competition. The same goes for the plastic and visual arts. During Dante's time, the "old-fashioned," "Roman" language is frequented and adopted the better to show the glory of the present vernacular. The Pisans seek to affirm themselves as more powerful sculptors than their ancient predecessors. The great architectures, which will lead up to Brunelleschi's cupola, rival the Roman ones for daring. Latin is the model for all this *ars* or *techne*—a model, however, to be surpassed!

Indeed, Latin grammar is noble, as it guarantees perfect order. But it cannot be understood by everyone—and Dante, the new intellectual, wishes precisely to be understood by all. The most serious problem, though, is that he could never express in Latin the dramas of the new times, nor represent in Latin the life of these cities, their conflict with both church and empire, the scandalous decadence of the Church, the catastrophe of the Imperial idea. The ideas and conflict of this epoch must find their own language, just as Augustus's new order had found it in Virgil. Both noble languages, yet only the former still living. Is Latin useless, then? Not at all. Latin remains an insuperable paragon of the synthesis of knowledge and eloquence, and as such it teaches one to seek and to pursue that synthesis in the vernacular. As William of Conches points out: "Wisdom without eloquence, though it does little good, at least does some. Eloquence without wisdom is harmful."[5] It is not enough for us to use the speech that we hold dear from infancy—as infancy is already inhabited by the form of language (*forma locutionis*); it is already, in a sense, a language. Is it imperative that we learn to speak well—not to be "literati," but so that we may be of worth to the city, whatever the field of our competence. *Grammar* is our model for how we should "arm ourselves" for the conversation-dialogue-conflict that shapes (*in-forms*) the human city.

The determination of signs (*determinatio signorum*), although based on human agreement (*ad placitum humanum*), must prove to be as fully formed, as orderly, and as harmonious as possible. Through such method—derived from the study of the Latin or grammar—not only can we achieve precision in communicating, and the minimization of the (never eliminable) risk of misunderstanding; most importantly, we are able to pursue the supreme goal of the communication of knowledge. For any learning (*mathema*), any knowledge (*scientia*), and any scientific community would be impossible without an illustrious vernacular that rivals Latin for clarity, and therefore that knows Latin so profoundly as to be able, eventually, to surpass it.

But then, will the vernacular not also become an artificial language? Impossible, as it taps into the "matrix," it is rooted in our infancy before any word is spoken. Together with the gift of freedom, God infuses into our souls that form of language (*forma locutionis*) that makes us able to assume, without any rule, whatever language in which our mother addresses us. (I am aware that Fenzi understands the expression *forma locutionis* to mean exclusively the first language spoken by Adam, which for Dante, as well as for the tradition before him, could only have been Hebrew.) The vernacular must be not artificial, but rather, so powerful as to be able to express any idea and communicate any content. To be able, in sum, to be poetry, in the original sense of *poiesis*—smith-like capability, tectonic force. Thus, "poetic" must be the foundation of the language spoken and understood by all; or rather, "poetic" must be its re-foundation, which will make it suitable for creating real communities of speakers. And poets will be the best wordsmiths of maternal speech.

However, is not this speech, too, unceasingly in flux? How can we give it shape? Does not this constant becoming reflect the nature of us humans, "highly unstable and variable animals" (*De vulg*. I, 9, 6)? How should we "cure" the infinite variety of languages, as well as the variety inherent in each singular language? Indeed, it is precisely the universal vicissitude of things that makes it necessary for us to seek what is "common," by building forms of understanding and communication that can belong to all precisely because they belong to no one. This is not an abstract task: quite the contrary, we best pursue this common element by immersing ourselves in the lived concreteness of the forms of existence that these languages represent. This is not something we sit down and artificially create: it is an impassioned chase from city to city, or rather, from neighborhood to neighborhood—that is, from life to life—to ferret out those forms that appear most stable, richest in history, most able to make our speech more vigorous and more persuasive. But also, more beautiful, more resounding and harmonious. In sum, an extraordinary impasto of historical conscience, experimentalism, and the quest for a "great form." And love for maternal speech.

In times when language is reduced to a mere means of exchanging information, when its symbolic form is mistreated, when the most plebeian parochialisms threaten to dissipate its universal communicative energy, and it seems as though we can defend against them only by embracing the rigorous formal-artificial idiom of the "exact sciences," Dante's advocacy for a vernacular that must make itself "illustrious" still maintains its innovative thrust. Indeed, *"loquor, ergo sum,"* I speak, therefore I am. But to be able to affirm this, my speech (*locutio*) must strive toward that wisdom, eloquence, and beauty whose traces and clues Dante investigates tirelessly, and with which he has built the *Commedia*'s supreme architecture.

Seven

On Dante's Political Theology

Dante's *prophecy*, to the extent that it seeks to be a prophecy, unfolds on two tightly interconnected levels: religious and political. This connectedness is precisely what makes the poet *a seer* and his poem *sacred*. Thus, poetic *fantasy* assumes a biblical language to communicate truths that could not be otherwise expressed. There can be no salvation for the city of man unless the authorities that represent those two dimensions manage to be *in actuality* (*energeiai*); that is, unless what they are in potency comes to a perfect fulfillment *in both*. They must understand in what their *form* consists, both for what makes them different and for what they have in common. Providence has distinguished, yet by no means separated, their goals. And these goals will be achievable as long as their respective domains are not confused.

The *health* [*salute*] of the earthly city would not be conceivable if those whose mission it is to "keep in shape" the flock in the hope of eternal *salvation* [*salvezza*] presumed to be the first guardians and foundation of that very *health*, and, by acting accordingly, proved themselves unworthy of *re-forming* the Church according to the form of living that Christ prescribed by his example. Nonetheless, this re-formation—and the militant Church in history is always "to-be-reformed" (*semper reformanda*)—appears to Dante essential to health on earth. It is not a quiet separation of spheres, whereby each party merely "tolerates" the other! For Dante, the Church will operate *according to the Word* not only by respecting the autonomy and *rationality* inherent in political power but also by recognizing what the *true* form must be which that power is called upon to assume.

Because such form is consistent with the universality of its task, the church will have to promote it through its very preaching. The "two Suns," Papacy and Empire, should not be opposed; rather, they should find a way to integrate and illuminate each other. For Dante, in other words, the Church must *wish* the Empire to be autonomous, not just tolerate its independence. In turn, the Empire must not simply approve but also actively endorse the value that the reform of the Church is destined to assume for the whole field of human relations. There is no neutrality of either Sun to the form of the other! The City is both city of man (*civitas homini*) and city of God (*civitas Dei*), and contains in itself all the dynamics that issue from such duplicity. In fact, we should not think of them as two cities, but rather as one two-personed city. A dual city, as dual is the nature of Christ himself: a "two-form animal" ("la biforme fera," *Purg.* XXXII, 96)! And the prophet reveals that those whose task it is to represent the City according to this dual nature must find in the difference of their respective missions the eschatological sense of mutual understanding and, even more, communion. In sum, the Church's universality, when conceived and lived in truth, cannot but demand an Empire; thus, a movement of authentic *re-formation* cannot stay neutral to that political end. The Empire, in turn, demands that the Church reform itself, if it wishes to operate effectively and carry out its idea. It is not just that it would be un-Christian for an Empire to remain indifferent to the lot of Peter's seat, to the misery in which it has sunk, to the apocalyptic crises it is going through; such an Empire would end up betraying its own very mission. Both a Church without an Empire and an Empire without a Church spell a City *in tatters*. This is the "state of affairs" that the prophet denounces and protests with all his might—in the *Commedia* as well as in the *Monarchia*.

The error consists in trying to reduce either authority to the other, in identifying them in one. The error lies in the preeminence of the abstract One, a notion that the *Commedia* opposes down to its very poetic structure: if nothing else, the tercet would suffice to express Dante's thought! We must safeguard the *two* within the one, even with all the dangers it entails; but then the unity of two makes three, that is, their very relation, the sign of their unity—a figure that, however, is also another "person," and that in turn, as soon as it is expressed, hints back at the preceding figure: A-B-A-B-C (the third)-B (again).

Peace results from the *free interconnection* of the two authorities. If "of necessity" ("per viva forza," *Purg.* XVI, 111) one wants to absorb the other into itself, eclipsing its value, *happiness on earth* will be impossible to attain. Only the two Suns together will be able to keep the Era "in shape." Besides, Dante knows very well that this connection could never mean, in the present age (*in hoc saeculo*), any definitive harmonization, or the establishment of a new "state of nature." The two Suns act upon each other also *fearing* each other "because, so joined, one need not fear the other" ("però che, giunti, l'un l'altro non teme," *Purg.* XVI, 112). Also, each one acts as a katechontic force to the other. The sword must fear the pastoral, and vice versa. If we fail to understand this thoroughly, we miss the fully political significance of Dante's prophecy. Is this prophecy not entirely pervaded by the hope that the providential intervention of *the Eagle* (i.e., the Empire) will not only "show Italy the righteous way" ("a drizzare Italia," *Par.* XXX, 137) but also drive out "he who on earth usurps my place, my place, my place" ("Quelli ch'usurpa in terra il luogo mio / il luogo mio, il luogo mio che vaca," *Par.* XXVII, 22–23), meaning, of course, Saint Peter? The Eagle may be responsible, with Constantine ("perhaps / offered with sound and kind intent," "forse con intenzion sana e benigna," *Purg.* XXXII, 137–138), for the heavy freight the Church's "small bark" ("navicella mia," *Purg.* XXXII, 129) has taken on; however, it is the very same Eagle whose upcoming return is announced by Beatrice; for the power that "will slay the whore / together with that giant who sins with her" ("anciderà la fuia / con quel gigante che con lei delinque," *Purg.* XXXIII, 44–45) belongs to the very same "eagle that had left its plumes within / the chariot" ("l'aguglia che lasciò le penne al carro," *Purg.* XXXIII, 38). Otherwise, the degenerate, *thieving* Church, by uniting itself with the new "giant," symbol of a regal anti-imperial power (a power, thus, incapable of ruling), will know no check to her vices, just as the latter will no longer find in the Church the formidable *katechon* which used to exercise its *prophetic* voice over the Church's dominion. The Two must remain distinct, and each must be ready to denounce whatever "sins" the other may commit in the fulfillment of its mission. Peace will be possible only when the Two are willing never to leave each other in peace!

Of course, this does not in any way exclude—in fact, it encourages—an autonomous movement of *re-formation* within each authority, whereby the Political may fully strive toward the Empire, and the Church toward the way of life that Christ embodied. Only the most radical will to *self-reformation* intrinsic to each of the two Suns can accomplish their harmony, founded on mutual respect, on both reverence and critical energy. Founded, in sum, on that truthful speech (*en parresia*) that renders conceivable a Peace *in the present age*. Just as an unreformed Church—popes and cardinals whose thoughts "are never bent on Nazareth" ("non vanno i lor pensieri a Nazarette," *Par.* IX, 137)—would never be able to understand the providential nature of the Empire, in the same way a political power opposing the notion of Empire will always strive to either appropriate the pastoral or reduce prophecy to silence. Then, a game of mutual desacralization must inevitably commence between a captive Church and an anti-imperial power—a perfectly veridical game indeed, as by that point *there will no longer be anything sacred* about either of them. The death of the Empire, thus, becomes an omen of the end of Christianity itself. It is in this perspective—in the anguish that such perspective is always on the verge of provoking in Dante—that we must understand the apocalyptic thrust of his poem (and it is precisely here, perhaps, where we should ultimately find its deepest connection to Humanism).

Dante is a prophet not only because he expresses supernatural truths, but above all because he knows the just relationship between the latter and the "intellect and art" ("con ingegno e con arte," *Purg.* XXVII, 130) that the Virgilian *ratio* (but is it merely *ratio*? We will see . . .) instilled and cultivated in him to perfection (wherefore Dante is "crowned" by Virgil, *Purg.* XXVII, 142). Are not the enemies of the Greyhound and the Eagle also the enemies of Saint Francis's highest poverty (*altissima paupertas*)? The spotted leopard of lust and fraud, the lion of arrogance and violence are the enemies, and especially the most horrid beast, the "restless" beast, the *damned wolf* that "can never sate her greedy will" ("che mai non empie la bramosa voglia"), which "mates" ("s'ammoglia") with all the human vices (*Inf.* I, 98–100), which with her "hungering . . . deep and never-ending" ("per la tua fame sanza fine cupa!," *Purg.* XX, 12) embodies envy and avarice to the highest degree. Wolves are the ultimate enemies, and they are both clergymen and lay people—those who turned Florence into the "plant" of Lucifer, the plant that "produces and distributes the damned flower" ("produce e spande il maladetto fiore," *Par.* IX, 130)—the same diabolical force that always leads Francis's flock astray—and those who disguised themselves in shepherd's clothes the better to torment the lambs. Dante's invective always combines the two perspectives. The eschatological tone and the polemic-political tone chime in unison, even as far as *inside* the Empyrean. In fact, the most dramatic political *pathos* erupts from the *blessed* soul of Beatrice. We might say that her words are precisely what provide the political-theological key of the *Monarchia*.

Upon awakening from his sleep, which is the image of the disciples' sleep on Mount Tabor, Dante sees Beatrice sitting "alone upon the simple ground" ("sola sedeasi in su la terra vera," *Purg.* XXXII, 94), the inflexible guardian of the Chariot of the Church—she stands at "the griffin's breast" ("al petto del grifon," *Purg.* XXXI, 113)—at the same time *rooted* in the Land of Eden. She is crowned by the seven virtues, cardinal and theological, in their unity without confusion. A foreshadowing of the heavenly City, indeed, where one is citizen "without end" ("sanza fine," *Purg.* XXXII, 101); but also, a symbol of the perfection of the earthly one, *Rome*, a Rome Christianly revisited and yet, also, always the historical one, of which Christ himself was a citizen ("cive / di quella Roma onde Cristo è romano," *Purg.* XXXII, 102–103). True, Christ is *the* citizen of the heavenly City, but being a *Roman* on earth is here assumed as the true image of the ultimate, eternal citizenship. The exaltation of Rome as providential paragon of the earthly City is fully in keeping with the overall religious and political design of Dante's prophecy.

If Christ were not *Roman*, the idea of Empire that we have hitherto delineated would not hold. It is His Announcement that entails for Dante the universal unity of humankind also in its political dimension. Even these basic considerations ought to suffice to understand what a colossal mistake it would be to "modernize" Dante's political philosophy. There is no autonomy of the Political, much less a modern notion of the state form (whose imminent affirmation Dante denounces and condemns). From this point of view, neither Marsilius of Padua nor William of Ockham is yet on the horizon. There dominates in Dante a theological-political finalism that is totally absent in Marsilius, where there is also no trace of Rome's idealization. The emerging reality of governance (*regnum*) ends up overwhelming any imperial utopia. So, on the one hand, Dante will undoubtedly appear as a pure *reactionary* to whoever might wish to read history in terms of a more or less linear, happy "progress" toward a peaceful, indifferent division of powers between rationality (the subject matter of "philosophy") and religious-superstitious tradition and customs (reduced to the private sphere of sentiment). If, on the other hand, we perceive, in all their dramatic complexity, the consequences of the work of mutual *desacralization* that political power and religious authority will carry out; if we understand the notion of the Empire in all its philosophical depth as the expression of the unity of the Possible Intellect (an Averroist notion, which Dante refines in a few essential points), that is as the only political form consistent with the creativity of a general intelligence not ascribable to anyone in particular; if we believe that every form of political power must be *contradicted* by an eschatological reservation of prophetic nature; and finally, if the horizon of political action continues to be *happiness on earth*—a never fully quenchable thirst, a thirst that "even as / it quenches hunger, spurs the appetite" ("saziando di sé, di sé asseta," *Purg.* XXXI, 128–129), but that ultimately is *the salt* of every definite goal—then, and only then, will we have put ourselves in a position to grasp the "timely-untimely" dramatics inherent in the project of the *Monarchia*, at least with regard to that general instance whereby the work fully resonates with the *Commedia*.

It is therefore impossible to isolate Dante's political discourse from its theological foundation—indeed, from its mystical vision. This very duality, while also the cause of its aporias and contradictions, is what ultimately constitutes its originality and richness. For Dante, it is not just a matter of establishing what the duties (*officium*) are of those who must guarantee "a kind of community self-sufficient for life," nor is it just about realizing a government (*regimen*) that be "directed to the common good" (John of Paris),[1] although his idea of Empire certainly includes all of the above. For Dante, the Empire cannot be reduced to practical activity (*operatio practica*), which is inherent in human being-there and aimed toward a specific end. The issue is infinitely more complex, in that it concerns the possible nexus or harmony between health [*salute*] and salvation [*salvezza*]; it concerns, in other words, the way in which these "two cities" can evolve from being simply "linked" and "fused together" (Augustine[2]) to reaching a communion that, in safeguarding each other's specificity, will eliminate any enmity between them. Although to different degrees (collaterally in the former, prominently in the latter), this very same issue runs through both the *Monarchia* and the *Commedia*, against the backdrop of the great historical, cultural, and existential drama that they jointly represent.

It is an issue that Dante addresses from a perspective radically opposed to Augustine's (an opposition that, however, he never acknowledges in the *Monarchia*, where he makes but a passing reference to Augustine and only about questions of hermeneutical method). In Dante, the "demon-adoring city,"[3] the "daughter of the first Babylon,"[4] the "city of confusion,"[5] becomes the *historical incarnation* of the idea of perfect republic (*respublica*), so perfect that it allows us to call the first citizen of the heavenly city by the name of *Roman*.

Respublica was precisely the name that Augustine refused to attribute to Rome[6]—a name that does not indicate any specific regime, but rather the establishment of a political order whereby everyone is given what is rightfully their due, and whose laws may be freely and gladly obeyed "with one heart" (*uno corde*). Recall the representation of Good Government in Ambrogio Lorenzetti's great series of fresco panels painted in Siena, a work contemporary to Dante's *Commedia*! The Empire, characterized by unity of rule, by no means contradicts *respublica*; on the contrary, it brings the latter's potency into act, by expressing its ultimate purpose: to be the exact opposite of private property (*res privata*). The Empire is that *respublica* ordained exclusively to the public good, that it, to render justice to everyone, by countering every vice with a corresponding virtue. Indeed, it is also for his implicit *republicanism* that Dante will be loved by humanists, including Ficino and Machiavelli (as different as they were from each other). For Augustine, instead, besides the obvious fact that "there is no authority except that which God has established" (Romans 13, 1), the Empire is but a solace from the hard work of living, created for the administration of the affairs of Babylon, at most a katechontic power against the effects of our wounded nature (*natura vulnerata*), and therefore a mark of our sinfulness, an institution made necessary by the spread of our conflicts. It is most certainly not, as it is in Dante, true medicine, indispensable for the health [*salute*] of body and mind, distinct-yet-inseparable from the salvation [*salvezza*] of the soul.

That Dante may conceive of the Empire in these terms is of course inevitable, as for him the City, realization of civility (*civilitas*), is not the product of artificial pacts, of pragmatically defined conventions, but rather the very expression of human nature. In this respect, Dante is faithful to Thomist doctrine: even if he had remained in the Edenic state, man would have lived socially (*socialiter*), and here would necessarily have been the need for someone (*aliquis*) to lead everyone else to the pursuance of the common good. Naturally, in the Edenic condition this *someone* is God himself (one is here reminded of the God of Plato's myth, who in the golden age would personally lead us to pasture); it will be now necessary to discover and realize the most consistent image of this someone, from both a *rational and a theological* standpoint. Governance (*regnum*), therefore, cannot be reduced to a remedy for the weakness (*infirmitas*) inherent in our fallen nature (*natura lapsa*); though our sinfulness may indeed make its presence more urgent, it is nonetheless our original nature that requires it. Being political is a foundational trait of our human being-there, yet this principle is by no means expressed by Dante in merely Aristotelian terms. The Edenic root of governance forces us to consider authority as contingent on nothing else but the divine will. And thus, the fact that governance is required by our very nature calls for its definition in logico-rational terms. We are required, in other words, to elaborate a science of the City (*scientia civitatis*) that be endowed with its own significance.

But Dante's interrogation goes even further. Is a *kingdom in act*—the Act of Kingdom (that is, the perfection of its potentiality) and thus the realization of human happiness in the *earthly* Paradise—at all conceivable by simply keeping its idea autonomous? Is it possible to limit the problem of the City (if the establishing of Joy on earth is the *final cause* that determines its very movement) merely to its political-juridical-institutional architecture? It seems to me that the *Commedia* does not contradict the *Monarchia*. On the contrary, it maintains its substance—or rather, it constitutes a further development and a radical questioning of the *Monarchia* itself. Let us see in what sense this is true.

Political power is itself full *auctoritas*, just as that *someone* who is destined by providence to lead us all to the common good is worthy of being called Augustus. These principles are founded on the correct use of reason and have been "entirely revealed to us by the philosophers" (*Mon.* III, 16, 9).[7] The cornerstones of the Christian faith confirm all this. And how could they ever be in contradiction with the *laws of nature*? "What is contrary to nature's intention is against God's will" (*Mon.* III, 2, 2). Reason (*ratio*) and faith (*fides*) unanimously set before man two goals to pursue, two beatitudes: the happiness that is "figured in the earthly Paradise" (as described in the final Cantos of the *Purgatorio*) and "the happiness in the eternal life," which we cannot access unless our virtue is helped along, and then transfigured, by God's light (*Mon.* III, 16, 7–8). Two ultimate goals ("duo ultima," *Mon.* III, 15, 6), two beatitudes. Does it mean, also, two truths? Not at all. The truth is one; the two Suns are lights from the Light (*lumina de lumine*). Both descend directly from God (*immediate a Deo*), but neither is absolute; rather, one is *relative* to the other. Nor is this just a matter of mutual "reverence" or of the fact—completely obvious to the devout—that "in some sense" the happiness of mortal life is "ordered towards immortal happiness," as the last lines of *Monarchia* appear—somewhat hastily—to conclude (*Mon.* III, 16, 17–18). Indeed, the entire context of the *Monarchia*, too, revolves around the question of the nonadventitious relationship (*relatio non adventitia*) that must be posited between the Two, so as not to cause religion to secede from faith, both being the very energies of the soul. To define each in its own sphere is a necessary task, and Dante appears satisfied that this task has been accomplished in the *Monarchia*. However, once a boundary is set, there inevitably arises the question of its overcoming. And this—it bears repeating—is already implicit in the fact that the two Suns, the two Ultimate, are by no means disconnected (*ab-soluti*) "from the summit of all being, that is from God" (*Mon*. III, 13, 1–2).

I like to think that Dante was concluding the *Monarchia* at the same time that he was composing the great lines with which Virgil "crowns" his pupil at the end of *Purgatorio* XXVII. The pilgrim's natural disposition to doing good (as God created man good) has been educated to perfection; his will has become "free, erect, and whole" ("libero, dritto e sano," *Purg*. XXVII, 140) and will never again have to obey laws and norms imposed from the outside. Dante's own "pleasure" ("piacere," *Purg*. XXVII, 131), by now regenerated, will be his "guide" ("duce," *Purg*. XXVII, 131). Has Dante, then, "through the teachings of philosophy" (*Mon*. III, 16, 8), finally reached his ultimate goal on earth? If that were the case, the following Cantos would already chronicle the second phase of his pilgrimage; that is, they would be preparing Dante to *transhumanize* himself, and would have no structural relationship to the preceding stages of his ascent. But this is obviously not true. Dante's will may now be stretched toward the good but is by no means already able to accomplish it; while by now well on the road to earthly beatitude, Dante's will cannot yet be capable of grasping it in all its plenitude. The scene of the earthly Paradise is that of the grandiose, inexhaustible symbolism that begins with the encounter with Matelda—*smile* of human happiness—and continues throughout the encounter with Beatrice, the baptism in the Lethe, the vision of the metamorphoses of the Chariot, and the concluding religious-political prophecy. By the time Virgil bids Dante farewell, his magisterial task accomplished, the pilgrim's initiation to the *true Earth* has only just begun.

At least two crucial experiences await Dante before he can claim to have reached the first of the two Ultimate Goals. The first: knowledge of history sub specie *aeternitatis*—a history that man has indeed lived and to some extent also (in Vico's sense) made, yet which is at last contemplated in its providential design, freed from the myriad contingencies that used to becloud our vision of it. This history is indissolubly sacred and profane: here is the great Procession of the first and second Pact, the symbol of the Alliance, which finds its center and its end in the unity of the Chariot of the universal Church—which is itself a Roman Chariot, inseparable from the memory of Rome: "Not only did no chariot so handsome / gladden Rome's Africanus or Augustus / himself" ("Non che Roma di carro così bello / rallegrasse Affricano, o vero Augusto," *Purg.* XXIX, 115–116). And around the chariot is also where the very real battle between Eagle, Fox, and Dragon is being fought: the Eagle that has erred, but that now can and must make amends; the Fox of heresies and schisms, equally damaging to both church and empire; the apocalyptic Dragon, represented by the Giant and the "ungirt . . . whore" ("una puttana sciolta," *Purg.* XXXII, 149), has transformed "the saintly instrument" ("'l dificio santo," *Purg.* XXXII, 142), and now sits on the Chariot, appearing certain of victory. There is no earthly Paradise for he who does not grieve over this human history, who does not strive to understand it from God's perspective and does not fight it in this apocalyptic moment as the prophet has always fought power when it "has gone astray" ("disvia," *Purg.* XVI, 82).

However, this first experience does not suffice for Dante to be allowed into the true Earth. He *witnesses* the revelations of Eden from the banks of the Water that, after splitting itself, goes on ceaselessly to nurture Lethe and Eunoe. Dante admires the scene, every bit as dumbfounded as Virgil, who is following him, although *here, in the earthly Paradise*, he will not be able to teach him anything else (even if Dante, by turning toward the Master, seems to wish he still would, despite the last words Virgil has spoken). Virgil has reached "the place past which [his] powers cannot see" ("dov'io per me più oltre non discerno," *Purg.* XXVII, 129) and eventually disappears without Dante even noticing, almost vanishing into thin air, overcome by the vision before which his *reason* proves utterly powerless. Yet not even Dante, though endowed by now with a will "erect and whole," has perfect discernment of what he is given to see. In order to tread the true Earth and become "pure and prepared to climb unto the stars" ("puro e disposto a salire a le stelle," *Purg.* XXXIII, 145), Dante must accomplish one last act, here in the only place of happiness (*locus felicitatis*) possible on earth: an act, therefore, that must absolutely not assume an exclusively religious, supernatural significance. In order to return to earth and truly teach—not just repeat—what he has seen, he must overcome the hardest challenge: that of confession and repentance. In other words, he must be able to *convert*, in the most *violent* meaning of the word: to wrest himself from his past being, *di-vert* it from what it was and *con-vert* it all toward the full knowledge of that to which it aspires. A sea of tears must wash away his errors, if he truly wishes to *reach into the future* (*infuturarsi*; see *Par.* XVII, 98).

There can be neither mercy nor forgiveness unless "the debt / of penitence that's paid when tears are shed" is discharged ("sanza alcuno scotto / di pentimento che lagrime spanda," *Purg.* XXX, 144–145). That is: achieving knowledge of the great symbols in which the sense of the human experience is articulated constitutes the other side of knowing ourselves, of remembering—at the center of our being-there—the image of the obstinacy with which we refused salvation for the sake of following "counterfeits of goodness" ("imagini di ben seguendo false," *Purg.* XXX, 131). Only when repentance strikes Dante so deeply that he falls, vanquished as if dead, does the figure *who belongs in the earthly Paradise*, Matelda, plunge the initiate into the Lethe, whereupon he will be able to forget his sins and replace the tremendous burden that they exert on his memory with the *anamnesis* of his nature's original goodness. The water of the Lethe is the water of *forgiveness*. Without a journey through confession, repentance, conversion, and forgiveness one cannot become a *citizen* of the earthly Paradise. It is a journey that we do not find described in the *Monarchia*. Might it perhaps be in contradiction with the philosophical teachings that must lead to the beatitude of this earthly life? Indeed, if *beatitude* is our very same goal on earth, one cannot see how else it could be pursued. Can one *rationally* conceive of a perfect government unless all citizens convert from envy and avarice—from the "holy hunger" ("sacra fame," *Purg.* XXII, 40) for the "damned flower" ("maladetto fiore," *Par.* IX, 130)—precisely to that justice of which Aristotle, "the master of the men who know" ("'l maestro di color che sanno," *Inf.* IV, 131), speaks: to act for the good of others, to aim for the common good, instead of wishing for more and disrespecting equality? ("There are many people who can exercise virtue in their own affairs but are unable to do so in their relations with others," *Nic. Eth.* V, 1, 1130a).[8] Neither the best laws nor the most valiant katechontic powers are worth anything if the citizens' ethos is not converted: "The laws exist, but who applies them now? / No one . . ." ("Le leggi son, ma chi pon mano ad esse?," *Purg.* XVI, 97). The reason for this state of affairs lies not merely in the sad condition in which the relations between the two Suns find themselves. Rather, this condition is precisely the most dramatic symptom of a bewilderment of anthropological proportions, of a radical inability to convert and forgive. What city could ever be conceived as long as such impotence persists?

The question is explicit in the *Commedia*, but it would indeed be a poor use of the argument from silence to affirm that it is excluded from the horizon of the *Monarchia*, and that Dante becomes aware of it only later, after the shipwreck of the hopes he had placed on "the noble Henry" ("l'alto Arrigo," *Par.* XVII, 82). Despite the undoubtable tension between these two works, they both elicit the need for a metapolitical consideration of Empire, a consideration called for by the very nature of the latter's architecture and purpose. Perhaps Beatrice does not await Dante at the end of the *Monarchia* because she is already quietly present at the beginning of it. There, she has already received the confession of he who had betrayed her by chasing "things deceptive" ("cose fallaci," *Purg.* XXXI, 55), by following a school that erred both theologically and ethically, and from whose figures Dante has been painfully freeing himself on his journey through *Inferno* and *Purgatorio*. In the *Commedia*, Beatrice is just as much the perfect citizen of the earthly Paradise as Dante's guide in the not-wild flight toward the mystical vision.

Besides, if the political dimension is inscribed in the very order of creation and is not in any way reducible to an architecture of conventional pacts and norms, the forms that a political regime assumes could not be considered extraneous to the *final cause* of the whole creation. That there needs to be political authority (and that this authority, to be fully effective, ought to be embodied in an Augustus) is not a consequence of the *wound* that our nature inflicted on itself, and for which, then, only an intermundane cure could be conceived. To be of effective value, political action—the Aristotelian praxis—will have now to reinsert itself into the Order of creation, broken by sin. This is the supernatural element! To attain earthly happiness through the teaching of philosophy entails a return into that Order that philosophy is in itself incapable of realizing—a return that takes on the existentially very concrete figures of conversion. This can never be underscored enough: Virgil is sent to Dante by grace of the three Ladies. Virgil becomes the guide of someone who has invoked—perhaps only with the voice of anguish—supernatural help, not the coming of the prophet of the *Aeneid*. The very peace of the earthly Paradise is not otherwise achievable, nor visible, because only that Light in heaven harmonizes subject and object, seer and seen. Ultimately, then, there are "two Peaces," as in Augustine, although the earthly one is intended by Dante as utterly opposed to Augustine's philosophy of history; two Peaces interwoven just like the two cities, and similarly forming one dual Being. Even for the greatest emperors, true Peace will be the one attained through that love of God that "suffers violence" ("violenza pate," *Par.* XX, 94), as much for the pagan Trajan as for the Christian Constantine, who also "has learned . . . the evil that derives / from his good act" ("conosce . . . il mal dedutto / dal suo bene operar," *Par.* XX, 58–59).

It therefore seems thoroughly consistent that at the center of supreme ecstasy Dante's mysticism should take on the tone of the harshest invective, that a nostalgia for the Empire should roil the mind and hearts of the blessed, that Rome should continue to be exalted, and never with more verve than in the canto of Justinian. All of this without the *Commedia* ever trying to correct the most overtly scandalous trait of the *Monarchia*: the implication that not only the Roman conquest occurred rightfully (*de iure*), but that the very condemnation of Christ, too, was juridically just, and that the value of his sacrifice is contingent on the right procedure followed in his sentencing (and rightfully also, we might add, was the revenge the "worthy Titus" ("'l buon Tito") took on the "wounds / from which the blood that Judas sold had flowed" ("vendicò le fóra / ond'uscì il sangue per Giuda venduto," *Purg.* XXI, 82–84). Guido Vernani had no difficulty in demonstrating the absolutely heretical nature of those assertions with respect to the whole exegetical and theological Catholic tradition, both Latin and Eastern.[9] Those are theses that Dante asserts with the force of syllogism, and yet that none of the blessed ever contradicts. Like it or not, they too are part and parcel of Dante's mysticism.

In further support of this viewpoint, let us consider the analogy between Dante's religious prophecy—which holds Saint Francis as an example: a prophecy, in other words, wholly founded on the *form of evangelical life* against any fixed rule, any centralist "statist" model—and his notion of Empire. Dante's Empire is *ex nationibus*—constituted by the European nations. The Eagle is one yet comprised of many fires and many eyes. The Empire is called upon to give unitary form to such multiplicity, not to suppress it. Whereas Marsilius of Padua will never see anything but the State, Dante raises the question of the *relation among nations*. And nation means, above all, language. The Dante of the *Monarchia* is the same Dante of the *De vulgari eloquentia*: the man who first acknowledges scientifically the nobility of vernaculars, while at the same time researching the affinities and differences between them—the man who recognizes the multiplicity and becoming of languages to be historically necessary, yet also attempts to establish a relationship between them, to put them in communication with one another—the same man, in other words, who conceives as the purpose of political science and praxis a communion among nations that may be superior to the "selfishness" of each nation.

Dante's Empire is not a form of domination that demands absolute mastery and hegemony over the crowd of nations—that is, in fact, rather what the State form will demand. Dante conceives of the Empire as a guide for the different political "idioms," as the *auctoritas* that makes each of them *illustrious*. The Empire expresses the idea of a common mundane authority that may act as the guardian of national differences and at the same time of their possible harmony. Was the Roman Empire a model for this form, did it bear any similarities to it? In this venue the question appears otiose; this is Dante's Rome, extraordinary precisely in its "untimely timeliness," in its radical opposition, almost *ante litteram*, to any notion of state absolutism, in its steadfast adherence to the notion of an *ontological* bond between the nobility of the vernacular, personal freedom, and the formation of the City. Such was the spirit in which Giuseppe Ungaretti, one of the great poets of the twentieth century, was reading Dante, in the midst of a historic crisis perhaps even more radical than that which the Florentine poet had survived: "In Dante, aggressive man and builder, a human harmony must be imposed on the earth." A notion by no means "plaintive of the past and the future as two lost paradises" must be imposed against the avarice that corrupts Italy and Europe whenever we make an idol of Shakespeare's universal whore. "No, it is not about protecting money, but Europe; we need Love, not money—is what Dante said."[10]

Eight

A Brief Note on the German Reception of Dante

The criticism that, from varied perspectives, has examined the relationship between the world of Germanic medieval literature and Dante has necessarily shunned the issue of the influence that the Italian poet may have exerted on German poetry and philosophy. Wolfram von Eschenbach and Walter von der Vogelweide lived a century before Dante; and while analogies and juxtapositions are certainly possible, they have no bearing on any vital themes in their works. And at any rate, no authentically groundbreaking work on the affinities between those great medieval poets was to appear on the scholarly scene until at least the eighteenth century.

We can safely affirm that the earliest evidence in German culture of a profound interest in Dante is found in the work of Swiss critic and poet Johann Jakob Bodmer, *Treatise on the Wonderful in Poetry* (*Abhandlung von dem Wunderbaren in der Poesie*, 1740, with Johann Jakob Breitinger). Bodmer sees in Dante—whom for this reason he places next to his beloved Milton—not only the "sacred fire," the "mania" of the poetic genius (a position close to that of Giambattista Vico, whom he might have known), but also the *educator*, the purveyor of a political *mission*. Thus, in the German-speaking world, Dante emerges as the paragon of a grandiose *epic*, in opposition to both the Baroque and an Enlightenment perceived as too cold and intellectualistic, devoid of religious strength.

The great season of Dante in Germany is the *Goethe-zeit*, between Romanticism and Idealism, though Goethe himself contributed little to it. It does not seem as though the bust and medal of Dante he owned were indications of his need to measure up to him. The words that Johann Peter Eckermann reports in his conversations show how, for Goethe, Dante remains something obscure, and indeed the German writer always keeps his distance from the theologico-philosophical world of the *Commedia* and the *pathos* therein expressed, just as his *Italian Journey* keeps its distance from the whole great Romanesque-Gothic season, from Cimabue to Arnolfo di Cambio, from Giotto to Francis of Assisi. In *Annalen 1821*, Goethe defines Dante's greatness as "gruesome, often atrocious" (*widerwärtige, oft abscheuliche*), at times even repulsive to his sense of Nature derived from Bruno and Spinoza.[1]

Nor is it all that clear—precisely in light of the abovementioned appraisal—whether the well-known episode narrated in the *Second Roman Visit* should be intended ironically (perhaps not coincidentally, the account is found in the chapter "Some Questions about Nature Which Intrigue and Perplex Me"). An intelligent young Italian man insists that it is impossible for foreigners to fully comprehend a genius like Dante. Goethe cuts him short by declaring himself in complete agreement, as he himself could never understand how one can develop an interest in the *Commedia*. "I thought the Inferno absolutely horrible (*ganz abscheulich*), the Purgatorio ambiguous (*zweideutig*), and the Paradiso a bore (*langweilig*). The young man was delighted, for my words seemed a proof of his assertions."[2]

Yet, in *Poetry and Truth*, Goethe would state that what he appreciates the most about the ancient schools is the overlapping (*in eins zusammenfielen*) of poetry, religion, and philosophy.[3] Indeed, a comparison between Dante and Goethe should take its bearings precisely from the *opposite* meaning they bestow on the *harmonizing* mission that, in both, poetry-*Dichtung* is called upon to represent. Goethe does not dare tackle the nexus of this comparison, as demonstrated also by his short work *Dante* (1826), which he wrote on the occasion of Karl Streckfuss's translation of the *Commedia*—and wherein, however, he evinces a keen understanding of the visual power of Dante's poetry.[4]

We owe the Schlegels, then, the revelation of Dante's crucial importance—not only in the field of arts and literature, and not merely for Germany, but for the entire European civilization. The scholarly work they initiate in the *Athenaeum* years (1798–1800) lays the groundwork for any subsequent research into the universal significance of the Florentine poet's work. The translation attempts and brief comments made by A. W. Schlegel in *Über des Dantes göttliche Komödie* (1796)—a work praised by

Herder—are but the prelude to the sustained, focused, truly epoch-making studies that F. Schlegel would devote to Dante in his *Letter on the Novel* and the *Discourse on Poetry* (*Brief über den Roman, Gespräch über die Poesie*), and in the *Fragments* (only a few of which were to be published in the literary magazine *Athenaeum*, the "organ" of Romanticism).

In those studies, Dante features as the "sacred founder and father of modern poetry," the "seed of the whole modern poetry," and "among all modern poets, the *only encyclopedic image of the epoch*. Dante, not Shakespeare." Dante as *modern*: this is the notion that marks the crucial turn in the appraisal of the Florentine poet! Which means, Dante as *romantic*, in the sense that the term will end up assuming in Schelling, and then in Hegel.[5]

From this perspective, the specific contents of the *Commedia*—that "obscurity" that repulsed Goethe—have no specific value in themselves. What counts is the perfect harmony achieved by its three main dimensions: the narrative, the dramatic, and the anagogical (here we should recall the few passages Johann Georg Hamann, the "Wizard of the North," wrote on Dante). The first should be intended as *mythos*—not *fabula* but *true* story; imagination, the ability to put the *Realissimum* into images. The second is *drama*, a dimension in which events affect not simply individuals but destinies as well.

The third expresses the eschatological dimension that dominates the whole European culture but that has been most powerfully expressed by the great medieval theological syntheses epitomized in Dante. These three dimensions feature in the poem in *absolute* form. Each one is present in its highest, unsurpassable form, and at the same time inseparable from the others. Together, they constitute the *transcendental* of modern poetry. In other words, every poetry of Modernity should be included a priori in the poetry of Dante, which would not only represent the former's chronological origin but also its very principle, the *arche* immanent in its whole development.

Modern poetry is characterized by the intertwining of genres, yet from the privileged perspective of the transformation of epos into novel. The novel is the artistic form of the Romantic, and the *Commedia*—as F. Schlegel peremptorily affirms—"is a novel."[6] It is the life of a person represented in all the problematic complexity of his experience; a character, that is, absolutely concrete in the liveliness of his suffering, empathizing, and questioning, who concentrates in himself and *embodies* every theologico-philosophical content, every allegory or symbol.

However, while in the evolution of the novel form the relation to essence is gradually lost—insofar as essence becomes the goal of an unappeasable nostalgia or need-to-be—the quest in Dante appears to achieve its end: it does not devolve into "adventure," nor is the end presented in the guise (*facies*) of *renunciation*. Precisely for this reason—because of the accord between its beginning and its end, and despite its departure from ancient drama—his work was called *Commedia*. Thus, by virtue of its relation to the world, "traveled" in the totality of its characters, Dante is, indeed, *epos*. Yet, at the same time, because of the centrality of the questioning subject, it is also already a novel—though the affirmation of essence over the multiplicity of mundane contents makes it still consistent with the form of *drama*.

The unrepeatable interweaving of these three dimensions makes Dante the *arche* of poetry in Christian Europe (*Europa oder Christenheit*[7]); in fact, it expresses this Europe's only possible *mythology*. All future poetry will be somehow forced to choose between drama—but only as *Trauerspiel* (mournful drama)—or epos—yet only in terms of an individual's *experience*, a bildungsroman wherein the "formation" is utterly intramundane. The motion that in Dante was directed toward ascending now spreads out over the horizon of historical becoming, in which essence is degraded to estimated value. The *Commedia* "becomes" the comedy of Wilhelm Meister's apprenticeship and journeyman's years (*Lehrerjahre* and *Wanderjahre*)—for the romantics, as is well known, the prototype of the contemporary novel. Although Dante's "transcendental" remains the backdrop upon which all other forms of European poetry must project themselves to reveal their meaning, none of them could represent the same ascending movement again.

Schlegel's interpretation of Dante, as well as the place he assigns to him in the history of European poetry, remain fundamental in German literary culture and aesthetics, at least until the advent of György Lukács's *The Theory of the Novel*. First Schelling, in *Philosophy of Art* and in the seminal "On Dante in Relation to Philosophy ("Über Dante in philosophischer Beziehung"—published in *Kritisches Journal der Philosophie*, which he founded and coedited with Hegel[8])—then Hegel himself, in his lessons on aesthetics, continue to move along the critical path inaugurated in *Aetheneum*. However, though the interpretive categories remain essentially the same, between Schelling and Hegel (and the Hegelian Lukács a century later) their significance changes radically.

For Schelling, Dante's epos creates a *rational myth* that fuses art, religion, and philosophy. Dante's discourse is not conducted through conceptual forms: it is *myth*. In it, philosophy and religion are determined within the concreteness of very real individualities, of figures and events all the more accurately drawn the more they are revelatory of universal destinies and values. In the *Commedia*, philosophy and religion show that they can shape their epoch as effectual historical forces. For Schelling, Dante is not merely a transcendental, unrepeatable as such. He is a true *exemplum* or *paradigm* for a future, really possible alliance between poetry, religion, and philosophy, with the purpose of representing the *myth* of a new Era, free from the abstractions that have hitherto imprisoned the highest forms of expression of human creativity by keeping them segregated from one another.

The dense, moving pages that Hegel devotes to Dante in the *Aesthetics* take up several of these motifs, yet from a somewhat "disenchanting" perspective. The destiny of the European novel does not allow for a return to any authentic epos, not even an epos that might be transfigured into a *myth* capable of shaping a civilization. The novel fulfills itself in the modern *bourgeois* epic; it is essentially *prose*, as the lives it represents are no longer fit for inclusion in the verse, the rhyme, or the grandiose architecture of the *Commedia*. The novel is the account of irreversibly *secularized* individualities, precisely to the extent that they deplore their situation and gain experience of themselves exclusively in their conflict with their world.

The cradle of the novel's world—as the "metaphysics of youth" of Lukács and Benjamin will point out—is the individual in his solitude. Yet Dante is still key to European Romantic poetry because his poetry reflects on itself and could not be otherwise. Both Schlegel and Schelling had already indicated this dimension, which becomes crucial in Hegel's analysis of the overall destiny of contemporary art. The poetry of Romanticism is intellectual in its essence—and it is precisely Dante who reveals its origin. Romantic poetry is not allowed to be naïve. It is poetry that thinks about itself, obliged to justify itself to the other forces—philosophical, religious, or political—of the time.

It is the very question that Dante asks himself from the beginning, and that goes on to reverberate throughout his pilgrimage: Could I really be the one to "gather" in myself all the wealth of my vision? Could my art have such a value? How can poetry "transhumanize" into prophecy (where prophecy means *preaching* to man in his temporal reality)? The creative existence discussed by Benjamin, who draws a parallel between Dante and Baudelaire, expresses itself in this indefatigable questioning: in no other poetry does this questioning feature more forcefully than in the *Commedia*.[9] Nonetheless, for Hegel, Dante's catholic epos cannot announce the coming of any God. Its *absolute* greatness consists in being able to represent "every singularity and particularity" *sub specie aeternitatis*.

It is true that the poem encompasses the "totality of the most objective life," but the figures of its very real world move on "indestructible bases," eternalized in the light of God's judgment.[10] Such a synthesis is either *the impossible* in the Age of the Novel or it is possible only in the forms of irony and nostalgia—a transformation whose "logical" conclusion Lukács describes in *The Theory of the Novel* (published in 1920 but certainly already in progress as early as the last years of the war).

The interventions of Schlegel, Schelling, and Hegel remain an essential contribution to Dante scholarship. The extent of Francesco de Sanctis's indebtedness to them, for example, is well known.[11] Yet their influence on subsequent German thought—if we except Lukács and, as we will see, Walter Benjamin—does not appear altogether remarkable. The "systematic" approach to Dante characteristic of both Romanticism and Hegel, as well as the exceptional role played in this period by the reference to the form of the *Commedia*, might well have prevented the critics of idealism from engaging in any sustained inquiry into the complexity of Dante's work. On the one hand, the *Commedia* is seen as a grandiose relic of a theological past, and on the other, simply as a vigorous testimony of ethical individualism. Perhaps only Marx (who concludes his preface to the first book of the *Capital* with a perfect Dantean hendecasyllable of his own creation!) loves Dante with a love somewhat akin to that of young Schelling.[12] In his introduction to the Italian edition of the *Communist Manifesto*, Engels provides an outline of the Dante reading that Marx intended to give: Dante is the genius that marks the end of the Middle Ages, and the emergence of new social and cultural forces more and more consciously locked in conflict with traditional orders and powers.[13] It is the very condition of exile—of one's foreignness to a present "master"—that produces the great works of literature, the ones that usher in new ages.

Obviously, for Marx, too, as for Hegel, Dante's poetry is altogether unrepeatable, as is the human and intellectual experience conveyed in it. The same goes for Nietzsche, who can indeed deem Leopardi a paradigm for a modern poetry—contemporary "thinking poetry" (*denkende Dichtung*)—but not Dante (though he does mention them together sometimes). This by no means detracts from the *synpatheia* he feels for Dante's work. Even though that kind of poetry could never flourish again—a poetry that "presupposes a significance not only cosmic, but also metaphysical of the objects of art" (*Human, All Too Human*, 220)—the "predilection for things problematic and strong" that characterizes *decisive* characters, which certainly Nietzsche would wish to represent, reaches its *ne plus ultra* precisely in the *Commedia* (*Posthumous Fragments*, Fall 1887).[14]

Dante is irremediably distant, but this distance is at the same time extreme nearness (something Benjamin also notices, apropos the relation between Dante and Beatrice, in a fragment from 1928–1929),[15] especially in an aspect that involves Nietzsche in every fiber of his being—Nietzsche the "experimenter," the "prophet" of Zarathustra, forced to live in this as yet *unaccomplished* epoch. In this respect, Dante is for Nietzsche a sort of "it must be" [*dover-essere*]: he teaches that, even when limits appear insuperable, even under the harshest constrictions or in times of deepest misery, one must find the strength to discover *immense spaces*. Within the most inexorable confines, one must learn to move as Bach did in the form of counterpoint, most freely [*liberissimamente*], and as Dante did in the enchainment of his tercets, in the formidable, hierarchic architecture of his *Commedia*.

It is, in sum, the strong taste of this "freedom under the law" that Nietzsche learns from Dante (*Posthumous Fragments*, April–June 1885;[16] Stefan George will approach Dante from an analogous perspective). He would find this taste again in Richard Wagner—as we read in a page of moving intensity that Nietzsche dedicates to his youthful (and never really waned) passion. After hearing for the first time in Monte Carlo the prelude of *Parsifal*, he writes to Peter Gast: "Has Wagner ever done anything better?" Every nuance of feeling (*nuance des Gefuhls*) is here conveyed in the most direct, succinct, epigrammatical form. A synthesis of emotions that many would deem irreconcilable are here perfectly accomplished: "It contains a synthesis of states which to many men, even 'higher men,' it would seem impossible to unite, and is of a commanding severity, of a 'loftiness' (*Höhe*) in the most terrifying sense of the word, and of an omniscience and penetration (*Mitwissen und Durchschauen*) that seem to transpierce one's soul with knives—and withal it is full of pity (*Mitleiden*) for that which it sees and orders there." Wagner pulled it off and—"This sort of thing is to be found in Dante, but nowhere else."[17] No equivalent can be found, though, either in subsequent German thought or poetry, for Nietzsche's "grasp" on the living body of Dante's art. Georg Simmel's long essay *Dantes Psychologie*—roughly contemporary with Wilhelm Dilthey's *Introduction to the Human Sciences* (*Einleitung in die Geisteswissenschfaten*, 1883, wherein Dante is discussed only for his theologico-political ideas)—is certainly not on a par with his other studies on Rembrandt and Goethe. In its essence, it is an attentive analysis of the fundamental tropes or terms in Dante's thought, yet one severely vitiated by misleading assumptions about the dualisms or pessimisms that would supposedly characterize it.[18]

Conrad Ferdinand Meyer, whose relationship with the classics is decidedly intense, wrote a fine novel, *The Monk's Wedding* (*Die Hochzeit des Mönchs*, 1884) set at the court of Cangrande della Scala with Dante as protagonist: a Dante who, at least in some respects, transcends the cliché of the strict judge, of the incorruptible scourge of human vices, inflexibly faithful to his ideal. Gerhardt Hauptmann, Thomas Mann's democratic "Father Hauptmann," would attempt his own failed *Commedia* in perfect tercets *The Great Dream* (*Der große Traum*, written in 1914 but published only in fragments in 1942), a mythological, esoteric, religious mishmash strongly influenced by fashionable fin de siècle speculations around Christ and Dionysus.

Only Stefan George can hold a candle to Nietzsche's notion of Dante as paradigm for a kind of "freedom under the law," but I consider George an extraordinary "case" in twentieth-century Germany. It may appear odd that even in authors who show knowledge and appreciation for Italian literature, like Hofmannsthal, the references to Dante are scarce and not very significant, if not totally missing, as in the case of Rilke, who speaks of Dante only to underscore the latter's great influence on the work of beloved sculptor Auguste Rodin. How can it be that some of the greatest representatives of early twentieth-century German literature, even those who were profoundly influenced by the great romantic-idealist *Kultur*, do not feel the strong bond with Dante that had otherwise "formed" their masters? It is indeed odd that within such a vast critical output as that of Thomas Mann, for instance—attested by the famous essay collection *Nobility of Spirit*—there should not be a place for Dante except for a short, insignificant passage written in 1921 for the six hundredth anniversary of the Florentine's death. What some scholar indicates as possible Dante "memories" in Mann's major novels are in fact little more than *topoi* of European literature. The same can be said about Herman Hesse, who ignores Dante altogether in his *Bibliothek der Weltliteratur*.

I think the reason should be chalked up to a precise distinction that runs through European cultural history, starting from the *Goethe-zeit*, which is also a *Kant-zeit*. On the one hand, those who see in Goethe the insuperable prototype for bourgeois *Kultur*, the representative who most profoundly and dramatically presages the tragic dangers run by a Europe bent on dissolving its values, cannot fail to perceive Dante's greatness; on the other hand, they cannot truly understand him, forced as they are to keep him at a cautious distance. To be Goethians in this sense—in the sense of measure and restraint—cannot be reconciled with the "transhumanizing" audacity of Dante's genius, with the authentically revolutionary thrust that animates his entire thought. The interpretation of Goethe, then, ends up deciding also on the position one assumes vis-à-vis the Florentine poet. Nietzsche loves Dante precisely insofar as his opinion of Goethe is the opposite of that of Thomas Mann.

Things are different for those authors who mercilessly and tragically reflect the end of the universal meaning—not only literary, but also ethical and political—of what Romanticism itself defined as the "great canon," the axis of Dante-Shakespeare-Goethe. They understand that an irreversible crisis has overwhelmed it, regardless of how one might have interpreted it. The leaderless journeys, the aimless pilgrimages have begun. Even the strictest judges, such as Karl Kraus, are doomed to get lost or go astray. No matter how one looks upon those "fathers," they represent "the way it was," a way that we might be able to save only through our adventurous self-experiments, by living through this crisis without consolation or illusion.

As Simmel observed about Dante: in modernity, keeping together—and at maximum tension—great form, a systematic will, and powerful psychological impulses (*logos* and *pathos*, we might say) becomes the very definition of *the impossible*. In Benjamin, Dante is well represented—thanks also to the influence of Eric Auerbach's early important works on the poet's realism[19] (we are not discussing here, of course, the German Dante scholars, critics, and historians of the Italian literature)—yet he is mostly present as a foil for the interpretation of Baudelaire. (I do not believe we should stress too much the "suspended" quotation in the French version of the *Theses on the Philosophy of History*.[20]) To my mind, Dante's lines as Benjamin transcribes or rewrites them cannot but refer to that relation of distance-nearness that infuses the pilgrim's vision of Beatrice before she entrusts the pilgrim (*homo viator*) to Saint Bernard.[21] In Musil and Kafka, Dante speaks merely by his absence. A poetry emerges around this time, but only with the aim of shattering that Romantic "canon" from within itself and exploding its contradictions: it is the poetry of Hölderlin, the exile *par excellence*, the stranger soul on earth.

As I mentioned earlier, Stefan George represents an extraordinary "case." His translation of several key passages of the *Commedia* (which came out in the second edition in 1921) no doubt constitutes an apex in contemporary German poetry. In a brief article published in *Die literarische Rundschau* on the occasion of the poet's sixtieth birthday, Benjamin recalls the great emotional impact that hearing George's translation of *Inferno* V had on him: "The voice that read it to me one morning in an atelier in Munich has continued to reverberate in me for many years."[22]

It is a translation that miraculously manages to preserve the rhythm and the musicality of Dante's tercets, letting them flow effortlessly from one another, with a language whose aulic tone does not detract from its force or clarity of communication. A true, great *laudatio* of the ancient Master, he who "for every coming people (therefore for us, too)" will signify the beginning of every New Poetry (*Neue Dichtung*—as George capitalizes it in the preface—*Vorrede*—to the first edition of his Dante translations).[23] In George's rendition, the "floral style" in which, for Benjamin, "the old bourgeoisie disguises the premonition of its own impotence"[24]—a style overwhelmingly present in *Das buch der hängenden gärten* and *Das jahr der seele* ("Come to the park they say is dead and you / Will see the glint of smiling shores beyond"),[25] gives way to an ascetic tension for the completeness—for the perfection—of the language.

Poiesis, the art of the "best craftsmen" (*miglior fabbri*) must be shown without ornament, in its naked tectonic power. While George's Dante is indeed—according to tradition—the leader of all solitary spirits fighting against their times, he is above all the unsurpassable master of what we might call, in Weber's parlance, the notion of *Dichtung als Beruf*, poetry as profession-vocation—perhaps the most indelible mark George has left on contemporary poetry. As his disciple Ludwig Klages states (in *Stefan George*, 1902), it is the "transparency as hard as crystal" of Dante's poetry that George wishes to infuse into the German one; this is the need, the determination that guides his soul.[26]

Ernst Robert Curtius, the great historian and philologist, and an admirer of George, helps us (in *Stefan George in Conversation*) to understand the motivation behind his "revelation" of Dante in a world that had in many ways forgotten both.²⁷ George was born in a family that over the course of two generations had assimilated to the French culture. In *The Seventh Ring* he elects Lotharingia, the kingdom of Middle France, as his true homeland. His German being will always look to France—and through France to the whole Romance-speaking Europe (*Romània*). A similar movement is also found in Hofmannsthal—although Romània to him is ultimately the spirit of his *Austrian* homeland. In any case, George's and Hofmannstahl's Mitteleuropa would be inconceivable without the Franco-Mediterranean world. In George's Rhine "shall run my fiery blood, my Roman breath."²⁸ And quintessentially Roman is the political meaning of Dante's Empire, as is the *earthly* Paradise itself for which he longs. In fact, Dante calls Romans the very denizens (*cives*) of Paradise! In this aspect, George's notion of Dante breaks sharply with the Romantic one, from a perspective that might evince some correspondence with Oswald Spengler. (Indeed, Romanticism has no place in the "synchronic" *Tables Illustrating the Comparative Morphology of History*—the summary of the *Decline of the West*.²⁹)

George's Dante starkly opposed the formidable prejudice against *latinitas* (and in favor of the Hellenic myth) that was a crucial component of contemporary German *Kultur* (and philosophy: it still features prominently in Heidegger). It was this very "Romanness"—the rigor and meter that it taught him—that made it impossible for George's *daimon* to ever become mired either in extreme reactionary stances or in the confused jumble of "conservative revolutions." True, his is a notion essentially on the wane, by now incapable of holding together "an order that was collapsing on all fronts" (Benjamin).³⁰ We would be hard-pressed, indeed, to find it in Musil or Kafka. It is a notion most pure in its solitude: yet one whose indelible memory is forever preserved in George's translations of Dante's *Commedia*.

Nine

Schelling's Dante

The importance of Dante's *opus* in Schelling's philosophy, at least between the *Oldest Systematic Program of German Idealism* (*Erstes Systemprogramm des deutschen Idealismus*, ca. 1795) and *Ages of the World* (*Weltalter*, 1811–1815), has been brilliantly argued long ago by Wolfram Hogrebe, and it is not my task here to repeat his observations.[1] I do believe that the relationship that binds Schelling to Dante can also stretch beyond those boundaries and constitute a privileged avenue for our understanding of crucial stages in the development of his philosophical system, as compared to that of Fichte or Hegel. In this venue, I will limit myself to pointing out how an investigation along this avenue might unfold.

I think it is impossible to find a preceding discussion on Dante that measures up to "On Dante in Relation to Philosophy" (1803), the essay Schelling published in the last number of *Kritisches Journal der Philosophie*. In many respects, Dante's greatness, his universal significance—beyond abstract categorizations, be they philosophical, theological, or aesthetical-artistic—for the whole European civilization, is a "discovery" of classical, and at least in part Romantic (think of Friedrich Schlegel), idealism. How important is the contribution of Vico's *New Science*? From a strictly historical-philological perspective, I cannot say. Certainly, neither Schelling nor Hegel would ever have subscribed to the notion of a "Tuscan Homer" who "sang only of histories"[2]—a notion, however, that Vico himself later revises: if Dante, "for lack of reflection . . . does not know how to feign," he is nonetheless "learned in the loftiest esoteric knowledge."[3]

Yet the centrality of the theme of *figure*, of Dante's *symbolic realism*, on which the interpretation of both German philosophers is predicated, may well have been inspired by Vico. In fact, the key notion of Schelling's 1803 essay appears fundamentally Vichian: the big events in European literature must not be read as fairytales; they are not important as works of fiction, but as *myths*, in the most primordial sense of the word, that is, as *facts*; they are narrations, true, but of facts that are *real*, and whose reality is more effectual than any mere contingent occurrence. Their quality resides not in the force of *invention* but, on the contrary, in their ability to *see and narrate* something that is *absolutely real*—real insofar as it proves *critical* in the life of a people, of a culture. Dante's *prophecy*, the prophetic language of his poetry, belongs precisely to this order of reality.

The principles already expressed in *Systemprogramm* return in Schelling's essay on Dante, wherein he wishes for a poetry-teacher of humanity whose mission is to create a new *mythology*. Schelling finds this grandiose mission concretely outlined in Dante's *Commedia*, where an epoch is represented in all its complex totality and communicates its values universally, that is, in a form that is understandable by anyone, so that an entire people can orient its life according to them. Is a future Dante possible? No, Hegel will later argue in the *Aesthetics*: because in the Romantic age—the age of disenchantment—every exposition of a myth becomes immediately an *interrogation* of its meaning, thereby turning into myth*ology*. Schelling's position on this point, however, is profoundly different, and not merely in the Jena years.

Both in the *Lessons on the Philosophy of Art* and in the above-mentioned essay, Dante appears as "the most universal representative of modern poesy,"[4] because in his "divine poem,"[5] through the representation of figures that assume universal value *by virtue of their very singularity*, he gives shape to his epoch. He creates a great myth, a myth that not only speaks to its age but consciously in-forms it with itself. We speak here not of classical myth, of course, but of a *rational myth* that weaves together art and religion and fuses them into such a perfect unity as to require a specific theory, a philosophy or aesthetics of its own.[6] The emphasis with which Schelling exalts his discovery of Dante ("the poem of all poems, the poesy of modern poesy itself"[7]) is all the more remarkable when we compare it to Hegel's sober considerations in *Aesthetics*—a radical *reassessment* of that notion of art derived precisely from the *Systemprogramm*. Already in Hegel's *Phenomenology of Spirit*, the growing tendency to a fusion of art, religion, and philosophy, which Schelling hailed as the destiny of the "new Age," will be indicated as the underlying reason for "the death of art."[8]

The way in which Schelling grasps the essential character of Dante's poetry will continue to bear upon the later development of his thought. The *necessity* of the artistic form, as it shows itself in the *Commedia*, lies in its giving birth to *universal individualities*. Concept and figure are not juxtaposed to find an agreement or "compromise" between them. The figure in its singularity is *extra-ordinary*, to the point of becoming universal and necessary, that is, *eternal*. All the figures in the *Commedia* are eternal, insofar as they are free from contingency and accidentality. Hegel will read Dante in an essentially allegorical-metaphorical sense. For Schelling, on the contrary, Dante expresses *symbols*. Not figures, that is, which point beyond themselves to universal meanings, relinquishing their individuality to give rise to the eternal; but rather, a universal-eternal that is *incarnate*, inseparable from this *being-there*, from its face and presence. In this sense, myth is the same as symbol. Symbol is precisely the *event* in which the energy of the presence that irrupts and strikes does not change, does not become, does not cease, but remains before us as the *indestructible*. And such is also the force of myth.

We still encounter the same tones in works from decades later. In Schelling's *Historical-Critical Introduction to the Philosophy of Mythology* (1842), we read that "philosophy still has to show the possibility of what from the standpoint of art has always been perceived as necessity," namely the possibility that "actual beings" may signify in themselves eternal and universal principles. "Every work of art stands all the higher the more it at the same time awakens the impression of a certain necessity of its existence, but only the eternal and necessary content overcomes, as it were, the contingency of the work of art."[9] Those *actual beings* are myths, that is, the gods of myth, the scope and character of their actions. Is it not, then, precisely the knowledge of mythology that prepares art's turn to a more substantial terrain? Is it not mythology that frees art from contingency, from indulging now in subjective feeling, now in a skeptical disenchantment (which nowadays rather seems to define it)? Does not this "wretched time, which laid waste to [the poet's] heart also, [and] does not allow him any faith in its forms and figures"[10] allow him to conceive and see those forms as *eternal figures*?

Those are roughly the same words that Schelling uses to illustrate the *epoch-making* character of Dante's poetry. It seems obvious that, even at the end of his quest, and differently from Hegel, Schelling does not consider that poetry just as an extraordinary "report" but rather as living example of an art capable of rising above any "fashion" and therefore capable of *mythopoetic imagination*.

It is possible to follow the presence of Dante and of this notion in all of Schelling's *oeuvre*, starting from the writings that mark his break with Fichte. Not that Fichte really suffered from the "unaesthetic" character that Schiller ascribed to him; quite the contrary. Luigi Pareyson has illustrated the importance for the philosophy of art (not just Romantic art) of the Fichtean idea of *productive imagination*.[11] This idea stands at the center of Fichte's works contemporaneous with Schelling's early production, such as On Spirit and Letter in Philosophy. Nonetheless, much as Fichte might wish for an alliance of art and philosophy against the men of letters, he will always consider a work of artistic genius to be, if not subordinated to the moral imperative, certainly charged with the *duty* of promoting it. For Fichte, Dante is an example of precisely this *Duty*; his studies on the poet, his translations of the *Purgatorio*, indicate that the essential content of the *Commedia* is to be found in the expression of Duty, or in the spirit's longing to eternalize itself through the eternal pursuit of Duty. Such a reading is, in some respects, opposite to Schelling's, for whom the symbol of myth does not allude or refer to something beyond itself, does not find its meaning beyond the actuality of its presence; on the contrary, it expresses that meaning immediately in the singularity of its own figure or *Gestalt*. The profound congeniality that ties Schelling and Goethe in the Jena years is predicated precisely on this notion of symbol: for Goethe, "True symbolism is . . . the living, momentary revelation of the unfathomable,"[12] and thus inimical, on this principle, to any allegorism.

Even the philosophy of nature, which would appear to develop in a sphere extraneous to Schelling's immense interest in Dante, continues to show the latter's inescapable influence. For example, the central idea of Schelling's *Statement* (*Darlegung*, 1806) on the relationship between nature and Fichte's *Doctrine of Science*, is that an intellect "abandoned" by reason is only capable only of reaching the *negative*, that is, of positing its opposite as absolutely other from itself. In the *Doctrine of Science*, opposition is not deemed to be *the very same movement of unity*, Life "that in itself moves, originates, and creates."[13] For Fichte (according to Schelling), "a knowledge of the in-itself or the absolute will always be impossible for human beings; we can only know our own knowledge, only depend upon it as ours, and remain in it."[14] Nature would then consist in nothing but affections of the I, that is, it could be considered only as something essentially profane, *not divine*, something perfectly dead in itself. Fichte's gaze—Schelling insists—is *mortifying* to nature; it is the gaze that asserts, "All that surrounds me are mere appearances, which are present for me only insofar as I wish them to be. They are nothing to me except what I make of them myself,"[15] and in this finds its highest Joy, that is, in the eternity of the I *as against* the nothing in itself of nature. But how—Schelling protests—can this be Joy? How can Fichte's *Way Towards the Blessed Life* be *Paradiso*?

Precisely in his 1806 work *The Way Towards the Blessed Life*, Fichte sets out to represent this Joy. Yet, according to Schelling, Fichte merely stops at the abstract exaltation of the I that does not live from and in the life of the All, and thus can see nothing beyond itself but *natura naturata, res extensa*. Indeed, one hears powerful echoes of Giordano Bruno (rather than Spinoza, as we will see) in these "attacks" on Fichte. One hears also, once more, an overt allusion to Dante: the only true Joy is the one expressed in the *Paradiso*, because therein, the entire creation is viewed *sub species aeternitatis*, every single figure is "judged" from this perspective, represented as the word of the all-vivifying Logos, redeemer of the whole nature. The *Paradiso* is not the Joy of the I, which would be the end of its itinerary, but rather the Joy of the individual figure that reconciles itself with the All and is expressed by the All in itself. This Dante accompanies Schelling every step of the way in his critique of Fichte's philosophy, and especially in his most hidden mystical accents.

For Schelling, Fichte's thought is characterized by a perfect idealistic dualism, just as Descartes's thought is characterized by a "real opposition" (*reellen Entgegensetzung*[16]) of matter and soul. It is a dualism that results in a sort of *gnosis*, whereby the I-Demiurge, free in itself—in the essence of its own spirit—from any external conditioning, reduces nature to the *object* (*ob-iectum*) of its will and re-creates it as no other than the I's own product. On the contrary, according to Schelling, the philosophy of nature must have value as a reconciliation of the subject with the *reality* of the natural cosmos in its own movement, in the forms proper to its production—starting with the *will to life* that is everywhere apparent, with its essential *effort* (*conatus*) not to yield to *time* (*chronos*), to resist the "law" of decay that rules its figures or creations.[17]

What is the human brain if not the highest of such creations, that is, the creation that more than any other is able to discover stronger and stronger levels of organization, more and more capable of *persisting in being*? Nature is not spirit in its being-other (and here the break with Fichte foreshadows all the issues that will also occasion the break with Hegel) but is *spirit in itself*, starting with what appears to us as nature's most simply material aspects, which we call "inanimate." Being does not equal being-thought. Life in every one of its fibers is an instance of *self-transcending* (understandable only spiritually), and not the *phenomenon* of the I, or the not-divine opposed to the freedom of the I. Every element of nature is *symbol* of material and spiritual. Does it express itself this way in myth? Does myth speak of *natura naturans*? Would *mythein*, then, be the speaking of the thing, the thing's very speech? And would then poetry represent the *ars* able to listen to *how the thing speaks itself*, and in some way to "imitate" it? Is this what the ultimate, unfathomable essence of the notion of *mimesis* consists of? These are the queries that, in Schelling, tie together—or might perhaps tie together—the philosophy of nature, the philosophy of mythology, and the philosophy of art.

If we read it from this perspective, the philosophy of identity in the *System of Transcendental Idealism* (1800) already exhibits certain crucial traits of Schelling's ensuing "philosophical empiricism." But this development is made possible by the formidable presence of Spinoza in the early Schelling (a presence that Fichte, in his polemical writings, already notes). God is *natura naturans* also in Spinoza, and therefore it can be said to be both Thought and Extension (or else there could only be *natura naturata*, which is *not* God). We cannot know how far its power reaches, or of what creations it is capable. We do know, however, that the two Attributes, Thought and Extension, are both infinite and inseparable, even though they proceed distinctly. Because each is infinite, they cannot limit each other. Because they are both *agents*, they cannot *suffer* each other's action. But only together do they constitute Substance, God, or Nature. The *res particulares*, the different ways in which Substance unfolds, represent, to different degrees, the Substance's *perfection*. And perfection and existence coincide. Every existing thing is perfect according to its own particular mode of existence, that is to say, according to the *energy* with which it realizes its *effort* to persist in being. Fichte affirms that every being offers itself only in relation to a knowledge, that we can say nothing about a being unless by predicating-knowing it. This is true; however, what he fails to understand—which constitutes the

Spinozian foundation of the philosophy of nature—is that knowledge itself is *a mode of being*.

The organ of knowledge is a being among beings, and precisely that organ whereby the spiritual essence of nature shows itself *empirically*. Thought must begin from this unity, which a philosophical system is called upon to *demonstrate*. A "reconciliation" between I and Nature will never be attainable as long as our starting point is to postulate their primordial opposition. The fundamental error is to start with the I alone: "Everything is only God's or the All's," aphorism 44 recites.[18] Schelling's aphorisms of 1805 are "enthusiastic" texts that display in every line the Spinozian foundation of Schelling's critique of any system that arises from abstraction and does not present itself as the expression of a synthesis of knowing and Being, of finite and infinite. In the abstracting intellect the thing appears separate from its essence, and thus accidental, not necessary; it is reason—for Spinoza, the ultimate degree of knowledge—that conceives it as eternal in act (*actu*), because it is inseparable from the All: "To present with the seriousness of science those laws in which, as an ancient put it, the immortal God lives, yet to grasp with the same love the particular, even the most singular, and thus to identify in a nonfinite way the universal and the particular is the spirit of true philosophy."[19]

In the *Munich Lectures on the History of Modern Philosophy*, thirty years after the works we have hitherto discussed, it is clear in what direction Schelling meant to develop his philosophy of identity, which is actually an original re-visitation of Spinozism in a somewhat Goethian light. That idea of Nature eternally springing and eternally creating, synthesis of finite and infinite, constitutes the point from which all ensuing systems have departed—without being able, however, to free themselves from it. In what sense should such emancipation have occurred, and still occur? In the sense of conceiving the *freedom* of that Substance. The Spinozian Substance does not include in itself the idea of freedom; in fact, it has by no means the power to be different from what it is. Its power, as it were, exists *without possibility*. But if Substance is Thought, and if Extension itself is *not* inert matter (*hyle*)—because the fact *that it thinks* is a fact of experience[20]—how can we conceive it in that *profound quiet* in which Spinoza conceives it? From Spinozism, and beyond its "grandiose features," we must arrive at a *system of freedom*.[21] This alone will be the *supreme system*: to think Substance itself as Freedom, "freeing" Spinoza, the great Accursed, from the deterministic-mechanistic chains of his view of the physical world, which betrayed, all in all, his very intuition of nature as *divine, eternal creation*.

The "supreme system" is called upon to found that passage from Spinoza's *Ethics* that has always felt to many critics as if Spinoza were pulling himself up by his own bootstraps: What necessity subsists in the transition from "De servitude humana" to "De libertate"? How can the *imbecility* of that subject—described in parts 3 and 4 as a slave to affects and passions—not only grasp intellectual love but also recognize it as its goal, and rejoice in it? If the subject is endowed with the *energy* of such a reason, then its nature must necessarily be free in itself, and it is merely a matter of educating it to the *anamnesis* of such primordial being-free. But that also entails that the nature of Substance itself must be free, not just in the sense of the absolute "unconditionedness" of the *Causa sui*. The freedom of reason, which belongs to our *nature*, and thus to Nature, does not exist *blindly*. It follows that even the *Causa sui* cannot be conceived as blind, because reason is no other than one of its modes, the unfolding of one of its Attributes. Schelling's philosophy of Revelation develops on the basis of these premises, and of this implicit-explicit confrontation with Spinoza. "Entweder Spinozismus, oder keine Philosophie" ("You are either a Spinozist or not a philosopher at all"[22]) is a motto that fits Schelling just as well as Hegel.

How can we fail to hear, once more, Dante's tones—"the signs of the old flame" ("conosco i segni de l'antica fiamma," *Purg.* XXX, 48)—in this development of Spinozism from "De servitude" to "De libertate"? Schelling criticizes in Fichte a gnostic idea of Knowledge and Science that absorbs into itself the *love for* Being's universal *animation*—that orderly restlessness that shows *in every thing*, to different degrees, both its provenance from the eternal Substance and its re-turn or re-conversion to it. And the *Commedia* is the great *myth*, consistent with the spirit of its age, capable of expressing such notions universally. Schelling criticizes in Spinoza the possibility of understanding the freedom of reason by segregating it from the nature of Substance. But the dynamics of human nature that explains the possibility of achieving *intellectual love* cannot but dwell also within Substance itself, or else we risk reducing it to an accidental contingency, or a spectral possibility.

And again, he must have thought of Dante: of the God of Love, of the God who *suffers* the force of Love. Then, the transcendence of our being-there to the Divine, the ek-static *nature* of our being-there (Dante's *transhumanizing*), ceases to appear to us as a mere exception, ceases to eschew any *rational systematization*, because the freedom that shines through in this *power* of ours has its eternal root in the Freedom of the Cause itself. What else could Dante's *rational myth* possibly be about, if not the expression of that *real* possibility (which philosophy is called upon to *found* discursively, but which by itself could never communicate to everyone)? Meaning, the *power* inherent in the finiteness of our being to "surmount" those virtues or abilities that belong to the things considered merely by their empirical connection and temporal duration, in order to express their participation in the All and conceive its very own individuality *sub specie aeternitatis*.

The individual, the *figure*, and its very *becoming*, do not annul themselves in the Goal, but rather realize themselves by "touching" it—they are *in act*. What annuls itself is the abstract egoity, what falls away is the abstract separateness between finite and infinite. Nothing, properly, annuls itself, except the imagination, or confused thought, that conceives the *res singularis* as separate from the eternal Substance, as a contingency oscillating between being and the potential to be. This is how Fichte conceives it, insofar as he assigns authentic substantiality only to the I. And in the end, this is how Spinoza, too, conceives it, because in the necessity and eternity of the *Causa sui* he cannot find any of the traits of the reason-love, which nonetheless should express one of its modes. But not Dante, not the *exemplum* that he represented, and that continues to bear on Schelling's thought: the myth, expressed within the terms and limits of the Christian West, of the nonaccidentality of the finite, of the eternity of the *individual* figure. The first push for a *system of freedom* has part of its roots in the *Commedia*.

Such filiation become even more manifest if one considers certain peculiar traits of the philosophy of nature, as it is forcefully expounded, for instance, in the abovementioned *Aphorisms*. Think of the relation between *light and gravity* as an essential element of *Natura naturans*. The universe is their copula. Each force is relative only to the Relation that unites them. Neither light nor gravity constitutes a finite domain. Their relation reigns everywhere, and yet the nature of light and gravity is perfectly determinable. Light and gravity are immaterial energy, but every being concretely and intimately participates in it. In fact, the life of every being is the direct expression of it. The universe in each of its parts is the *explication* of the immaterial relation between light and gravity, of the conflict (*polemos*) whereby light tends to "rise" above the force of gravity, to "emancipate" itself from it, as gravity, in turn, tends to reassert its control over light. For Schelling, the problem of discerning the *law* capable of explaining such conflict, the harmony-conflict between the two great Powers, is inherent in every philosophy of nature.

How not to hear, in the very urgency in which it is expressed, the memory of Dante's symbolism? Does it not also consist precisely in the unfathomability of the principle whereby our being-there, while it cannot *overcome* the spirit of gravity absolutely, is nonetheless capable of *light*, that is, capable of harmonizing the *spirit* of gravity with the *spirit* of light? Dante's poetry, in this perspective, could become the model for a *rational myth* not only in terms of the relation between art, religion, and philosophy but also in terms of the relation between the latter three and the science of nature itself. It is also indisputable, however, that Schelling understands, and exalts, the "scientist" Goethe from this same perspective: the separation between philosophical and scientific considerations of nature is a mere intellectual abstraction. The more science frees itself from its deterministic paradigms, the more it is, so to speak, "physics writ large," the more its principles become philosophical, the more—*iuxta propria principia*—overcomes the opposition of thought and being, of matter and spirit, of finite and infinite. Indeed, every science ought to be free to develop according to its own methods and to analyze different dimensions of being. However, the more it *is* science, the more it will be *con*-science; that is, the more it will have knowledge of existing only insofar as it exists *in relation* to the others, and within the relation of each one to the All.

But if science and philosophy proceed from the idea of the unity of Substance to the point of positing in it the finite appearance of a being—thus demonstrating that Substance *is*, that it is a *concrete totality*, then poetry—Dante teaches—sees the infinite in the finite and resolves the infinite in figure. The road is the same, traveled from opposite ends that are also necessarily conjoined. Science, philosophy, and art are all *Queens*—as they are called in Dante's *Convivio*, insofar as they are all "studious" and images of the universal *Poiesis*, of Nature qua Acting, creating eternally at the beginning. *Poiesis* means science, philosophy, and art, very concrete forms of *making* that see, represent, know *Natura naturans* insofar as they are "born together" [*con-nate*] and *con-crescent* with it (*gignosko*, "to know," and *gignomai*, "to come into being," share the same root). It is in their action—which the higher it is, the more it detaches itself from suffering, without however ever being able to eliminate it—that nature and spirit meet. But there is nothing consoling about this encounter, and nothing could be farther from domestic bliss.

There is *conflict* (*agon*) between mind and body, just as between gravity and light. In every being, creation and action have a restless heart. And yet only this is *real*: the energy, which is manifested in every being, which only occurs in a being, even as it always transcends this being. As Goethe puts it in *One and All*: "And with effect to make creation new, / Its weaponized rigour soon enough undo, / Action eternal, vivid, rose" ("Wirkt ewiges, lebendiges Tun").[23] The name of reality is Action. Only *das Wirkliche* is real. No knowledge has a monopoly on it. Science, philosophy, and art *make, create*. To separate them—or to absorb them into an undifferentiated One—is to fail to understand *Reality*. For Schelling, only a system capable of expressing their common principle (*arche*) together with the laws of their Relation is worthy of being called *supreme*. Only the greatest minds can lead us down this path—a path whose oblivion would spell the end of philosophy—and among the fixed stars, Dante's journey, his experience (*Erfahrung*) will continue to endure through the twists and turns of Schelling's philosophical quest.

Notes

Notes to the Introduction

1. As a matter of fact, St. Bernard did nothing but raise an everyday experience to its mystical level and, conversely, bring back a symbol to its material origin. It is well known that breast milk squeezed into the eyes can cure bacterial conjunctivitis in infants.

2. Richard Dawkins, *The God Delusion* (London: Bantam Press, 2006), 77–79.

3. All quotes from the *Divina Commedia* throughout the volume are from Dante Alighieri, *The Divine Comedy: Inferno; Purgatorio; Paradiso*, trans. Allen Mandelbaum (New York: Everyman's Library, 1995).

4. On Cacciari's political philosophy, see Massimo Cacciari, *The Unpolitical: On the Radical Critique of Political Reason*, ed. and with intro. Alessandro Carrera, trans. Massimo Verdicchio (New York: Fordham University Press, 2009); Massimo Cacciari, *Europe and Empire: On the Political Forms of Globalization*, ed. and with intro. Alessandro Carrera, trans. Massimo Verdicchio (New York: Fordham University Press), 2016; and Alessandro Carrera, "The Transcendental Limits of Politics: On Massimo Cacciari's Political Philosophy," in *Contemporary Italian Political Philosophy*, ed. Antonio Calcagno (Albany, NY: SUNY Press, 2015), 119–138.

5. This reading was possibly influenced by Edith Wharton's admiration for Francesca and her rejection of Beatrice as an embodiment of repressed Victorian femininity (which Beatrice isn't). See Kathleen Verduin, "Edith Wharton, Adultery, and the Reception of Francesca Da Rimini," *Dante Studies* 122 (2004): 195–236.

6. For an engaging discussion on the challenges of teaching Dante today, see the essays collected under "Forum: Dante and Pedagogy," coordinated by Kristina Olson, *Dante Studies* 137 (2019): 124–209.

7. See also the chapter on Francis' *hilaritas* in Massimo Cacciari, *Dell'inizio*, rev. ed. (1990; repr., Milan: Adelphi, 2011), 660–674.

8. Man is abandoned and, we might say, overcome, but this is precisely what Nietzsche did not understand about Christian "nihilism," namely, that it does not necessarily entail hatred and annihilation.

9. On the one hand, this is Francis' superego, expressed in his injunction to enjoy poverty. Insofar as the Kingdom is already yours, you *must* be happy in your poverty, it is your *duty*. On the other hand, the Kingdom is still *in time*, on its way to ending time, and therefore still a work in progress. However, as I already pointed out, to apply modern psychology to the Middle Ages is indeed a daunting task.

10. See Giorgio Agamben, *The Highest Poverty: Monastic Rules and Form-of-Life*, trans. Adam Kotsko (Stanford, CA: Stanford University Press, 2013), 144.

11. *Dante: Convivio: A Dual-Language Critical Edition*, ed. and trans. Andrew Frisardi (Cambridge: Cambridge University Press, 2018), 201.

12. Maria Corti was among the first to suggest that Ulysses could be a symbol of radical Aristotelianism, a sort of "bad brother," we might say, to Siger of Brabant, in *Dante a un nuovo crocevia* (Florence: Sansoni, 1981), 85–97.

13. "Autonomy" (of the political, of science, and of different disciplines, each with its own "language") is a key word in the history of neo-Marxism and the Italian political debate of the 1970s—and a notion that Cacciari has investigated at length in his works from that period.

14. Guido Cavalcanti, *Rime*, ed. Marcello Ciccuto, intro. by Maria Corti (Milan: Rizzoli BUR, 1978), 98. Dante Alighieri, *Vita nuova*, in *Opere minori, Tomo I, Parte I*, ed. Gianfranco Contini and Domenico De Robertis (Milan: Ricciardi, 1984), 172.

15. And not just we, the modern: "Dante criticism has been divided on the subject of Ulysses essentially since its inception." There is the "pro-Ulysses group" and the group "that emphasizes the Greek hero's sinfulness." Teodolinda Barolini, *The Undivine Comedy: Detheologizing Dante* (Princeton, NJ: Princeton University Press, 1992), 49. Equally distant from moralistic condemnation and romanticization, J. Freccero regards Ulysses as a mirror in which Dante contemplates his own intellectual pride and the dangers associated with it. See John Freccero, *Dante: The Poetics of Conversion*, ed. and with intro. Rachel Jacoff (Cambridge, MA: Harvard University Press, 1986), 1–28 and 136–151.

16. Cacciari has already raised the issue of the "exhaustion of hell" in Massimo Cacciari, *The Necessary Angel*, trans. Miguel E. Vatter (Albany, NY: SUNY Press, 1994), 67–82.

17. See Alessandro Carrera, *La consistenza della luce: Il pensiero della natura da Goethe a Calvino* (Milan: Feltrinelli, 2010), 57–63.

18. See Massimo Cacciari, "Empire and *Katechon*: A Question of Political Theology," in Cacciari, *Europe and Empire*, 145–155; and Massimo Cacciari, *The Withholding Power: An Essay on Political Theology*, trans. Edi Pucci, intro. Howard Caygill (London: Bloomsbury, 2018).

19. See Alessandro Passerin d'Entrèves, *Dante as a Political Thinker* (Oxford: Clarendon Press, 1952), and Charles Till Davis, "Dante and the Empire," in *The Cambridge Companion to Dante*, ed. Rachel Jacoff (Cambridge: Cambridge University Press, 1993), 67–79. Indeed, recent scholarship tends to stress continuity

and similarity rather than divergence. For Teodolinda Barolini, "*Monarchia* and *Paradiso* coincide in fundamental respects." Maria Luisa Ardizzone detects a pattern of continuity/discontinuity in relation to the notion of Possible Intellect that she subsumes under the notion of complementarity as it is used in contemporary physics (the same object described from many points of view). See Teodolinda Barolini, "Dante Squares the Circle: Textual and Philosophical Affinities of *Monarchia* and *Paradiso*," and Maria Luisa Ardizzone, "Wireless Communications: Continuity and Discontinuity between *Convivio* and *Monarchia*," both in *Dante as Political Theorist: Reading Monarchia*, ed. and with intro. Maria Luisa Ardizzone (Newcastle upon Tyne, UK: Cambridge Scholars, 2018), 34 and 237.

20. For this use of the notions of "metapolitics" as "event," see Alain Badiou, *Metapolitics*, trans. and with intro. Joseph Barker (New York: Verso, 2005).

21. See Anthony K. Cassell, *The Monarchia Controversy: An Historical Study with Accompanying Translations of Dante Alighieri's* Monarchia, *Guido Vernani's "Refutation of the 'Monarchia' Composed by Dante," and Pope John XXII's Bull "Si fratrum"* (Washington, DC: The Catholic University of America Press, 2004), 81, 188–189. It is remarkable, however, that Pascal makes a similar point: "Jesus Christ would not be slain without the forms of justice, for it is much more ignominious to die by justice than by an unjust sedition" (*The Thoughts of Blaise Pascal*, trans. from the text of M. Auguste Molinier, by C. Kegan Paul [London: George Bell and Sons, 1901], 229).

22. "This is true symbolism, where the particular represents the general, not as dream and shadow, but as a live and immediate revelation of the unfathomable." Johann Wolfgang von Goethe, *Maxims and Reflections*, trans. Elisabeth Stopp, ed. with intro. and notes Peter Hutchinson (London: Penguin, 1998), 30 (in this and other editions, the number of the *Maxim* is not 752 but 314).

23. Two recent volumes bear witness of the continuous interest in Dante from Italian philosophers: Carlo Sini, *Dante. Il suono dell'invisibile* (Naples: Orthotes, 2019), and Giorgio Agamben, *The Kingdom and the Garden*, trans. Adam Kotsko (Kolkata, India: Seagull Books, 2020). As a final note, I wish to thank Amanda Pascali for compiling the index of names with great care.

Notes to Chapter 1

1. Giovanni Pozzi, "Sul Cantico di frate Sole," in Pozzi, *Alternatim* (Milan: Adelphi 1996), a groundbreaking discussion of Francis' lexicon and the "theology of the hymn."

2. See Erich Auerbach, "Figura," in Auerbach, *Studi su Dante* (Milan: Feltrinelli, 1963), 176–226, and, in the same volume, "Francesco d'Assisi nella Commedia," 227–240.

3. There is a real need for the *body* of Christ, as expressed in Saint Francis, *Admonitions* I (*Of the Lord's Body*), in *The Writings of Saint Francis of*

Assisi, trans. with intro. and notes by Father Paschal Robinson (Philadelphia, PA: Dolphin Press, 1906), 23–24.

4. That Henry Thode's enthusiasm, in *Franz von Assisi* (1885), upon discovering in Francis the origins of Renaissance art should be taken with extreme caution is the commonplace warning of any "sedentary philology" (in Warburg's parlance), one which nonetheless detracts nothing from the pioneering importance of the book. See the fine Italian edition *Francesco d'Assisi e le origini del Rinascimento in Italia*, ed. Luciano Bellosi (Rome: Donzelli, 1993).

5. Dante Alighieri, *The Divine Comedy: Inferno; Purgatorio; Paradiso*, trans. Allen Mandelbaum (New York: Everyman's Library, 1995). All the quotes from the *Divine Comedy* here and elsewhere are in Mandelbaum's translation [translator's note].

6. The complex character of Giotto's workshop has been convincingly emphasized by Bruno Zanardi in his meticulous, though otherwise questionable, analysis. See *Giotto e Pietro Cavallini* (Milan: Skira, 2002). On the attribution of the Assisi paintings (and for conclusions different from Zanardi's), see Alessandro Tomei, "La decorazione della Basilica di San Francesco ad Assisi come metafora della questione giottesca," in Tomei, *Giotto e il Trecento*, vol. 1 (Milan: Skira, 2009).

7. Giovanni Boccaccio, *The Decameron*, "Sixth Day," "Fifth Story," trans with intro. and notes by G. H. McWilliam (London: Penguin, 1995), 729. On the role of Giotto in humanism, see Michael Baxandall, *Giotto and the Orators: Humanist Observers of Painting in Italy and the Discovery of Pictorial Composition* (New York: Oxford University Press, 1986).

8. Giovanni Previtali, among others, discusses this issue—with serious invitations to caution—in his classic monograph, *Giotto e la sua bottega* (Milan: Fabbri, 1967). See also Giovanni Fallani, *Dante e la cultura figurativa medievale* (Bergamo: Minerva Italica, 1971).

9. For the interpretation of this much-debated passage of *Inferno* X, I follow Antonino Pagliaro in *Saggi di critica semantica*, 3rd ed. (Messina-Firenze: D'Anna, 1976), 355–374. For *Purgatorio* XI, I follow the reading of Enrico Malato in *Studi su Dante: "Lecturae Dantis," chiose e altre note dantesche* (Rome: Salerno Editrice, 2006), 460–484.

10. However, Chiara Frugoni has recently redeemed Enrico Scrovegni in *L'affare migliore di Enrico: Giotto e la cappella Scrovegni* (Turin: Einaudi, 2008).

11. See *Le immagini del francescanesimo: Atti del XXXVI Convegno Internazionale di Studi Francescani* (Spoleto, Italy: Fondazione Centro Italiano di Studi sull'Alto Medioevo, 2009), which includes an important essay by Chiara Frugoni on the Assisi cycle ("Rappresentare per dimenticare?"). We owe Frugoni, as is well known, the crucial study on the "invention" of the stigmata (*Francesco e l'invenzione delle stimmate: Una storia per parole e immagini fino a Bomaventura e Giotto* [Turin: Einaudi, 1993]) as well as numerous other essays on Francis and Giotto, which have been a constant reference in the present study. On the issue of the stigmata, see also Arnold Ira Davidson's remarkable essay "Iconografia e

filosofia delle stimmate di Francesco," in *Ascetismo, digiuni, anoressia*, ed. Paolo Santonastaso and Gerardo Favaretto (Paris: Masson, 1999); and Klaus Krüger, "Un santo da guardare," in Maria Pia Alberzoni et al., *Francesco d'Assisi e il primo secolo di storia francescana* (Turin: Einaudi, 1997).

12. Hans Urs von Balthasar founds his interpretation of Bonaventure as a "theological aesthetics" precisely on the "painting" of the stigmata, in *Gloria: Una estetica teologica*, vol. 2, trans. Giuseppe Ruggieri et al. (Milan: Jaca Book, 1978).

13. Quoted in Peter W. Lowen, *Music in Early Franciscan Thought* (Leiden, Netherlands: Brill, 2013), 233 [translator's note].

14. For Henri De Lubac, it could even be maintained that Bonaventure's confutation of Joachimism "is at the same time, to a certain degree, an asseveration." See De Lubac, *La posterità spirituale di Gioacchino da Fiore*, vol. 1, *Dagli spirituali a Schelling*, trans. Francesco Di Ciaccia (Milan: Jaca Book, 1981), 173. But see also Giovanni Miccoli's justified insistence in *Francesco d'Assisi: Realtà e memoria di un'esperienza cristiana* (Turin: Einaudi, 1991) on the harshness of Bonaventure's struggle against the Joachimite current proliferating within the Order.

15. Saint Francis of Assisi, *The Earlier Rule*, accessed June 24, 2021, Commission on the Franciscan Intellectual-Spiritual Tradition, https://www.franciscantradition.org/francis-of-assisi-early-documents/the-saint/writings-of-francis/the-earlier-rule/90-fa-ed-1-page-75.

16. Saint Francis of Assisi, *The Testament*, accessed June 24, 2021, https://www.franciscantradition.org/francis-of-assisi-early-documents/the-saint/writings-of-francis/the-testament/141-fa-ed-1-page-125.

17. Rue du Fouarre ("Street of Straw"), in the Latin Quarter, was the street of Paris where the schools of philosophy were located, including the one at which Siger taught. See *Paradiso* X, 136–138: "It is the everlasting light of Siger / who when he lectured in the Street of Straw, / demonstrated truths that earned him envy" [translator's note].

18. This is how Étienne Gilson interprets the presence of Siger in the *Paradiso*; *Dante et la philosophie*, 3rd ed. (Paris: Vrin, 1939). It is a philosophy free from any apprehension about how to agree with theology, and therefore not inimical to it. Nonetheless, it remains extraordinary and disquieting that Dante should welcome into the *Paradiso* this philosophy, which at any rate *is not his own* (not even at the time of the *Convivio*), and even more that he should have Bonaventure welcome it. On the anti-Aristotelian polemics by the Franciscan masters, see Gian Luca Podestà, "Maestri e dottrine del XIII secolo," in Alberzoni et al., *Francesco d'Assisi*.

19. Anthony K. Cassell, *The Monarchia Controversy: An Historical Study with Accompanying Translations of Dante Alighieri's "Monarchia," Guido Vernani's "Refutation of the 'Monarchia' Composed by Dante," and Pope John XXII's Bull "Si fratrum"* (Washington, DC, Catholic University of America, 2004), 152–153.

20. Angelus Silesius, *The Cherubinic Wanderer*, trans. Maria Shrady (New York: Paulist Press, 1986), 74.

21. Giovanni Miccoli (*Francesco d'Assisi*) shows how the theme of Francis' incomparability is utilized by Bonaventure to repress the eschatologism of the most extreme pauperistic currents. There is but one Christ, and but one perfect imitator of Him, Francis. However, as is made manifest by the Assisi cycle, the "unique" Francis must be made inseparable from the Order he has founded. Precisely this will become a dominant preoccupation.

22. However, it is precisely the Franciscans who, in polemic against Thomist "concordism," draw a distinction between theology and philosophy, attaching the greatest importance to the science of nature. See Bruno Nardi's essential overview of this matter in "L'aristotelismo della scolastica e i francescani," in Nardi, *Studi di filosofia medievale* (Rome: Edizioni di storia e letteratura, 1979), 193–211.

23. On the complex events that occurred between the visit to Innocent III, the Council of 1215, and the approval of the Rule by Honorius III, against the letter of the dictates of that very Council, see Herbert Grundmann's clear summary in *Movimenti religiosi nel Medioevo*, trans. Maria Ausserhofer and Lea Nicolet Santini (Bologna, Italy: il Mulino, 1974), 93–96.

24. Thomas of Celano, *The Life of Saint Francis by Thomas of Celano (Vita prima)*, ch. 21, accessed June 29, 2021, https://franciscantradition.org/francis-of-assisi-early-documents/the-saint/the-life-of-saint-francis-by-thomas-of-celano/675-fa-ed-1-page-234. Other translations of Thomas of Celano's lives of Saint Francis have been used as well; see note 27 [editor's note].

25. "Die großen Erotiker des Ideals, die Heiligen der transfigurirten und unverstandenen Sinnlichkeit." Friedrich Nietzsche, *Nachgelassene Fragmente, 1885–1887* (Fall 1887, 10, 51), ed. Giorgio Colli and Mazzino Montinari (Munich: Neuausgabe, 1999), 479.

26. "Verliebt, populär, Poet," (Nietzsche, *Nachgelassene Fragmente,* [9, 19] 347); translation slightly modified.

27. Tommaso da Celano, *Vita seconda di San Francesco d'Assisi*, ch. 125, accessed June 29, 2021, www.santuariodelibera.it/FontiFrancescane/framevitaseconda.htm. Thomas da Celano's second biography of Saint Francis of Assisi is also known in English as *The Remembrance of the Desire of a Soul*, with reference to Isaiah 26:8. See *The Francis Trilogy of Thomas of Celano: The Life of Saint Francis, The Remembrance of the Desire of a Soul, The Treatise on the Miracles of Saint Francis*, ed. J. A. Wayne Hellman, Regis J. Armstrong, and William J. Short, foreword by Regis J. Armstrong, O.F.M. Cap. (Hyde Park, NY: New City Press, 2004) [editor's note].

28. Saint Bonaventure, *The Life of St. Francis of Assisi: A Biography of St. Francis of Assisi and Stories of His Followers* (1867), ed. with a preface by Cardinal Henry Edward Manning (Charlotte, NC: Tan Books, 2010), 40–46. Two translations of Saint Bonaventure's *The Life of St. Francis of Assisi* have been used. From now on, the 1867 Cardinal Manning edition will be indicated as Bonaventure, *Life of St. Francis* (1867), and the 1904 edition (London: Dent,

no translator named, see note 42) will be later indicated as Bonaventure, *Life of St. Francis* (1904) [editor's note].

29. Saint Francis of Assisi (attributed to), *Exhortation to the Praise of God*, "Laudate eum caelum et terra. Laudate omnia flumina Dominum . . . Omnes creaturae benedicite Dominum. Omnes volucres caeli laudate Dominum," accessed June 24, 2021, https://www.franciscantradition.org/francis-of-assisi-early-documents/writings-of-francis/the-undated-writings/exhortation-to-the-praise-of-god/154-fa-ed-1-page-138.

30. The Franciscan enjoyment of God (*frui Deo*) does not reject, like Augustine, the notion of usefulness (*uti*). While the former is, indeed, disinterested joy, it is God himself who, through his creatures, gives himself as also *usefulness* (*utilitas*) to those who thereby enjoy Him.

31. Leo Spitzer bases on this point his interpretation of the *Canticle*; see "Nuove considerazioni sul Cantico di Frate Sole," in Spitzer, *Studi italiani*, ed. Claudio Scarpati (Milan: Vita e Pensiero, 1976), 43–71.

32. For all these cultural, political, religious, theological events, see Raoul Manselli's groundbreaking research in Manselli, *Da Gioacchino da Fiore a Cristoforo Colombo* (Rome: Istituto storico italiano per il Medioevo, 1997). On the eschatology of Thomas and Bonaventure within the context of the philosophical debate between the twelfth and thirteenth centuries, see Tullio Gregory, *Mundana sapientia* (Rome: Edizioni di storia e letteratura, 1992).

33. Bonaventure, *Life of St. Francis of Assisi* (1867), 108.

34. On the importance of the beardless image of Francis, see Luciano Bellosi, *La pecora di Giotto* (Turin: Einaudi, 1985).

35. Quoted (but to be taken with a pinch of salt) in Ernesto Buonaiuti, *Storia del cristianesimo* (1942–1943), 3rd ed., vol. 2 (Milan: Dell'Oglio, 1979), 469.

36. "The opposite operation to the one carried out by some 'companions,' and certainly by Brother Leo"—that is, the intention to obliterate the debates arisen over the new formulation of the Rule, as well as the dissentions within the Order (Miccoli, *Francesco d'Assisi*, 293)—seems to me to have been pursued in a far more transparent way in Assisi's paintings than in Bonaventure's *Legenda*.

37. "Et non dicant fratres: haec est alia regula, quia haec est recordatio, admonitio, exhortatio et meum testamentum, quod ego frater Franciscus parvulus facio vobis fratribus meis benedictis." Francis, *Testament*, https://www.franciscantradition.org/francis-of-assisi-early-documents/writings-of-francis/the-testament/143-fa-ed-1-page-127.

38. Giorgio Agamben has written important pages on the relationship between "order" and life in monasticism. See Giorgio Agamben, *The Highest Poverty: Monastic Rules and Form-of-Life*, trans. Adam Kotsko (Stanford, CA: Stanford University Press, 2013).

39. On Francis' mission in the Holy Land, see the recent research done by Franco Cardini, "Francesco e il sultano. La storia e il messaggio," in *Francesco d'Assisi: Otto secoli di storia 1209–2009*, ed. Giuseppe Chili (Bologna: Fondazione

del Monte di Bologna e Ravenna, 2009); and Chiara Frugoni, *Francesco e le terre dei non cristiani* (Milan: Edizioni Biblioteca Francescana, 2012).

40. Thomas of Celano, *The Life of Saint Francis (Vita prima)*, accessed June 24, 2021, https://franciscantradition.org/francis-of-assisi-early-documents/the-saint/the-life-of-saint-francis-by-thomas-of-celano/684-fa-ed-1-page-243.

41. Thomas of Celano, *Life of Saint Francis (Vita prima)*, https://franciscantradition.org/francis-of-assisi-early-documents/the-saint/the-life-of-saint-francis-by-thomas-of-celano/686-fa-ed-1-page-245.

42. Bonaventure, *The Life of St. Francis by Saint Bonaventura*, no translator named (London: Dent, Aldine House, 1904), accessed June 24, 2021, https://archive.org/details/lifesaintfranci02bonagoog/page/n154.

43. Bonaventure, *Life of St. Francis* (1904), https://archive.org/details/livessfrancisas00howegoog/page/n366.

44. Bonaventure, *Life of St. Francis* (1904), https://archive.org/details/lifesaintfranci02bonagoog/page/n164.

45. Thomas of Celano, *Life of Saint Francis (Vita prima)*, https://franciscantradition.org/francis-of-assisi-early-documents/the-saint/the-life-of-saint-francis-by-thomas-of-celano/624-fa-ed-1-page-183.

46. "Et ipse Dominus conduxit me inter illos et feci misericordiam cum illis"; Francis, *Testament*, https://www.franciscantradition.org/francis-of-assisi-early-documents/writings-of-francis/the-testament/140-fa-ed-1-page-124. Both Bonaventure and the Assisi cycle deviate sharply from the spirit of the *Testament*.

47. Thomas of Celano, "The First Life of S. Francis," in *The Lives of S. Francis of Assisi by Brother Thomas of Celano*, trans. Alan George Ferrers Howell, LL.M. (London: Methuen, 1908), 66, accessed June 26, 2021, https://archive.org/details/livessfrancisas00howegoog/page/n90/mode/2up?q=houses.

48. "Omnibus comune nec proprium ulli." Dante, *De vulgari eloquentia*, I, 18, 2, ed. and trans. Steven Botterill (Cambridge: Cambridge University Press, 1996), 43.

49. Saint Thomas Aquinas, *Summa contra gentiles*, Priory of the Immaculate Conception at the Dominican House of Studies, Washington, DC, accessed June 24, 2021, https://dhspriory.org/thomas/ContraGentiles3b.htm#13.

50. "Illa celsitudo altissimae paupertatis." Saint Francis of Assisi, *The Later Rule*, accessed June 24, 2021, https://www.franciscantradition.org/francis-of-assisi-early-documents/the-saint/writings-of-francis/the-later-rule/119-fa-ed-1-page-103.

51. Martin Heidegger, "Die Armut," *Heidegger's Studies* 10 (1994): 5–11.

52. Friedrich Nietzsche, *Thus Spoke Zarathustra: A Book for All and None*, ed. Adrian Del Caro and Robert B. Pippin, trans. Adrian Del Caro (Cambridge: Cambridge University Press 2006), 216–217.

53. Thomas of Celano, *The First Life of S. Francis*, accessed June 24, 2021, https://archive.org/details/livessfrancisas00howegoog/page/n126; translation slightly modified.

54. That Dante, on the contrary, did not know it is the thesis advanced by Umberto Cosmo in the fine study *Con Madonna Povertà: Studi francescani* (Bari, Italy: Laterza, 1940).

55. Here a long discussion should ensue on the concept of analogy in medieval Aristotelianism and in Thomas Aquinas. In this venue, I can only refer the reader to the brilliant pages Enzo Melandri devoted to this matter in his masterwork *La linea e il circolo: Studio logico-filosofico sull'analogia* (Bologna: Il Mulino, 1968), now reissued with an introductory essay by Giorgio Agamben (Macerata, Italy: Quodlibet, 2004), 92–94.

56. See Carlo Michelstaedter, *Persuasion and Rhetoric*, trans. Russell Scott Valentino and Cinzia Santini Blum (New Haven, CT: Yale University Press, 2004) [translator's note].

57. "Qui vere pauper est spiritu, se ipsum odit et eos diligit qui eum percutiunt in maxilla," in Saint Francis, *Admonitions* XIV, https://www.sacred-texts.com/chr/wosf/wosf03.htm.

58. It would be opportune, here, to address the question of Francis' notion of poverty vis-à-vis that which unfolds with powerful mystical "logic" in the Dominican Meister Eckhart. While the sermon *Loved by God and Men* (*Dilectus Deo et hominibus*) certainly shows the veneration that the great Master felt for the fool (*pazzus*) of Assisi, the distance between them remains immense. Both in the aforementioned sermon and in the fundamental *Blessed Are the Poor* (*Beati pauperes*), being-poor coincides with the radical resolution of the "being-there" into Being, or rather, in what is *beyond* Being. Perfectly poor are, therefore, not only those who affirm all things to be nothing but also those who succeed in freeing themselves from the very God-Being, a stance in clear contradistinction to Franciscan mysticism (and, a fortiori, to its versions in Dante and in Giotto). It is nonetheless essential to keep Eckhart's position in mind if we wish to understand the perspective that Francis inaugurates (and Francis' relationship to Eckhart equals Saint Clare's relationship to Marguerite Porete).

59. Saint Francis of Assisi, *The Praises of God and the Blessing*, accessed June 24, 2021, https://www.franciscantradition.org/francis-of-assisi-early-documents/writings-of-francis/the-praises-of-god-and-the-blessing/125-fa-ed-1-page-109.

60. Francis, *Later Rule*, https://www.franciscantradition.org/francis-of-assisi-early-documents/writings-of-francis/the-later-rule/120-fa-ed-1-page-104.

61. Francis, *Earlier Rule*, https://www.franciscantradition.org/francis-of-assisi-early-documents/the-saint/writings-of-francis/the-earlier-rule/85-fa-ed-1-page-70.

62. Saint Francis of Assisi, *The Admonitions*, Franciscans, accessed June 24, 2021, https://www.franciscans.ie/the-writings-of-st-francis/#7.

63. Ephrem Longpré, "Les *Distinctiones* de Fr. Thomas Pavie, O.F.M.," *Archivum Franciscanum historicum* 16 (1923): 3–33.

64. Jacques Le Goff insists on the "maternal" aspects of Franciscan spirituality in his fine study *Saint François d'Assise* (Paris: Gallimard, 1999). But

the essential on this "language" had already been said by Giovanni Pozzi in his introduction to *Scrittrici mistiche italiane*, ed. Giovanni Pozzi and Claudio Leonardi (Genoa, Italy: Marietti, 1998); and later by Pozzi and Beatrice Rima in their "Introduzione a Chiara d'Assisi," in Chiara d'Assisi, *Lettere ad Agnese: La visione dello specchio* (Milan: Adelphi, 1999).

65. Saint Francis of Assisi, *Later Admonition and Exhortation*, accessed June 24, 2021, https://www.franciscantradition.org/francis-of-assisi-early-documents/the-saint/writings-of-francis/later-admonition-and-exhortation/64-fa-ed-1-page-49.

66. Francis, *Testament*, https://www.franciscantradition.org/francis-of-assisi-early-documents/writings-of-francis/the-testament/142-fa-ed-1-page-126.

67. On Saint Clare of Assisi, see Chiara Frugoni's fine book *Storia di Chiara e Francesco* (Turin: Einaudi, 2011).

68. Erich Auerbach masterfully comments on Francis' letter in *Mimesis: The Representation of Reality in Western Literature*, trans. Willard R. Trask (Princeton, NJ: Princeton University Press, 1953), 165–173.

69. "Et si millies postea coram oculis tuis peccaret, dilige eum plus quam me." Saint Francis of Assisi, accessed June 24, 2021, *Letter to a Certain Minister*. https://oll.libertyfund.org/titles/assisi-the-writings-of-saint-francis-of-assisi.

70. Quoted in Krijn Pansters, *Spiritual Growth and the Virtues in Franciscan Literature and Instruction of the Thirteenth Century* (Leiden: Brill, 2012), 130.

Notes to Chapter 2

1. In addition to the classic references (from Giorgio Padoan, *Il pio Enea, l'empio Ulisse: Tradizione classica e intendimento medievale in Dante* [Ravenna, Italy: Longo, 1977], to Maria Corti, *Percorsi dell'invenzione: Il linguaggio poetico e Dante* [Turin: Einaudi, 1993]), see the ample documentation contained in Mario Aversano's comment *Dante Cristiano: La "selva," Francesca, Ulisse e la struttura dell'Inferno* (Rome: Il Calamaio, 1994).

2. "And that because of false brethren unawares brought in . . . ," Galatians 2:4 (KJV).

3. See L. Annaei Senecae, *Ad Lucilium Epistulae morales*, LXXXVIII, 7, with intro. and commentary by R. D. Reynolds (Oxford: Clarendon Press, 1965).

4. See Romano Guardini, *La "Divina Commedia" di Dante: I principali concetti filosofici e religiosi*, ed. Oreste Tolone, in *Opera Omnia*, vol. 29/2 (Brescia, Italy: Morcelliana, 2012), in particular part 6, *Il religioso, Cristo, Dio*.

5. See Mario Fubini, "Il peccato di Ulisse," in Fubini, *Il peccato di Ulisse e altri scritti danteschi* (Milan: Ricciardi, 1966), 1–36, in particular 5–7.

6. Virgil, *Aeneid*, trans. Frederick Ahl, intro. Elaine Fantham (Oxford: Oxford University Press), 10.

7. See the addendum at the end of this chapter.

8. Here and elsewhere, the quotes from the *Convivio* are taken from *Dante: Convivio: A Dual-Language Critical Edition*, ed. and trans. Andrew Frisardi (Cambridge: Cambridge University Press, 2018) [translator's note].

9. This interpretation of this page from *Il Convivio* has been aptly illustrated by Alessandro Raffi, *La Gloria del volgare: Ontologia e semiotica in Dante dal "Convivio" al "De Vulgari"* (Soveria Mannelli, Italy: Rubbettino, 2004).

10. See Bruno Nardi, "La tragedia d'Ulisse," in Nardi, *Dante e la cultura medievale* (Bari, Italy: Laterza, 1942), 89–99, in particular 98.

11. See Étienne Gilson, *Dante et la philosophie*, 3rd ed. (Paris: Vrin, 1939), 109–110.

12. "Of all the good things to be done, what is the highest." Aristotle, *Nicomachean Ethics*, 1, 4, 1095a 15–16, trans. and ed. Roger Crisp (Cambridge: Cambridge University Press, 2004), 5.

13. Aristotle, *Nicomachean Ethics*, 1, 3, 1094b 14, 4.

14. See Ruedi Imbach, "Ulisse come figura di filosofo," in Imbach, *Dante, la filosofia e i laici*, trans. Pasquale Porro (Genoa, Italy: Marietti, 2003), 185–212.

15. Gilson, *Dante*, 262–263.

16. See Antonino Pagliaro, "Il disdegno di Guido," in Pagliaro, *Saggi di critica semantica* (Messina, Italy: D'Anna, 1953), 355–379; and Enrico Malato, "Il 'disdegno' di Guido: Chiosa a Inf. X 63: 'Forse cui Guido vostro ebbe a disdegno'" (1991), in Malato, *Studi su Dante: "Lecturae Dantis," chiose e altre note dantesche* (Rome: Salerno Editrice, 2006), 425–459.

17. See Gennaro Sasso, *Dante, Guido, e Francesca* (Rome: Viella, 2008).

Notes to Chapter 3

1. Guido Cavalcanti, *Rime*, ed. Marcello Ciccuto, intro. Maria Corti (Milan: Rizzoli BUR, 1978), 98. See also *The Poetry of Guido Cavalcanti*, trans. Lowry Nelson (New York: Garland, 1986).

2. Gregory Palamas, *The Triads*, ed. and intro. John Meyendorff, trans. Nicholas Gendle, pref. Jaroslav Pelikan (Mahwah, NJ: Paulist Press, 1983).

3. Quoted in Norman Russell, "Theosis and Gregory Palamas: Continuity or Doctrinal Change?" *St. Vladimir Theological Quarterly* 50, no. 4 (2006): 360.

Notes to Chapter 4

1. On the power of the imagination (*vis imaginativa*) in Dante, in its scholastic and mystical sources, both Christian and Islamic, see the important essay by Mira Mocan, *La trasparenza e il riflesso: Sull'alta fantasia in Dante e nel pensiero medievale* (Milan: Mondadori, 2007).

2. The Way of Beauty (*via pulchritudinis*) is at the center of Anna Maria Chiavacci Leonardi's studies on Dante; see especially *Le bianche stole: Saggi sul Paradiso di Dante* (Florence: SISMEL-Edizioni del Galluzzo, 2010).

3. Giuliana Carugati insists, instead, on the incompleteness of this vision in *La scrittura mistica della "Commedia" di Dante* (Bologna, Italy: il Mulino, 1991).

4. On the possible relationships between the last Dantean visions in the *Paradiso* and great contemporary paintings, see Carlo Maria Ossola's fascinating discussion in *Viaggio a Maria* (Rome: Salerno Editrice, 2016).

5. In the wake of Erich Auerbach's seminal essay, I believe that the most exhaustive recent discussions of the last Canto and the prayer to Mary are those offered by Piero Boitani in *Il tragico e il sublime nella letteratura medievale* (Bologna: il Mulino, 1992); and by Marco Ariani in "La mistica preterizione: Il 'dicer poco' dell'ultimus Cantus," in *Cento Canti per cento anni: Lectura Dantis Romana*, ed. Enrico Malato and Andrea Mazzucchi (Rome: Salerno Editrice, 2015), 971–1011.

6. Marco Ariani rightly calls attention to Dante's expressions that "humbly" limit the power of his vision, but this does not change the essential point: "Unlike the mystic, blinded by the inaccessible light, the poet stares intrepidly into the abyss until his eyes wear out, as he is obliged to figure the unfigurable, forced to wrest from oblivion the scattered fragments of his vision" (*La mistica preterizione*, 986). Along the same lines, Piero Boitani notes that "Dante cannot limit himself to defining God as ineffable: he must describe Him in some way"; *Il tragico e il sublime*, 325 [quotes translated from the Italian text; translator's note].

7. On the sign of *folgore* (or *fulgore*), see Ariani, *La mistica preterizione*, 1004–1008.

Notes to Chapter 6

1. *Nuova edizione commentata delle Opere di Dante*, vol. 3, *De vulgari eloquentia*, ed. Enrico Fenzi with the collaboration of Luciano Formisano and Francesco Montuori (Rome: Salerno Editrice, 2012).

2. All the quotes are from Dante, *De vulgari eloquentia*, ed. and trans. Steven Botterill (Cambridge: Cambridge University Press, 1996) [translator's note].

3. The presence or absence of a quasi-Chomskyan generative grammar in Dante has been the subject of a long controversy after the publication of Maria Corti's *Dante a un nuovo crocevia* (Florence: Sansoni, 1981), in which the author advanced the hypothesis of a direct influence of radical Aristotelian Boethius of Dacia and the *Modistae* on Dante's philosophy of language. By and large, Dante scholars were not favorable to Corti's thesis, which nonetheless stirred a long and intense debate and was supported by Umberto Eco in *The Search for the Perfect Language*, trans. James Fentress (London: Blackwell, 1995). The recent scholarship tends to separate Dante's "natural language" from the assumption

that human language be based on an "innate structure." Costantino Marmo, for instance, does not deny that Dante might have referred to an "innate human ability to structure and generate languages" that was downgraded after Babel. He does deny, however, that Dante could have learned such idea from the *Modistae*, where the consistency of grammar is founded on its relationship with reality and not on an innate or deep structure. See Costantino Marmo, "Had the *Modistae* Any Influence on Dante? Thirty Years after Maria Corti's Proposal," in *Dante and Heterodoxy: The Temptations of 13th Century Radical Thought*, ed. Maria Luisa Ardizzone, conclusion by Teodolinda Barolini (Newcastle upon Tyne, UK: Cambridge Scholars Publishing, 2014), 1–17 (p. 16). The controversy, however, has not been settled yet [editor's note].

4. "In contemporary scholarly usage 'Romania' is taken to mean the sum total of the countries in which Romance languages were spoken." Ernst Robert Curtius, *European Literature and the Latin Middle Ages*, trans. Willard R. Trask, with a new afterword by Peter Godman, Bollingen Series, vol. 36 (1948; repr., Princeton, NJ: Princeton University Press, 1990), 30 [editor's note].

5. "Sapientia sine eloquentia prodest, sed parum—eloquentia vero sine sapientia . . . obest." Wilhelm von Conches, *Philosophia I, Prologue* 1, 17, in *Ausgabe des 1. Buchs von Wilhelm von Conches Philosophia*, ed. Gregor Maurach (Pretoria: University of South Africa, 1974). See also Joan Cadden, "Science and Rhetoric in the Middle Ages: The Natural Philosophy of William of Conches," *Journal of the History of Ideas* 56, no. 1 (1995): 1–24 (4–5) [editor's note].

Notes to Chapter 7

1. Arthur P. Monahan, *John of Paris On Royal and Papal Power: A Translation, with Introduction, of the "De potestate regia et papali" of John of Paris* (New York: Columbia University Press, 1974), 8.

2. Saint Augustine, *The City of God, Books I–VII*, vol. 1, I, 35, trans. Demetrius B. Zema and Gerald G. Walsh (Washington, DC: The Catholic University of America Press, 1950), 72.

3. Saint Augustine, *The City of God, Books XVII–XXII*, vol. 3, XVIII, 41, trans. Gerald G. Walsh and Daniel J. Honan (Washington, DC: The Catholic University of America Press, 1954), 150.

4. Augustine, *City of God*, XVIII, 22, 113.

5. Augustine, *City of God*, XVIII, 51, 171, with reference to Isaiah 24:10, "The city of confusion is broken down" [editor's note].

6. Augustine, *City of God*, XIX, 21, 232.

7. The quotes from the *Monarchia* are from Dante, *Monarchy*, ed. and trans. Prue Shaw (Cambridge: Cambridge University Press, 1996) [translator's note].

8. Aristotle, *Nicomachean Ethics*, ed. and trans. Roger Crisp (Cambridge: Cambridge University Press, 2004), 83.

9. See Guido Vernani, "The Refutation of the Monarchia composed by Dante (1327–1334)," in Anthony K. Cassell, *The Monarchia Controversy: An Historical Study with Accompanying Translations of Dante Alighieri's Monarchia, Guido Vernani's "Refutation of the 'Monarchia' composed by Dante," and Pope John XXII's Bull "Si fratrum"* (Washington, DC: The Catholic University of America Press, 2004), 174–197.

10. Giuseppe Ungaretti, "Cause dell'attuale crisi" (1931), in *Vita d'un uomo: Saggi e interventi*, ed. Mario Diacono and Luciano Rebay (Milan: Mondadori, 1974). "In Dante, uomo aggressivo ed edificatore, un'armonia umana va imposta sulla terra" (258); "lamentosa del passato e del futuro come di due paradisi perduti" (259); "No, non si tratta di salvare il denaro, ma l'Europa. Ci vuole 'Amore,' come diceva Dante, non denaro" (261).

Notes to Chapter 8

1. Johann Wolfgang von Goethe, *Goethes Sämtliche Werke in 40 Banden*, vol. 30, *Annalen* (Stuttgart, Germany: J. C. Cotta, 1856), 360. Unless otherwise indicated, all the notes are the editor's or the translator's.

2. Johann Wolfgang von Goethe, *Italian Journey, 1786–1788*, trans. W. H. Auden and Elizabeth Mayer (New York: Pantheon Books), 1982, 367.

3. "With the most ancient men and schools I was best pleased, because poetry, religion, and philosophy were completely combined into one." Johann Wolfgang von Goethe, *Autobiography of Goethe: Truth and Poetry Related to My Life* (book 6, part 2), trans. John Oxenford, accessed June 28, 2021, http://www.thefloatingpress.com, from an 1848 edition, 372.

4. See *Die göttliche Komödie des Dante Alighieri übersetzt und erläutert von Karl Streckfuß*, part 1, *Die Hölle* (Halle, Belgium: Hemmerde und Schwetschke, 1824). Streckfuss sent the translation to Goethe in July 1824 with a personal dedication note. See also Goethe's commentary and amendment of Streckfuss' translation of *Inferno* XI, 97–105, and *Inferno* XII, 1–10, 28–45, and 80–82, in *Dante Alighieri: Die Göttliche Komödie: Deutsch von Johann Wolfgang Goethe* (Elsa Verlag, 2020), Creative Commons digital publication, accessible at http://www.academia.edu.

5. The quotes from August and Friedrich Schlegel are taken from their collected works and are translated by the author: *August Wilhelm von Schlegel's Sämtliche Werke*, 12 volumes, ed. Eduard Böcking (Leipzig, Germany: Weidmann, 1846–1847); August Wilhelm Schlegel, *Kritische Ausgabe der Vorlesungen*, ed. Ernst Behler and Frank Jolles (Paderborn, Germany: Schöningh, 1989); *Kritische Friedrich-Schlegel-Ausgabe*, ed. Ernst Behler, Jean Jacques Anstett, and Hans Eichner (Paderborn: Schöningh, 1958).

6. "Dante's Komödie ist ein Roman," in *Kritische Friedrich-Schlegel-Ausgabe*, 16:91.

7. The author refers to Novalis' well-known 1799 essay *Die Christenheit oder Europa* (published posthumously in 1826). Commonly regarded as a manifesto of reactionary Romanticism, it is nonetheless remarkable in its call for a united Europe, free from the grips of nationalism.

8. See chapter 9 of this volume.

9. "*Les Fleurs du mal* bears a hidden resemblance to Dante in the emphatic way it traces the itinerary of a creative life. There is no other book of poems in which the poet presents himself with so little vanity and so much force." Walter Benjamin, *The Writer of Modern Life: Essays on Charles Baudelaire*, ed. Michael W. Jennings (Cambridge, MA: The Belknap Press, 2006), 158.

10. The author quotes here from Walter Binni, *I classici italiani nella storia della critica*, vol. 1 (Florence: La Nuova Italia, 1960), 59.

11. See my "De Sanctis europeo," *Archivio di storia della cultura* 33 (2020): 143–158 [author's note].

12. "I welcome every opinion based on scientific criticism. As to the prejudices of so-called public opinion, to which I have never made concessions, now, as ever, my maxim is that of the great Florentine: 'Segui il tuo corso, e lascia dir le genti.'" Karl Marx, *Capital: A Critique of Political Economy*, vol. 1, trans. Ben Fowkes, intro. Ernest Mandel (Harmondsworth, UK: Penguin, 1976), 93. Marx's line "Follow your path, and let these people talk" alters *Purgatorio* V, 13: "Vien dietro me, e lascia dir le genti" ("Come, follow me, and let these people talk").

13. "The *Manifesto* fully acknowledges the revolutionary role played by capitalism in the past. The first capitalist nation was Italy. The conclusion of the feudal Middle Ages and the beginning of the modern capitalist era are marked by a grandiose figure: it is Dante, an Italian, the last medieval poet and at the same time the first poet of modernity. As in 1300, a new era is underway today. Will Italy give us a new Dante, who will announce the birth of this new era, the proletarian era? *London, 1 February 1893*" ("Il *Manifesto* riconosce appieno il ruolo rivoluzionario giocato nel passato dal capitalismo. La prima nazione capitalistica è stata l'Italia. La conclusione del Medioevo feudale e l'inizio della moderna era capitalistica sono segnate da una figura grandiosa: è un italiano, Dante, l'ultimo poeta medievale e insieme il primo poeta della modernità. Come nel 1300, una nuova era è oggi in marcia. Sarà l'Italia a darci un nuovo Dante, che annuncerà la nascita di questa nuova era, l'era proletaria? *Londra, 1° febbraio 1893*"). Friedrich Engels, "Al lettore italiano" ("To the Italian Reader"), trans. from the original French Filippo Turati, in Karl Marx and Friedrich Engels, *Manifesto del Partito Comunista*, trans. Pompeo Bettini (Milan: Uffici della "Critica sociale," Tipografia degli Operai, 1893). Engels wrote the preface in French at Turati's request.

14. The quotes are taken from Friedrich Nietzsche, *Human, All Too Human: A Book for Free Spirits*, §220, trans. R. J. Hollingdale, intro. Richard Schacht (Cambridge: Cambridge University Press, 1986), 102, and the German edition of the posthumous fragments: *Herbst 1887, Fragment 5 [41]* on Wagner's prelude to *Parsifal*, Dante, and Lionardo [sic]; 5 [91] on Dante, Michel Angelo [sic], and Napoleon; 7 [7] on Dante and Goethe; 7 [39] on *Inferno* III, 5–6, "my maker was . . . the primal love" ("fecemi . . . il primo amore"). Friedrich Nietzsche, *Nachgelassene Fragmente, 1885–1887: Kritische Studienausgabe in 15 Bänden*, KSA, vol. 12, ed. Giorgio Colli und Mazzino Montinari (Munich: Deutscher Taschenbucher Verlag–De Gruyter, 1967–1977; repr., Munich: Neuausgabe, 1999), 198–199, 223–224, 284, 308.

15. "The *Divine Comedy* is nothing but the aura surrounding the name of Beatrice, the most powerful representation of the idea that all the forces and figures of the cosmos arise from the name born of love." Walter Benjamin, "Platonic Love," in *Short Shadows (I)*, in *Selected Writings*, vol. 2, part 2, 1927–1930, ed. Michael W. Jennings, Howard Eiland, and Gary Smith, trans. Rodney Livingstone et al. (Cambridge, MA: The Belknap Press, 2005), 268.

16. Friedrich Nietzsche, Aphorism n=10081 id='VII.34[25]' kgw='VII-3.149' KSA='11.429'; Aphorism n=10148 id='VII.34[92]' kgw='VII-3.170' KSA='11.450'. However, one should not forget Nietzsche's about-face in *Ecce Homo*, where he claims that his *Zarathustra* is superior to any other poem ("Dante is just another one of the faithful and not one who first *creates* truth"), and in *Twilight of the Idols* ("Dante: or the hyena who writes poetry in tombs"). See Friedrich Nietzsche, *The Anti-Christ, Ecco Homo, Twilight of the Idols, and Other Writings*, ed. Aaron Ridley and Judith Norman, trans. Judith Norman (Cambridge: Cambridge University Press, 2005), 129 and 192.

17. Friedrich Nietzsche, "Letter to Peter Gast, January 21, 1887," in *Selected Letters of Friedrich Nietzsche*, trans. Anthony M. Ludovici, "Selected Letters of Friedrich Nietzsche, Wikisource, the free online library, accessed December 20, 2020. See also *Friedrich Nietzsches Gesammelte Briefe*, vol. 4 (no. 201), ed. Elisabeth Förster-Nietzsche, Peter Gast, Fritz Schöll, and Curt Wachsmuth (Berlin: Schuster und Loeffler, 1902–1909), 490.

18. Georg Simmel, "Dantes Psychologie," in *Zeitschrift für Völkerpsychologie und Sprachwissenschaft*, ed. V. M. Lazarus and H. Steinthal, 15 vols., part 1: numbers 1–2; part 2: numbers 3–4 (Berlin: Ferd. Dümmler / Harrwitz & Gossmann, 1884) 18–69, 239–276, available online at "Georg Simmel: Dantes Psychologie," socio.ch, accessed December 20, 2020. See also Wilhelm Dilthey, *Introduction to the Human Sciences*, ed. Rudolf A. Makkreel and Frithjof Rodi (Princeton, NJ: Princeton University Press, 1989), 185–188.

19. Erich Auerbach's studies from the 1920s are gathered in the seminal *Dante: Poet of the Secular World* (1929), trans Ralph Manheim (Chicago, IL: University of Chicago Press, 1961), which would profoundly influence Romano

Guardini's own works on Dante, collected in *La Commedia di Dante: I principali concetti filosofici e religiosi*, ed. Oreste Tolone (Brescia, Italy: Morcelliana, 2012). Given the scope and complexity of the issues upon which they touch, discussion of Guardini's contributions—as well as Urs von Balthasar's chapters on Dante in *The Glory of the Lord: A Theological Aesthetics*, vol. 3, trans. Andrew Louth et al. (San Francisco, CA: Ignatius Press, 1986)—lies beyond the scope of this article [author's note].

20. "La vérité immobile qui ne fait qu'attendre le chercheur ne correspond nullement à ce concept de vérité en matière d'histoire. Il s'appuie bien plutôt sur le vers de Dante qui dit: 'C'est une image unique, irremplaçable du passé qui s'évanouit avec chaque présent qui n'a pas su se reconnaître visé par elle.'" Walter Benjamin, *Gesammelte Schriften* vol. I, part 1, ed. Rolf Tiedemann and Hermann Schweppenhäuser (Frankfurt am Main: Suhrkamp, 1974), 1261. The reference to Dante, which does not seem to correspond to any specific line in the *Commedia*, appears only in Benjamin's own French version of his *Theses on the Philosophy of History*. Our translation: "The immobile truth which just waits for the seeker does not correspond at all to this concept of truth in matters of history. Rather, it relies to Dante's line that says: 'It is a unique, irreplaceable image of the past that vanishes with each present that has failed to recognize itself as targeted by it.'"

21. On this matter, however, see the fine essay by Marco Maggi, *Walter Benjamin e Dante* (Rome: Donzelli, 2017) [author's note]. According to Sigrid Weigel, whom Maggi quotes (*Walter Benjamin e Dante*, 69–71), Benjamin might have had *Par.* XXXIII, 140–141, in mind: "But then my mind was struck by light that flashed / and, with this light, received what it had asked" ("Se non che la mia mente fu percossa / da un fulgore in che sua voglia venne") [editor's note].

22. "Es war der fünfte Gesang der 'Hölle,' in dem die Stimme, die ihn eines hellen Vormittags in einem Münchner Atelier mir las, durch Jahre in mir fortwirkte." Walter Benjamin, "Über Stefan George," *Literarische Rundschau*, July 13, 1928. See also *Gesammelte Schriften* vol. 2, part 1 (Frankfurt am Main: Suhrkamp, 1977), 623–624. Benjamin's 1928 article on Stefan George is not included in the four-volume English edition of Benjamin's *Selected Writings* (Cambridge, MA: The Belknap Press, 1999–2006).

23. Dante, *Stellen aus der Göttlichen Komödie*, trans. Stefan George (Berlin: Verlag der Blätter für die Kunst, 1909); then in Stefan George, *Dante: Die göttliche Komödie: Gesamt-Ausgabe der Werke*, vol. 10/11 (Berlin: Bondi, 1932).

24. Walter Benjamin, "Stefan George in Retrospect" (1933), in Benjamin, *Selected Writings*, vol. 1, part 2, *1931–1934*, ed. Michael W. Jennings, Howard Eiland, and Gary Smith, trans. Rodney Livingstone et al. (Cambridge, MA: The Belknap Press, 2005), 707.

25. Stefan George, *The Works of Stefan George*, trans. Olga Marx and Ernst Morwitz, 2nd ed. (Chapel Hill: University of North Carolina Press, 1974), 81.

26. The quote is translated from the Italian edition, Ludwig Klages, L'anima e la forma, ed. Giampiero Moretti and Pietro Tripodo, trans. Pietro Tripodo and Filippo Segato (Rome: Fazi, 1995; electronic ed., 2013), which includes Klages' *Stefan George* and several poems by George.

27. Ernst Robert Curtius, "Stefan George in Conversation" (1911), in Curtius, *Essays in European Literature*, trans. Michael Kowel (Princeton, NJ: Princeton University Press, 1973), 107–128.

28. "Mein römischer hausch." Stefan George, *The Seventh Ring* (1907), quoted in Ernst Robert Curtius, *European Literature and the Latin Middle Ages*, trans. Willard R. Trask, with new intro. Colin Burrow (Princeton, NJ: Princeton University Press, 1953), 10.

29. Oswald Spengler, *The Decline of the West: Form and Actuality*, trans. Charles Francis Atkinson (New York: Knopf, 1927). The "Tables" are the last section of the volume (pages not numbered).

30. Walter Benjamin, "Stefan George in Retrospect," 706–707.

Notes to Chapter 9

1. Wolfram Hogrebe, "Schelling und Dante," *Deutsches Dante-Jahrbuch* 62, no. 1 (1987): 7–32.

2. *The New Science of Giambattista Vico*, trans. Thomas G. Bergin and Max H. Fisch (Ithaca, NY: Cornell University Press, 1948), 271.

3. *New Science of Giambattista Vico*, 279.

4. Friedrich Wilhelm Joseph Schelling, *The Philosophy of Art*, trans. Douglas W. Stott (Minneapolis: University of Minnesota Press, 1989), 239.

5. Schelling, *Philosophy of Art*, 74.

6. Herein begins a line of thought of crucial importance to modern European culture—even beyond art and philosophy. The Wagnerian project finds in this context its philosophical and political origin.

7. Schelling, *Philosophy of Art*, 239.

8. I cannot discuss here the meaning of this all too famous expression of Hegel's. I have written about it extensively in several essays. To be sure, it is not meant to indicate a chronological end, but rather a *fulfillment* of the forms, both classical and Romantic, of representation or artistic *mimesis*.

9. F. W. J. Schelling, *Historical-Critical Introduction to the Philosophy of Mythology*, trans. Mason Richey and Markus Zisselsberger (Albany, NY: SUNY Press, 2007), 168.

10. Schelling, *Introduction*, 169.

11. Luigi Pareyson, *Fichte* (Milan: Mursia, 1976).

12. Quoted in Schelling, *Philosophy of Art*, 314n103, as Goethe's *Maxim* no. 752. However, in other editions such as Johann Wolfgang von Goethe,

Maxims and Reflections, trans. Elisabeth Stopp, ed. with intro. and notes Peter Hutchinson (London: Penguin, 1998), and *Massime e riflessioni*, trans. and intro Barbara Allason (Turin, Italy: De Silva, 1943), the number is not 752 but 314 [editor's note].

13. F. W. J. Schelling, *Statement on the True Relationship of the Philosophy of Nature to the Revised Fichtean Doctrine: An Elucidation of the Former*, trans. Dale E. Snow (Albany, NY: SUNY Press, 2018), 48.

14. Schelling, *Statement*, 21.

15. Johann Gottlieb Fichte, *Early Philosophical Writings*, trans. Daniel Breazeale (Ithaca, NY: Cornell University Press, 1988), 206.

16. F. W. J. Schelling, "Propädeutik der Philosophie," in *F. W. J. von Schellings Sämtliche Werke*, sect. 1, vol. 6 (CD-ROM, Total Verlag, 1997), 2231.

17. I have mentioned the importance of Schelling's idea of the relationship between art and myth for the Wagnerian musical drama. Now we should speak of the subterranean influence of Schelling's philosophy of nature on Schopenhauer's system, much as the latter might try his hardest to erase every trace of it (as he also tries to conceal his obvious indebtedness to Spinoza).

18. "Schelling's Aphorisms of 1805," trans. Fritz Marti, *Idealistic Studies* 14, no. 3 (1984): 237–258 (250).

19. "Schelling's Aphorism of 1805," 245.

20. Exactly what Leopardi also asserts [author's note]. "That matter thinks is a fact. It is a fact because we ourselves think." Giacomo Leopardi, *Zibaldone*, 4288, 18 September 1827, ed. Michael Caesar and Franco D'Intino, trans. Kathleen Baldwin et al. (New York: Farrar, Straus and Giroux, 2013), 1913 [editor's note].

21. This is the aim of all of Schelling's attempts at a system after the *Philosophical Investigations on the Essence of Freedom* (1809), revolving around a "reevaluation" of the category of the *possible*.

22. Georg Wilhelm Friedrich Hegel, *Lectures on the History of Philosophy: Medieval and Modern Philosophy*, trans. E. S. Haldane and Frances H. Simson (Lincoln: University of Nebraska Press, 1995), 283.

23. J. W. Goethe, *The Collected Works in 12 Volumes*, vol. 1, *Selected Poems*, ed. and trans. Christopher Middleton (Princeton, NJ: Princeton University Press, 1994), 243.

Chapter Sources

San Francesco in Dante e Giotto (Milan: Adelphi, 2012; 2nd rev. ed. 2015).
"Il 'peccato' di Ulisse," *Rivista di Studi Danteschi* 8, no. 1 (2013): 24–42.
"L'*Aisthesis Theia* di Dante," *Lettere Italiane* 68, no. 3 (2015): 519–528.
"L'ineffabile concreto: Sugli ultimi Canti della *Commedia*," in *Humana Feritas: Studi con Gian Mario Anselmi*, ed. Loredana Chines, Elisabetta Menetti, Andrea Severi, and Carlo Varotti (Bologna, Italy: Pàtron, 2017), 105–111.
"Il Paradiso: L'*amore* intellettuale di Dante," *Robinson*, literary supplement, *La Repubblica*, 212 (Dec. 24, 2020): 2–3.
"Latino e volgare nel *De vulgari eloquentia*," *Latinitas*, new series, only volume (2013): 83–86.
"Sulla teologia politica di Dante," in *L'anti-Babele: Sulla mistica degli antichi e dei moderni*, ed. Giovanni Gaeta, Isabella Adinolfi, and Andreina Lavagetto (Genoa, Italy: il melangolo, 2017), 265–280.
"Brevi note sul Dante di Germania," *Humanitas* 76, no. 1 (2021): 33–43.
"Il Dante di Schelling," in *Libertà e natura: Prospettive schellinghiane*, ed. Emilio Carlo Corriero (Turin, Italy: Rosenberg & Sellier, 2017), 115–124.

Index

Aeneas, 11, 23, 63, 65, 76
Agamben, Giorgio, 9, 158n10, 159n23, 163n38, 165n55
Andrea di Bonaiuto, 40
Angela of Foligno, Saint, 4, 58
Angelico, Fra (Guido di Pietro), 57, 58
Angelo of Clareno, 41
Anger, Kenneth, 4
Anthony of Padua, Saint (Anthony of Lisbon), 44
Aquinas, Saint Thomas, 4, 6, 27–33, 40–41, 48–49, 60, 77–78, 163n32, 165n55
Ardizzone, Maria Luisa, 159n19, 169n3
Ariani, Marco, 168n5–7
Aristotle, 2, 10, 14, 17, 68–69, 71, 73–77, 129, 167nn12–13, 170n8
Aristotelianism (Radical Aristotelianism), 10, 32, 158n12, 168n3
Arnolfo di Cambio, 44
Arrigo VII. *See* Henry VII
Assisi (city and Basilica, symbolism of the city), 23–27, 30–31, 35, 39, 59
Assisi (frescoes in the Basilica), 5–8, 21, 23, 25, 27, 31, 39–49, 57–59,
160n6, 160n11, 162n21, 163n36, 164n46
Auerbach, Erich, 59, 105, 141, 159n2, 166n68, 168n5, 172n19
Augustine of Hippo, Saint, 2, 16, 28, 37–38, 62, 71, 84, 124–125, 130, 163n30, 170nn2–6
Augustus (as name for all Roman Emperors), 126, 130
Augustus, Caesar (emperor) (Gaius Octavius), 116, 128
Averroism (Averroist philosophers, influenced by Averroes [Abū l-Walīd Muḥammad Ibn ʿAḥmad Ibn Rušd]), 10, 65, 75–78, 124
Aversano, Mario, 166n1

Badiou, Alain, 159n20
Balthasar, Hans Urs von, 161n12, 173n19
Barlaam of Calabria (Barlaam of Seminara, Barlaam the Calabrian), 91, 92
Barolini, Teodolinda, 158n15, 159n19, 169n3
Baudelaire, Charles Pierre, 12, 138, 141, 171n9
Beatrice (Beatrice Portinari), 3, 6, 11, 13, 17, 30–31, 37, 56, 58,

Beatrice (Beatrice Portinari) (*continued*)
    73–74, 78, 80–82, 84, 87–90, 94, 96–101, 108, 110–111, 121, 123, 128, 130, 139, 141, 157n5, 172n15
Bellosi, Luciano, 160n4, 163n34
Benjamin, Walter, 18, 137–139, 141–143, 171n9, 172n15, 173nn20–22, 173n24, 174n30
Benvenuto Rambaldi da Imola, 25
Berlinghieri, Bonaventura (*also* Master of Lucca), 26, 42
Bernard, Saint (Bernard of Clairvaux), 3, 5, 30, 100, 106, 110, 142, 157n1
Binni, Walter, 171n10
Boccaccio, Giovanni, 23, 77, 160n7
Bodmer, Johann Jakob, 133
Boethius of Dacia (Boetius de Dacia), 168n3
Boitani, Piero, 168nn5–6
Bonaiuti Treves, Alarico, 28
Bonaventure, Saint (Bonaventura da Bagnoregio, Giovanni di Fidanza), 4, 6, 7, 26–33, 38–49, 58, 60, 161n12, 161n14, 161n18, 162n21, 162n28, 163n28, 163nn32–33, 163n36, 164nn42–44, 164n46
Boniface VIII (Benedetto Caetani), 34, 40, 48, 60
Boorman, John, 12
Botterill, Steven, 164n48, 168n2
Breitinger, Johann Jakob, 133
Brunelleschi, Filippo (Filippo di ser Brunellesco di Lippo Lapi), 116
Bruni, Francesco, 113
Buonaiuti, Ernesto, 163n35

Cadden, Joan, 169n5
Cardini, Franco, 163n39
Carugati, Giuliana, 168n3
Cassell, Anthony K., 159n21, 161n19, 170n9

Cavalcanti, Guido (sometimes referred as Guido), 10–11, 24, 64, 73–74, 76–82, 90, 158n14, 167n1, 161nn16–17; *Donna me prega*, 11, 90
Cavallini, Pietro, 23, 160n6
Celestine V, Pope (Pietro Angelerio, Pietro da Morrone), 41
Chiara d'Assisi. *See* Clare of Assisi, Saint
Chiavacci Leonardi, Anna Maria, 168n2
Chomsky, Noam, 115, 168n3
Christianity, 34, 51, 122
Cicero (Marcus Tullius Cicero), 2, 61
Cimabue (Cenni di Pepo), 23–25, 134
Clare of Assisi, Saint, 43, 47, 49, 58–59, 165n58, 166n67
Clement V, Pope (Raymond Bertrand de Got), 40
Coleridge, Samuel Taylor, 12
Compagni, Dino, 77
Compilatio Florentina, 60
Conches, Wilhelm von (William of Conches), 116, 169n5
Constantine I, Roman Emperor (Constantine the Great), 121, 131
Convivio (also *Conv.*), 10, 30, 66–68, 71, 74, 76–78, 113, 154, 158n11, 159n19, 161n18, 167nn8–9
Corti, Maria, 158n12, n14, 166n1, 167n1, 168n3, 169n3
Cosmo, Umberto, 165n54
Curtius, Ernst Robert, 169n4, 174nn27–28

Damian, Peter (Pier Damiani, Petrus Damianus), 65
Davis, Charles Till, 159n19
Dawkins, Richard, 4, 157n2
Deleuze, Gilles, 12
De Sanctis, Francesco, 138, 171n11

Descartes, René, 1, 149
Diomedes (*Diomedes of Thrace*), 63
Dionysius the Areopagite, 15, 87, 100
Divine Comedy, 3–4, 12–14, 17, 25, 157n3, 160n5, 172n15
Dominic, Saint (Dominic de Guzmán), 4, 27–33, 41, 43, 57
Duccio (Duccio di Buoninsegna), 92

Eckermann, Johann Peter, 134
Eckhart, Meister (Eckhart von Hochheim), 165n58
Eco, Umberto, 168n3
Eliot, Thomas Stearns, 4
Empire (idea of Empire in Dante), 5–6, 8, 16–18, 21, 27, 40, 100, 116, 120–125, 128, 130–132, 143, 159n19
Engels, Friedrich, 138, 171n3
Eschenbach, Wolfram von, 133
Ethics (*Nichomachean Ethics*), 74–75, 167nn12–13, 169n8
Euripides, 61

Farinata degli Uberti, 10, 73
Fenzi, Enrico, 113, 117, 168n1
Fichte, Johann Gottlieb, 145, 148–150, 152–153, 174n11, 175n15
Ficino, Marsilio, 125
Fiore, Joachim de. *See* Joachim de Fiore
Formisano, Luciano, 168n1
Francis of Assisi, Saint (Giovanni di Pietro di Bernardone), 4–8, 21–60, 122, 131, 134, 157n7, 158n9, 159n1, 159n3, 160n4, 160n11, 161nn15–16, 162n21, 162n24, 162n27, 163n34, 163n37, 163n39, 164n46, 164n50, 165nn57–62, 166n65, 166n68; *Canticle of the Sun* or *Canticle of Creatures*, 7–8, 21, 37–39, 57–58, 163n31; *Earlier Rule*, 30, 56, 161n15, 165n61; *Later Rule*, 50, 56, 164n50, 165n60; *Letter to a Certain Minister*, 59, 166n69; *Testament*, 30, 41, 43, 58, 161n16, 163n37, 164n46, 166n66
Freccero, John, 158n15
Frisardi, Andrew, 158n11
Freud, Sigmund, 4, 12
Frugoni, Chiara, 160n10, 164n39, 166n67
Fubini, Mario, 64, 166n5

Gast, Peter (Johann Heinrich Köselitz), 139, 172n17
George, Stefan Anton, 18–19, 139–140, 142–143, 163nn22–25, 174nn26–28
Gilson, Étienne Henri, 74, 161n18, 167n11, 167n15
Giotto (Giotto di Bondone), 5–8, 23–27, 35–37, 39, 42, 47–50, 53–54, 56, 59–60, 92, 134, 160nn6–7, 160n11, 165n58
Godman, Peter, 169n4
Goethe, Johann Wolfgang von, 18, 19, 133–134, 135, 140, 141, 148, 154–155, 159n22, 170nn1–4, 172n14, 174n12, 175n23
Gregorius Magnus (Saint Gregory the Great, Pope), 62
Gregory IX, Pope (Ugolino di Conti, Hugolino of Ostia), 45
Gregory, Tullio, 163n32
Grundmann, Herbert, 162n23
Guardini, Romano, 62, 166n4, 173n19
Guido I da Montefeltro, 59
Guinizzelli, Guido, 24

Hamann, Johann Georg, 135
Harnack, Adolph von, 51
Harry VII. *See* Henry VII

Hauptmann, Gerhart Johann Robert, 140
Hegel, Georg Wilhelm Fredrich, 19, 135–138, 145–148, 150, 152, 174n8, 175n22
Heidegger, Martin, 11, 51, 143, 164n51
Henry VII (Harry VII, Arrigo VII), Holy Roman Emperor, King of Germany, 11, 95, 130
Hercules (Pillars of Hercules), 62, 65–66
Herder, Johann Gottfried, 135
Hildegard of Bingen, 3
Hofmannsthal, Hugo von, 143
Hogrebe, Wolfram, 145, 174n1
Hölderlin, Friedrich, 51, 142
Homer, 61, 145
Honorious III, Pope (Cencio Savelli), 33–34, 44–45, 48, 162n23
Horace (Quintus Horatius Flaccus), 61
Hugh of Saint Victor, 106

Imbach, Ruedi, 77, 167n14
Inferno, 15, 25, 88, 102, 107, 130, 134
Inferno (also *Inf.*) by Cantos: I, 122; II, 23; III, 41, 172n14; IV, 67, 129; V, 12, 37, 79, 109, 142; VII, 37; X, 11, 74, 79–81, 160n9, 167n16; XI, 170n4; XII, 170n4; XV, 49; XVI, 24–25; XIX, 31, 41, 49; XX, 23; XXVI, 25, 61–67, 69–70, 75–76; XXVII, 30, 41, 59
Innocent III, Pope (Lotario dei Conti di Segni), 6, 26, 31, 33–36, 42, 44–45, 48, 162n23

Jacoff, Rachel, 158n15
Jacopone da Todi, 27
Jesus Christ, 17–18, 23, 36, 42, 44–45, 52–54

Joachim de Fiore, 6, 28–29, 32, 40–41, 101, 161n14
John of Paris, 124, 169n1
John XXII, Pope (Jacques Duèze), 49
Joyce, James, 83
Justinian I, Eastern Roman Emperor (Justinian the Great), 131

Kafka, Franz, 142–143
Klages, Ludwig, 142, 174n26
Kraus, Karl, 141

Lacan, Jacques, 12
Lawrence, Saint (Saint Laurence), 106
Le Goff, Jacques, 165n64
Leonardi, Claudio, 166n64
Leopardi, Giacomo, 12, 138, 175n20
Longhi, Roberto, 23
Longpré, Ephrem, 165n63
Lorenzetti, Ambrogio (Ambruogio Laurati), 125
Lukács, György, 51, 136–138
Luke (Gospel of), 32, 52

Machiavelli, Niccolò, 125
Maggi, Marco, 173
Malato, Enrico, 11, 80, 160n9, 167n16, 168n5
Mandelbaum, Allen, 4, 157n3, 160n5
Mandelstam, Osip, 83
Mann, Thomas, 140–141
Manselli, Raoul, 28, 163n32
Marmo, Costantino, 169n3
Marsilius of Padua (Marsilio da Padova, Marsilio dei Mainardini), 18, 123, 131
Martello, Carlo (Carolus Martellus, Carolus Tudes), 86
Martini, Simone, 92
Marx, Karl, 138, 171nn12–13
Mary (Holy Mary, Saint Mary), 3–5, 96, 100–101, 107, 111, 168n5

Index

Masaccio (Tommaso di Ser Giovanni di Simone), 47
Master of Lucca. *See* Bonaventura Berlinghieri
Matthew (Gospel of), 50, 58
Matthew of Acquasparta, 40
Matthew of Paris, 43
Mazzucchi, Andrea, 168n5
Melandri, Enzo, 165n55
Mengaldo, Pier Vincenzo, 113
Meyendorff, John, 167n2
Meyer, Conrad Ferdinand, 140
Miccoli, Giovanni, 161n14, 162n21, 163n3
Michelangelo (Michelangelo Buonarroti), 172n14
Michelstaedter, Carlo, 54, 165n56
Middle Ages, The, 1–4, 8, 10, 13, 62, 115, 138, 158n9, 171n13
Milton, John, 12, 133
Mocan, Mira Veronica, 167n1
Monahan, Arthur P., 169n1
Monarchia (also *Mon.*), 16, 17, 18, 25, 30, 75, 77–78, 120, 123–124, 126–127, 129–131, 159n19, 159n21, 161n19, 169n7, 170n9
Montuori, Francesco, 168n1
Musil, Robert, 142–143

Nardi, Bruno, 69, 162n22, 167n10, 28
Neoplatonism, 14, 61, 84
Nicholas III, Pope (Giovanni Gaetano Orsini), 39
Nicholas IV, Pope (Girolamo Masci), 39, 40, 48
Nietzsche, Friedrich, 7, 8, 17–18, 38, 51–52, 91, 138–141, 158n8, 162nn25–26, 164n52, 172n14, 172nn16–17
Novalis (Georg Philipp Friedrich Freiherr von Hardenberg), 171n7

Oedipus, 4
Olivi, Peter John (Pietro di Giovanni Olivi), 8, 40–41
Olson, Kristina, 157n6
Ossola, Carlo Maria, 168n4

Padoan, Giorgio, 166n1
Pagliaro, Antonino, 11, 80, 160n9, 167n16
Palamas, Gregory, 14, 15, 91–92, 167nn2–3
Pansters, Krijn, 166n70
Paradiso, 6, 13, 25, 37, 40, 56, 88, 91–93, 97, 105, 107, 134, 149, 159, 161nn17–18, 168n4
Paradiso (also *Par.*) by Cantos: I, 37, 63, 87, 92; II, 87, 89; III, 57; IV, 14, 83–84, 91–92, 101, 106; V, 86; VII, 84, 100; VIII, 86; IX, 83, 107, 122, 129; X, 5–6, 27, 37, 41, 49, 77–78, 161n17; XI, 5–6, 27, 31, 33–35, 41, 49–50, 78; XII, 5–6, 27, 31–33, 41, 48; XIII, 5–6, 27, 41, 78; XIV, 13, 88–89; XVII, 129–130; XVIII, 83; XX, 105–106, 131; XXI, 65, 83, 85, 100, 103, 107; XXII, 14, 37, 84, 94; XXIII, 95–97; XXVI, 115; XXVII, 11, 31, 94–95, 98, 111, 121; XXVIII, 15, 37; XXIX, 15, 108; XXX, 83, 87, 95, 98–100, 107, 111, 121; XXXI, 22, 37, 99, 101–102, 110–111; XXXII, 100; XXXIII, 66, 85–86, 90, 95, 98, 100–103, 173n21
Pareyson, Luigi, 148, 174n11
Pascal, Blaise, 159n21
Passerin D'Entrèves, Alessandro, 17, 159n19
Paul, Saint (Saul of Tarsus), 23, 29, 63, 89, 97, 99
Pelikan, Jaroslav, 167n2

Peter, Saint, 8, 31, 33, 57, 60, 84, 94, 120–121
Petrarch (Francesco Petrarca), 5, 91
Plato (Plato's Cave, Platonic Love), 2, 3, 71, 76, 91, 95, 98, 125, 172n15
Porete, Marguerite, 165n58
Portinari, Beatrice. *See* Beatrice
Pound, Ezra, 4, 83
Poverty (Franciscan virtue), 5, 6–9, 31, 33–35, 40, 45, 47–60, 122, 158nn9–10, 163n38, 165n58
Pozzi, Giovanni, 159n1, 166n64
Purgatorio, 17, 88, 97, 126, 130, 134, 148
Purgatorio (also *Purg.*) by Cantos: V, 171n12; XI, 24–25, 160n9; XIV, 36; XVI, 121, 128, 129; XVIII, 63, 80–81; XX, 122; XXI, 131; XXII, 129; XXVI, 4; XXVII, 17, 122, 127–128; XXIX, 128; XXX, 129, 152; XXI, 123–124, 130; XXXII, 9, 16, 120–121, 123, 128; XXXIII, 25, 30, 121, 128

Raffi, Alessandro, 167n9
Rembrandt, Harmenszoon van Rijn, 140
Revelation, Book of, 42
Richard of Saint Victor, 106
Rilke, Rainer Maria, 140
Rima, Beatrice, 166n64
Rodin, François Auguste René, 140
Roman Empire, 16, 18, 123, 132
Rome, 9, 16, 23–24, 31, 61, 94, 105, 123, 125, 128, 131–132
Rumohr, Karl Friedrich von, 49
Russel, Norman, 167n3

Sabatier, Paul, 51
Salomon (Solomon, Jedidiah, King of Israel), 28
San Damiano (Monastery near Assisi), 46–47, 56, 58
Santa Croce (Basilica in Florence), 26, 40, 42, 48, 59
Sasso, Gennaro, 81, 167n17
Scaevola, Gaius Mucius, 106
Schelling, Friedrich Wilhelm Joseph von, 18–19, 135–138, 145–155, 174nn4–5, 174n7, 174nn9–10, 174n12, 175nn13–14, 175nn16–19, 175n21
Schiller, Johann Christoph Friedrich von, 19
Schlegel, August Wilhelm von, 134, 135–138, 148, 170n5
Schlegel, Karl Wilhelm Friedrich, 19, 134, 138, 145, 170n5
Schopenhauer, Arthur, 175
Scipio (Publius Cornelius Scipio Africanus), 31, 94
Scotus Eriugena, Johannes, 1–2
Scrovegni (Chapel), 36, 160
Scrovegni, Enrico, 25, 160
Seneca, Lucius Annaeus (Seneca the Younger), 61–62, 166n3
Shaw, Prue, 169n3
Sibyl (Cumaean Sibyl), 102
Siger of Brabant (Sigerus, Sighier, Sigieri, Sygerius de Brabantia), 4, 6, 29, 41, 158n12, 161nn17–18
Simmel, Georg, 18, 140–141, 172n18
Sini, Carlo, 159n23
Sophocles, 2, 4
Spengler, Oswald, 143, 174n29
Spinoza, Baruch, 19, 78, 134, 149–153, 175n17
Spitzer, Leo, 163n31
Statius (Publius Papinius Statius), 61
Stigmata (of Saint Francis), 26, 30, 33, 42, 160n11, 161n12
Stigmatization (Giotto's Louvre predella and Assisi fresco), 35, 41, 45

Streckfuss, Karl (Adolf Friedrich Karl Streckfuß), 134, 170n4
Subiaco ("Holy Grotto"), 23, 26
Sultan, the (al–Malik al Kāmil), 21, 31, 33–34, 43–44, 58, 163n39

Thomas of Celano, 31, 35–36, 38, 43, 45, 53, 162n24, 162n27, 164nn40–41, 164n45, 164n47, 164n53
Thomas of Pavia (Thomas Tuscus, Thomas Pavie), 58, 165n63
Tito (Titus Caesar Vespasianus, Roman Emperor), 131
Torriti, Jacopo, 23
Trajan (Caesar Nerva Traianus, Roman Emperor), 105, 131
Trissino, Gian Giorgio, 113
Turati, Filippo, 171n13

Ubertino of Casale, 29, 40–41, 58
Ulysses (*Odysseus*), 61–79, 158n12, 158n15
Ungaretti, Giuseppe, 132, 170n10

Verduin, Kathleen, 157n5
Vernani, Guido, 18, 131, 159n21, 161n19, 170n9
Vico, Giambattista (Giovan Battista Vico), 115, 127, 133, 145–146, 174n2, 174n3
Villani, Giovanni, 26
Virgil (Publius Vergilius Maro), 61–64, 73, 80–81, 116, 122, 127, 128, 130, 166n6
Vita nuova, 5, 11, 76, 80, 158n14
Vogelweide, Walter von der, 133
Vulgari eloquentia, De (also *De vulg.*), 14, 24, 48, 113–118, 131, 164n48, 167n9, 168n1, 168n2

Wagner, Richard, 172n14, 172n16, 174n6, 175n17
Weigel, Sigrid, 173n21
Wharton, Edith, 157n5

Zarathustra (Zoroaster), 51, 139, 164n52